DATA BANK ON INDIAN HISTORY

DATA BANK
ON
INDIAN HISTORY

Compiled and Edited by
Arvind M. Dwivedi

ANMOL PUBLICATIONS PVT. LTD.
NEW DELHI - 110 002 (INDIA)

ANMOL PUBLICATIONS PVT. LTD.
4374/4B, Ansari Road, Daryaganj
New Delhi-110 002
www.anmolbooks.com

Data Bank on Indian History

First Edition 2001
ISBN 81-261-1004-X

PRINTED IN INDIA

Published by J. L. Kumar for Anmol Publications Pvt. Ltd., New Delhi-110 002 and Printed at Mehra Offset Press, Delhi.

CONTENTS

PREFACE

Today, we are living in the age of competitions. Gone are the days when the degrees were enough to get a job. Now the thorough study of any subject is required to get through in any competitive examination. The objective multiple choice type questions are asked almost in all the competitions. In order to meet the increasing demand of the aspirants, we have prepared the Data Bank on Indian History and feel pleasure on presenting the same before you. It is concise, comprehensive and dependable which has a wide coverage of the syllabus.

The proportion, of questions from History in General study has get tremendous increase in the recent past. Near about 20% questions are asked from this portion. In the present data bank we have touched all the concerns of syllabus as well as the latest pattern of questions asked in UPSC, SSC, LIC, GIC, CDS, NDA and other examinations. We have taken utmost care in preparing the questions with particular gradation and level of the various examination.

We shall feel grateful to the readers if they send us their valuable comments so that further improvements may be made in the subsequent editions of the book.

—Arvind M. Dwivedi

1

INDUS VALLEY CIVILIZATION AND HARAPPAN CULTURE

INDUS VALLEY CIVILIZATION

1. The Harappan Civilization was mainly concentrated in:
   (a) Punjab, Rajasthan and Gujrat
   (b) Punjab, Rajasthan and U.P.
   (c) Haryana, Rajasthan and Delhi
   (d) Gujarat, Haryana and Western U.P.

2. Which one of the following is not one of the Harappan sites related to the maritime activities of the Harappan people?
   (a) Lothal (b) Balakot
   (c) Sokta Koh (d) Desalpur.

3. Two most important Harappan crops were:
   (a) Wheat and barley
   (b) Sesamom and mustard
   (c) Rice and peas
   (d) Cotton and sugarcane.

4. Three most common features of all Indus Valley sites are:
   (a) Use of baked bricks and pottery, elaborate drainage system and occurrence of harsh or jungle animals;
   (b) Climate, flora, fauna and artificial irrigation
   (c) Desert, rivers, and zoological features
   (d) Buildings, town planning and burial system.

5. One of the Harappan deities not represented in later Hindu religion is:
   (a) Pashupati Siva (b) Seven mothers
   (c) Compound creatures (d) Chanhudaro.

6. At which of the following places has a brick dockyard connected to the gulf of Cambay by a channel been discovered?
   (a) Lothal (b) Suktagender
   (c) Amri (d) Chanhudaro.

7. The term 'Late Harappan' which is gaining currency now stands for:
   (a) Declining phase of the culture
   (b) Use of iron by the Harappans
   (c) The post-urban phase of the culture
   (d) Regional variation in the culture.

8. Which of the following finds helps us most to understand the religious and social life of the Indus Valley age?
   (a) Burial grounds
   (b) Terracotta Figures
   (c) Furniture and pottery
   (d) Remains of houses and other buildings.

9. From the scattered skeletal remains of the Harappans found at different sites. The most appropriate conclusion to be drawn would be that there was:
   (a) Some kind of military assault
   (b) Mass execution of human sacrifice
   (c) Casual burial of human bodies
   (d) Malaria or any other pathogenic condition.

10. One of the most plausible reasons which made the Harappans move away from their urban settlements was;
   (a) Foreign invasion
   (b) Hydrologic changes
   (c) Ecological changes
   (d) Demographic changes.

11. The largest number of Harappan sites in post-Independence India have been discovered in:
    (a) Gujarat (b) Rajasthan
    (c) Punjab and Haryana (d) N.W. Uttar Pradesh.

12. In which of the following respects have the various sites marked uniformity?
    (a) Agriculture practices (b) Crafts
    (c) Town planing (d) Seals.

13. The Mature Harappan civilization appears to have lasted for around --------------centuries:
    (a) Four (b) Five
    (c) Seven (d) Three.

14. Which of the following was not the likely purpose of the great bath in the citadel at Mohenjodaro?
    (a) Community bathing
    (b) Swimming exercise and water sports
    (c) Some elaborate ritual of vital importance, including a corporate social life
    (d) Storage of water to be used during drought or emergency.

15. Almost all Harappan towns had large granaries because:
    (a) Taxes were paid in kind, and therefore granaries acted as a sort of public treasuries
    (b) Surplus produce of the countryside was stored in the towns
    (c) Foodgrains were started for the purpose of trade
    (d) All the above.

16. The doors, windows and ventilators of the houses in the Harappan towns did not open towards the roads but towards the backlanes in order to save the houses from:
    (a) Pollution
    (b) Noise of the main road
    (c) Both (a) and (b) above
    (d) Thiefs and robbers.

17. The use of lime and costly burnt bricks instead of sun-dried bricks, by the Indus Valley people for construction purposes is a proof of:
    (a) A moist climate on account of the close proximity of the civilization to the river valleys
    (b) Advanced technology
    (c) Better planning
    (d) Knowledge of the manufacture of lime.

18. The Harappan towns and cities were divided into large --------------blocks.
    (a) square (b) Rectangular
    (c) Circular (d) Semi-Circular.

19. From which of the following sites excavated recently have three stages of Harappan occupation been noticed/
    (a) Rojaidi (b) Desalpur
    (c) Surkotda (d) All the above.

20. On that basis has the time span of the Harappan Civilization now been fixed between 2300 B.C. and 1750 B.C.?
    (a) Latest finds in Rajasthan, Gujrat, Chandigarh, Haryana, Madhya Pradesh etc.
    (b) Radio-carbon dating (R-14)
    (c) Common pottery designs and other antiquities
    (d) Details of links between the Harappan Civilization and the Ancient Civilization of west Asia.

21. Which of the following does not indicate close links between the Indus Valley and other contemporary west Asian civilizations?
    (a) Indus Valley seals had been found from Sumer, Elam and Mesopotamia
    (b) Trade between the Indus Valley and Sumer was carried on by land and partly by sea
    (c) Literacy and archaeological evidence of brisk trade between Harappan and Mesopotamian towns
    (d) Harappan economy was dependent on imports from west Asia.

22. The Harappan people conducted brisk trade with
    (a) Afghanistan (b) Mesopotamia
    (c) Bahrain (d) All the above.

23. Which of the following was not one of the distinctive features of Harappan culture?
    (a) Rectangular town planning
    (b) Absence of canal irrigation
    (c) Use of iron side by side with copper or bronze for implements
    (d) The great granaries of Mohenjodaro and Harappan.

24. Which of the following is not one of the similarities between Harappan culture and the other Ancient Civilizations of Sumer, Mesopotamia and Egypt?
    (a) Organised city life
    (b) Burial system and religious beliefs
    (c) Potter's wheel
    (d) Domestication of animals.

25. Which of the following is not a characteristic feature of the Harappan pottery?
    (a) Well-fired red ware
    (b) Painted black designs
    (c) Vegetal and geometric patterns
    (d) Red and black polished ware.

26. Which of the following was not a feature of internal trade of the Harappans?
    (a) Trade was multifaceted
    (b) It was operated on regional as well as inter-regional level
    (c) It had a guild system coupled with nomadic trade
    (d) It was purely a barter trade.

27. The most important industry of the Harappans at-Lothal and Chanhudaro was:
    (a) Shipbuilding (b) Bead-making
    (c) Handlooms (d) Metallurgical industries.

28. Copper used most widely by the Harappans was obtained from:

(a) Baluchistan (b) Khetri mines
(c) Mesopotamia (d) Both (a) and (b) above.

29. Which of the following is not one of the proofs of maritime activities of the Indus Valley people?

(a) The discovery of a dockyard at Lothal
(b) The drawing of a ship on a seal
(c) Discovery of a large number of articles which were not produced or found in the country
(d) Commercial links of the Harappans with the west Asian countries.

30. The most important item of import for the Harappans was:

(a) Metals and Precious stones
(b) Foodgrain
(c) Textiles
(d) Pottery.

31. In the Harappan buildings mostly burnt bricks were used, not stones because:

(a) Without iron tools stone-cutting was difficult
(b) Bricks provided better flood defence
(c) Bricks were ideally suited for the moist climate
(d) Stone was not readily available.

32. The Indian script which appears to be the closest to the Harappan script is:

(a) Brahmi (b) Dravidian
(c) Kharosthi (d) Devanagri.

33. An animal engraved on most of the Harappan seals is the:

(a) Humpless bull or unicorn
(b) Elephant
(c) Bison
(d) Tiger.

34. From a large number of seals discovered from almost all the Harappan sites it appears that they were used for -------------purposes.
 (a) Ritualistic and Religious
 (b) Commercial
 (c) Both (a) and (b) Above
 (d) Symbolic.

35. Rows of distinctive fire altars with the provision of ritual bathing have been found at:
 (a) Mohenjodaro
 (b) Harappa
 (c) Kalibangan
 (d) Lothal.

36. In which of the following respects is there considerable variation in the Harappan Civilization?
 (a) Town Planning
 (b) Brick sizes
 (c) Weights and measures
 (d) Size of dwellings.

37. The site that played the role of Harappan trading station was:
 (a) Harappa (b) Kalibangan
 (c) Lothal (d) Surkotda.

38. The cereal not known to have been grown by the Harappan people was:
 (a) Barley (b) Pulses
 (c) Rice (d) Wheat.

39. Which of the following is not a feature of the religious life of the Indus Civilization?
 (a) Pipal and Scasia trees were regarded as celestial plants
 (b) The tree of life figures with great frequency on the seals
 (c) The Indus deities like the Vedic deities were predominantly male
 (d) None of these.

40. Which of the following features of modern Hinduism is not derived from the Harappan cults?
    (a) Shakti Worship
    (b) Worship of Siva as Pashupati
    (c) Worship of Siva-linga in the form of conical and cylindrical stones
    (d) Dedication of temples to a particular deity.

41. The deification/worship of which of the following was not part of the religion of the Indus Valley people?
    (a) Mother Goddess
    (b) Forces of nature
    (c) Trees and their spirits
    (d) Certain animal chimeras and their authropie figures.

42. Harappan people had a common burial system which is proved by:
    (a) The earth burials with the head of the dead normally laid towards the north
    (b) The burial of commonly used items with the dead
    (c) Both (a) and (b) above
    (d) The burial of the dead body in the sitting posture.

43. Children's toys and playthings found during excavations do not include:
    (a) Carts and chariots
    (b) Animals with revolving or moving heads
    (c) Marbles
    (d) Chess boards.

44. Harappan weapons were made of:
    (a) Stone (b) Copper
    (c) Bronze (d) All the above.

45. Which of the following was not one of the tools and implements used by Indus Valley people?
    (a) Needles and razors
    (b) Sickles and plough

(c) Forks and spoons
(d) Grinding stones for flouring wheat, pestles and querns.

46. Which of the following toilet and cosmetic objects were not perhaps known to Indus Valley people?
(a) Copper mirrors
(b) Ivory combs
(c) Antimony rods
(d) Hair dyes.

47. The common households utensils of the Harappan people were made of:
(a) Stone
(b) Faience
(c) Well-baked painted pottery
(d) Copper.

48. The metal most widely used by the Indus Valley people was:
(a) Copper (b) Bronze
(c) Gold and Silver (d) Tin.

49. On the basis of available evidence the Harappan Civilization contributed two important things which were:
(a) Growing wheat and cotton
(b) Knowledge of mathematics and decimal system
(c) Copper and bronze smelting technology
(d) Making soak-pits and earthen pipes.

50. Traces of which of the following has not found in the Indus civilization?
(a) Mustard (b) Barley
(c) Sugar-cane (d) Sesamum.

ANSWERS

1.	(a)	2.	(d)	3.	(a)	4.	(a)
5.	(d)	6.	(a)	7.	(c)	8.	(b)

9.	(a)	10.	(b)	11.	(a)	12.	(c)
13.	(b)	14.	(d)	15.	(d)	16.	(c)
17.	(a)	18.	(b)	19.	(d)	20.	(b)
21.	(d)	22.	(d)	23.	(c)	24.	(b)
25.	(d)	26.	(d)	27.	(b)	28.	(d)
29.	(b)	30.	(a)	31.	(d)	32.	(b)
33.	(a)	34.	(c)	35.	(c)	36.	(d)
37.	(c)	38.	(b)	39.	(c)	40.	(d)
41.	(b)	42.	(c)	43.	(d)	44.	(d)
45.	(c)	46.	(d)	47.	(c)	48.	(b)
49.	(a)	50.	(c)				

2
VEDIC ERA AT A GLANCE

1. The four fold division of society is expressly mentioned in:
   (a) Yajurveda
   (b) Purusa-Sukta of Rigveda
   (c) Hiranyagarbha-Sukta
   (d) Satapatha Brahmana.

2. In the early Vedic Period the Aryan and Dasyus or Dasas were the two main classes in society. Which of the following was not one of the basic points of difference between the two?
   (a) Language
   (b) Religion
   (c) Food eating habits
   (d) Physiognomy and colour.

3. In the Vedic period the people called Pani, were:
   (a) Those who controlled trade
   (b) Cattle breeders
   (c) Cowherds
   (d) Ploughmen.

4. The standard unit of value, used as medium of exchange during the Vedic period was:
   (a) Cow
   (b) Necklet of gold
   (c) Both (a) and (b) above
   (d) Pana.

5. The sage who is said to have Aryanised South India was:
   (a) Vishwamitra (b) Agastya
   (c) Vashishtha (d) Yagyavalkya.

6. Which of the following social practices was not pursued during the Vedic period?
   (a) People could change their occupations
   (b) Intermarriages were allowed
   (c) Food cooked by the Shudras was not taken
   (d) Sati was totally unknown.

7. The Jana during the Vedic period refers to:
   (a) District (b) Tribe
   (c) Villages (d) People.

8. The name Aghnya mentioned in many passages of the Rigveda applies to
   (a) Priest (b) Women
   (c) Cows (d) Brahmanas.

(a) The staple food of the Vedic Aryans was:
   (a) Barley and rice
   (b) Milk and its products
   (c) Rice and pulses
   (d) Vegetables and fruits.

10. Who of the following was not a learned women scholar credited with the composition of Vedic hymns?
   (a) Vishwavara (b) Apala
   (c) Ghosha (d) Swayamvara.

11. The most common crime mentioned in the Rigveda was:
   (a) Murder (b) Kidnapping
   (c) Cattle lifting (d) Robbery.

12. The ward *dampati* used in the Rigvedic period designates:
   (a) Husband and wife
   (b) Mistress as well as master of the house
   (c) Newly wedded couple
   (d) Head of the family.

13. What did the term niyoga with reference to women, stand for in the Vedic society?
    (a) The performance of Vedic sacrifices by a woman independently
    (b) The vow of celibacy taken by a woman of aristocratic society
    (c) Cohabitation of a childless widow with her husbands brother until the birth of a son
    (d) Symbolic self-immolation of a widow at the death oi her husband.

14. The high moral and ethical order of the Vedic society is proved by the fact that
    (a) Crimes were very rare
    (b) Crimes were highly respected
    (c) To speak the truth was considered a religious duty
    (d) All the above.

15. Which of the following statements about the Vedic family is not correct?
    (a) The basic unit of the Aryan tribal society was the patriarchial family
    (b) The birth of a son was especially welcome, for the sons presence was essential at important ceremonies
    (c) The society of marriage had been recognised and the tie of marriage was a binding force all through life
    (d) Child marriage was not restricted.

16. In the Vedic homes the fire was kept burning continuously because it was:
    (a) Personification of sacrificial fire
    (b) Second in importance to Indra
    (c) Messenger between the gods and devotee
    (d) All the above.

17. Which of the following dates regarding the composition / age of the Rigveda is most widely accepted?
    (a) 1000 B.C. (b) About 4500 B.C.
    (c) 1500 B.C. (d) 1500 B.C. to 1000 B.C.

18. Who was the famous Vedic scholar to propound the above date?
    (a) Max Muller (b) Jacobi
    (c) Oldenburg (d) Winternitz.

19. Which of the following Vedangas contains the Srautra the Grihya and the Dharma Sutras?
    (a) Shiksha (b) Kalpa
    (c) Nirukta (d) Chhandas.

20. Who of the following was not the Vedic sungod?
    (a) Savitri (b) Vishnu Urukrama
    (c) Savita (d) Vishvakarma.

21. Which of the following contains the famous Gayatri mantras?
    (a) Rigveda
    (b) Yajurveda
    (c) Samaveda
    (d) Brihad aranyaka Upanishad.

22. In the Vedic literature God Indra is called Purandara destroyer of forts because:
    (a) Aryans had to fight with the enemies living in fortified places.
    (b) Aryans had expertise in breaking the forts
    (c) Aryans introduced the technology of fortification
    (d) Aryans had to make assaults against the fortified Harappan towns.

23. The concept, "The world is God and God is my soul," was propounded in the:
    (a) Rigveda (b) Brahmanas
    (c) Brahmasutra (d) Upanishads.

24. An inscription of 1400 B.C. which describes the Vedic gods was found in Asia Minor at
    (a) Cilicia (b) Boghaz-koi
    (c) Hitti (d) Euphratide.

25. The Rigvedic hymns can be treated as being historically fairly authentic because:
    (a) They give a chronological account of the historical events.
    (b) They are the earliest of the Vedic literature
    (c) Their composition was contemporary with the period described
    (d) The events described in them are corroborated by Avesthan Crathas.

26. Which of the following are known as Brahmanas?
    (a) The original texts of the Vedas
    (b) Explanatory prose manuals relating to prayer and sacrificial ceremony
    (c) Books dealing with worship and contemplation meant for wood-dwelling permits
    (d) Commentaries appended to the Aranyakas dealings with philosophical questions.

27. The Veda which is partly a prose work is:
    (a) Atharvaveda (b) Samaveda
    (c) Yajurveda (d) Rigveda.

28. Which of the following Vedas was the earliest composition?
    (a) Rigveda (b) Samaveda
    (c) Yajurveda (d) Atharvaveda.

29. Which of the following does not form part of the Vedas or the shruti?
    (a) Samhitas (b) Brahmanas
    (c) Upanishads (d) Puranas.

30. The Aryans expansion of India did not lead to:
    (a) Opening of new geographic areas
    (b) Emergence of predominantly agrarian economy
    (c) Discovery of the rich iron deposits in Magadha leading to great improvement in technology
    (d) Emergence of caste system based on specialisation in particular crafts or branch of knowledge.

31. The Vedic hymns constantly refer to the wars between Sudas, the ruler of the Aryan. Tribe of Bharatas and the non-Aryan prince—
    (a) Purandara (b) Divodasa
    (c) Nasatya (b) Mitanni.

32. Which of the following was not one of the distinguished tribes of the later Vedic period?
    (a) Bharatas (b) Kurus
    (c) Panchalas (d) Videhas.

33. Which of the following was the centre of Aryan activity in the later Vedic period?
    (a) The Aryavarta
    (b) From the Yamuna to the western border of Bengal
    (c) The Punjab and Delhi region
    (d) Uttarapatha.

34. Which of the following was largely instrumental in accelerating the process of Aryan expansion?
    (a) The desire of the priest to cause Agni to taste newlands.
    (b) The hasty withdrawal of demoralised aborigines
    (c) ·e of improved implements of irons
    (d) The denudation of forests by floods on account of geomorphological changes.

35. Which of the following did not form part of the Aryans knowledge of Indian geography in the later Vedic period?
    (a) The "two seas"
    (b) Several Himalayan peaks
    (c) The deccan up to the Krishna Valley
    (d) The entire Gangetic Valley.

36. In what sense may the Aryan subjugation of the earlier inhabitation be regarded as a backward step?
    (a) The Harappans were culturally for more advance than their conquerors

(b) The Aryans destroyed the well built cities and it took them many years to rebuild them
(c) The Harappanans had a script which Indo-Aryans did not have and it took them many years to develop one.
(d) The Aryans invasion destroyed the economic structure of the country.

37. The chief opponents of the Aryans were the indigenous people of non-Aryan origin known as Panis and Dasas or Dasyus. The factor which enabled the Aryans to emerge victorious in the struggle against the indigenous tribes was:
(a) Lack of unity among the indigenous tribes
(b) Better organisation among the Aryans.
(c) Superior military equipment of the Aryans
(d) Cultural superiority.

38. The main cause of the tribal wars among the early Aryans settlers, the most famous of which is referred to as the battle of ten kings in the Rigveda was:
(a) Intrigues of the purohitas
(b) Exhibition of prowess
(c) Foreign invasions
(d) Cattle and land disputes.

39. The geographical knowledge of the early Aryans did not extend beyond:
(a) Indus (b) Ganga
(c) Yamuna (d) Ghaggar.

40. The main focus of the Rigvedic culture was
(a) The Indo-Gangetic valley
(b) The Punjab and Delhi region
(c) The Indus Valley
(d) The region between the Swat and the Indus.

41. Which of the following correctly describes the land of the seven rivers where the initial Aryans settlements were located?
(a) The Indus Valley regions
(b) The Punjab and Delhi region

(c) The region from eastern Afghanistan to the upper valley of the Ganges

(d) The land of the Indus and its principle tributaries.

42. According to the theory of double invasion of India by the Aryans the first group inhabited the Punjab, and the second group pushed its way through Gilgit and Chitral and settled in the midland country

(a) Dr. Giles

(b) Dr. Hoernle

(c) Sir George Grierson

(d) C.V. Vaidya.

43. Which of the following is regarded as the original home of Indo-Iranians?

(a) The area between Dnieper and the Urals

(b) The two sides of Vistula River

(c) The plains of the Oxus and Jaxortes

(d) Sapta-Sindhava.

44. Immediately before coming to India the Indo-Aryans formed part of which of the following Indo-Europeans tribes?

(a) Hittite (b) Tocharion

(c) Indo-Iranian (d) Lithuanian.

45. On what evidence is South Russia, Central Asia regarded as the original home of the Aryans?

(a) Anthropological

(b) Philological

(c) Racial

(d) Archaeological.

46. Which of the following is now most widely regarded as the original homeland of the indo-Europeans as Aryans?

(a) India

(b) Central Europe

(c) South Russia or Central Asia

(d) The plains of Oxus.

47. The Aryans come to India as:
    (a) Invaders
    (b) Immigrants
    (c) Refugees
    (d) Merchants and nomads.

48. Who of the following was the first to suggest that the striking similarity between Sanskrit on the one hand and Greek, Latin etc., on the other, could be due to descent from a common parent language?
    (a) Max Muller (b) Sir William Jones
    (c) Monier Williams (d) P. Coeurdoux.

49. Which of the following is not considered an Indo-Aryan language?
    (a) Avesta (b) English
    (c) Arabic (d) Persian.

50. The term 'Aryan' as 'Indo-Aryan' and the 'Indo-European' primarily denotes a
    (a) Linguistic concept
    (b) Cultural concept
    (c) Racial concept
    (d) Ethnological concept.

51. Match the following Vedic Gods with their actual status or functions

(A)	Pushan	I	God of Heaven and Father of Surya
(B)	Savitri	II	Mother of Surya
(C)	Aditi	III	God of light
(D)	Dyaus	IV	God of marriage

	A	B	C	d
(a)	(IV)	(III)	(II)	(I)
(b)	(IV)	(II)	(III)	(I)
(c)	(I)	(III)	(IV)	(I)
(d)	(I)	(II)	(III)	(IV).

52. In the Rigveda the name Aghnya-not killed was applied to,
(a) Brahmin (b) Cow
(c) Women (d) Priest.

53. In the Rigveda the term duhitr used for the daughter literally means
(a) The milker of the cow
(b) The one whose is unwelcome
(c) Curse to parents
(d) Who is to be donated in marriage.

54. The most well-known variety of grain grown by the Vedic Aryans was known as
(a) Vrihi (b) Yava
(c) Mugda (d) Ikshu.

55. The 'Wedding Hymn' describing the oldest marriage ritual is found in the
(a) Rigveda (b) Yajurveda
(c) Samveda (d) Grihyasutras.

56. The Rigvedic concept of Rita denotes the
(a) Cosmic order or law prevailing in nature
(b) Ethical and moral order
(c) Both (a) and (b) above
(d) Amalgamation of " All gods" into "one".

57. The famous 'Frog Hymn' in the Rigveda throws light on the Vedic.................system.
(a) Sacrificial (b) Ecological
(c) Education (d) Agricultural.

58. Like the Vedic Aryans the custom of sacrificial tree was also followed by the ancient
(a) Romans (b) Greeks
(c) Iranians (d) All the above.

59. Which of the following functionaries was also known as the 'King maker' (raja-kartri)?
(a) Purohita (b) Mahishi
(c) Gramani (d) Ganapati.

60. The head of which of the following was supposed to be known as Ganapati or Jyeshtha?
   (a) Family (b) Tribe
   (c) Tribal Republic (d) Sabha.

61. Which of the following statements about the elaborate Judicial system of the later Vedic period is not correct?
   (a) The king played a very large part in the administration of justice
   (b) Certain cases were referred to the tribe for adjudication, and the judicial work of the tribal assembly was entrusted to a small body of sabhasadas or assessors
   (c) Petty cases in the village were decided by the gramyvadin or village judge.
   (d) Private Vengeance in criminal cases was prohibited.

62. Which of the following descriptions of the Later Vedic official is not correct?
   (a) Samagrahitri.......Treasurer
   (b) Kshattri........Chamberlain
   (d) Adhikrita........Superintendent of Police.

63. Which of the following statements about the administrative system of the later Vedic period is not correct?
   (a) On account of an assured income from the taxes the king could appoint many officers.
   (b) We hear of twelve ratnins, the forerunner of the latter day council of ministers
   (c) The beginnings of a regular system of provincial government may be traced in references to the sthapati and the shatapati
   (d) There was a secretarial charget with the responsibility of maintaining the records.

64. Which of the following statements about the administrative system of the Early Vedic period is not correct?
   (a) The king was assisted by a number of functionaries of whom the two most important were purohita and the senani

(b) Gramani was the head of the village only for civic purposes
(c) Forts and strongholds were under purapati
(d) The Vedic king had a system of espionage and also employed dutas or messengers.

65. Among the various units of the tribal kingdom (rashtra) of the Vedic society, which one of the following was the basic unit?

(a) Vish (b) Jana
(c) Kula (d) Grama.

66. Which of the following was not one of the reasons for the gradual weakening of the tribal assemblies in the Later Vedic Period?

(a) Increase in the royal power
(b) In large territorial states ordinary people could not travel long distances to attend their meetings
(c) The assemblies acquired an aristocratic character which took away most of their effectiveness
(d) They also surrendered some of their activities to the new officials called ratnins.

67. Which of the following statements about the tribal assemblies in the Early Vedic period is not correct?

(a) The king's authority was substantially limited by the tribal assemblies especially the sabha and samiti
(b) Sabha was a council of the elder members of the tribe perhaps women also attended it
(c) Samiti was a general tribal assembly and less exclusive than sabha
(d) These assemblies performed only political functions.

68. Which of the following statements about the system of taxation and revenue administration in the later Vedic period is not correct

(a) Settled life and stable agriculture led to the production of surplus which could be collected by the king in the form of taxes

(b) The king received regular contributions from the people in the shape of bali and shulka
(c) One-sixth of the produce of the land was payable to the king
(d) An official called bhagadugha collected the royal share of the produce.

69. Which of the following statements about the concept of king-ship in the later Vedic period is not correct?
(a) Kingship ceased to be elective and became here ditary
(b) A glamour was created around the king and in the rituals he was sometimes also represented as a god
(c) Some kind of class alliance between the priests and the warriors developed
(d) The king was invariably a kshatriya.

70. Differences in grade and status of kings are clearly hinted at in the later Vedic literature, but their exact hierarchy is difficult to determine, which of the following was not one of the designations adopted by the kings of this period?
(a) Raja (b) Ganapati
(c) Bhja (d) Virat.

71. Which of the following was not one of the important kingdoms of the later Vedic period
(a) Kuru-Panchala (d) Gandhara
(c) Kosala (d) Videha.

72. Which of the following was not one of the reasons for the growth in royal power in the Later Vedic period?
(a) Amalgamation of tribes
(b) Increase in the size of kingdoms
(c) Successful leadership of the kings in war
(d) Development of better military warheads.

73. Which of the following statements about the kings of the Early Vedic period is not correct
(a) The king was primarily a military leader who fought for cows and not for territory
(b) He rules over his tribe (jana) and not over particular regions

(c) Very likely he owed his office to the choise of the people

(d) He had an important role to play in the religious order also.

74. What was the main reason for the evolution of kingship in Vedic society?

(a) Patriarchal organisation of society
(b) The stress of war
(c) The desire to conquer new territories
(d) To provide organisation in society.

75. What was the normal of government in the Vedic period?

(a) Monarchy (b) Oligarchy
(c) Republic (d) Democracy.

76. The most important functionary who assisted the Vedic King, was:

(a) Purohita (b) Senani
(c) Gramani (d) Vrajapati.

77. A branch of Vedic science, which has been highly appreciated and revived by the modern scientists recently, is Vedic

(a) Medicine (b) Mathematics
(c) Astronomy (d) Space Sciences.

78. Various social rituals and the performance of several ceremonies or samskaras from conception to cremation have been described in the:

(a) Dharma-sutras (b) Srauta-Sutras
(c) Grihya-Sutras (d) Upanishads.

79. The coronation oaths of the king and the coronation songs provided in the Atharvaveda point to the fact that the Vedic King.

(a) Did not wield absolute power
(b) Was expected to promote material wellbeing of the people
(c) The kingdom was regarded as a trust, not a possession
(d) All the above.

80. Which of the following was not one of the reasons why the status of the carpenter in the Vedic period was as high as that of the test pilot in modern times?
   (a) Carpentry was reserved for craftsmen of Aryan origin
   (b) He was the maker of the chariot upon the quality of which victory in war depended
   (c) He was also the maker of the plough, the mainstay of agricultural operations
   (d) The increasing availability of wood from the forest made carpentry a lucrative profession.

81. Which of the following was not among the crafts and professions practised during the Rigvedic period?
   (a) Carpentry (b) Weaving
   (c) Tanning (d) Ivory work.

82. The famous 'Battle of Ten Kings' mentioned in the Rigveda was fought between.
   (a) King Sudas of Bharatas and the host of Ten kings
   (b) The Kurus and the Panchalas
   (c) The Kurus and the Ten kings of Bharatas
   (d) The Bhartas and the Tristu.

83. Which of the following was the most important effect of the change from pastoral to agricultural economy?
   (a) More permanent settling down of the tribes
   (b) Creation of a wider range of occupations
   (c) Increase in wealth and prosperity
   (d) Improvement in dietary habits.

84. Which of the following statements about the agricultural practices of the Rigvedic Aryans is not correct?
   (a) Canals were excavated to help agriculture, and the use of manure was also known
   (b) They also possesses some knowledge of the seasons which promoted agriculture
   (c) There are references to ploughing, sowing, reaping, threshing and windowing
   (d) The agricultural profession was not regarded as a respectable one.

85. During the Rigvedic period the purpose of worshipping was to.
   (a) Secure spiritual upliftment
   (b) Gain material well-being
   (c) Both (a) and (b) above
   (d) None of these.

86. The advent of the Aryans in India is associated with the introduction of.
   (a) Iron and horse
   (b) Superior crops such as sugarcane and pulses
   (c) Both (a) and (b) above
   (d) Tribal republics.

87. Which of the following statements about the later Vedic religion is not correct?
   (a) The lustre of the older gods was gradually dimmed, prajapati the Lord of created being, became the most important deity
   (b) Among the common people, Rudra and Vishnu became popular
   (c) The monothestic and monistic tendencies of the Rigvedic period suffered a decline
   (d) The popular superstitious belief in spirits, imps, spells, incantations and witchcraft found a place in the sacred canon.

88. Which of the following statements about the Vedic system of education is not correct?
   (a) Theoretically education was open to all dvijas, though the Vedas tended to become an exclusive preserve of the Brahmans
   (b) Apart from Arithmetic, Grammar and Prosody the Vedas constituted the main subject of study
   (c) The Aryans had a developed system of writing
   (d) Education was given free.

89. Which of the following regarding the social-life of the Vedic people is not true?
    (a) Social divisions were based on occupations
    (b) The members of one family could adopt different occupations
    (c) Slavery, including women slaves, was known
    (d) The society was not egalitarian.

90. The tax which the kings used to collect from the people in the Vedic period was called:
    (a) Bali (b) Vidatha
    (c) Varman (d) Kara.

91. A Rigvedic painted greyware site excavated recently in Haryana is
    (a) Alamgirpur (b) Bhagwanpur
    (c) Hastinapur (d) Kurkshetra.

92. Which of the following statements about the Vedic conception of life after death is not correct
    (a) Life after death was envisaged in terms of punishment for evil and reward for excellence or goodness
    (b) Sinners went to the House of clay, and those to be rewarded to the World of the Fathers
    (c) In some of the later hymns there is a hint of metempsychosis
    (d) The idea of the transmigration of souls was also clearly developed.

93. The famous Vedic saying, "War begins in the minds of men", is stated in the
    (a) Rigveda
    (b) Samaveda
    (c) Atharveda
    (d) Mundaka Upanishad.

94. Which of the following was not one of the results of sacrificial rituals?
    (a) They undermined the importance of the Rigvedic gods

(b) The wasteful expenditure incurred on these ceremonies led to deterioration in the economic condition of the people
(c) The priests became the chief beneficiaries of the sacrifices and consequently gained in power
(d) They also led to the decimation of the cattle wealth.

95. In the later Vedic period on account of rising royal pretensions and priestly ambitions, there took place a great development in the sacrificial cult. Which of the following was not one of the important and elaborate sacrifices of this period?
(a) Agnihotra
(b) Rajasya
(c) Vajapeya
(d) Ashvamedha.

96. In the Vedic period, the institution of kingship was created as a result of:
(a) National insecurity due to absence of a leader
(b) Repeated defiants of the Aryans against the non-Aryans
(c) Tribal wars amongst Aryan tribes
(d) All the above.

97. In the Atharveda, the two popular Vedic bodies (the sabha and samiti) have been called as the.
(a) Collective conscience of the people
(b) Two chambers of legislature
(c) Twin daughters of Prajapati (the creator)
(d) Unity of heart and mind.

98. Which of the following abstract deities of the Vedic religion has been admired most in the Rigveda?
(a) Sraddha (faith)
(b) Apsaras (Water-nymphs)
(c) Gandharvas (aerial spirits)
(d) Usha (goddess of dawn).

99. Which of the following gods was believed to belong to the terrestrial plane?

(a) Rudra (b) Varun
(c) Agni (d) Savitri.

100. The universe was divided into three main planes, namely, terrestrial plane, mid-plane and celestial plane. Which of the following gods was believed to belong to the highest plane i.e. The celestial plane or the Realm of light

(a) Indra (b) Agni
(c) Vishnu (d) Soma.

101. To which of the following solar deities is the famous Gayatri mantra addressed?

(a) Mitra
(b) Pushan
(c) Savitri
(d) Vishnu urukrama.

102. Varuna, the highest Vedic deity, was originally regarded as

(a) The Lord of waters
(b) The Upholder of the cosmic order
(c) The Lord of the Realm of light
(d) The Lord of the Realm of Air.

103. The earliest Iron Age occupation in India has been associated with

(a) Painted Greyware
(b) Black and red ware
(c) Ochre coloured pottery (O C P)
(d) Northern black polished ware.

104. The Indo-Aryan languages of India have been classified by Grierson and other scholars into.

(a) Non-sanskritic or pre Vedic
(b) Sanskritic or Vedic
(c) Both (a) and (b) above
(d) Outer and inner language.

105. Which of the following was not a judicial punishment in the Vedic period?
   (a) Tying a criminal to a stake
   (b) Subjecting the criminal to fire and water ordeal
   (c) A debtor was punished with a period of servitude under the creditor
   (d) Monetary compensation to the relative of a person killed/murdered.

106. Which of the following statements about the judicial system of the Vedic period is not correct?
   (a) There were no regular legal institutions of custom and law
   (b) The king and his chief priest were the arbiters, perhaps advised by certain elders of the community
   (c) Punishment was in terms of fines, the usual payment for killing a man being a hundred cows
   (d) Capital punishment was usually awarded in case of more heinous crimes like patricide, regicide etc..

107. The Vedic God incharge of right, truth and moral order (rita) was:
   (a) Dyaus (b) Varuna
   (c) Indra (d) Prajapati.

108. The term Dvija (twice born) in the Vedic period referred to
   (a) Brahmanas (b) Kshatriyas
   (c) Vaishyas (d) All the above.

ANSWERS

1.	(b)	2.	(c)	3.	(a)	4.	(c)
5.	(b)	6.	(c)	7.	(b)	8.	(c)
9.	(a)	10.	(d)	11.	(c)	12.	(b)
13.	(c)	14.	(d)	15.	(d)	16.	(d)
17.	(d)	18.	(d)	19.	(b)	20.	(d)
21.	(a)	22.	(a)	23.	(c)	24.	(b)
25.	(c)	26.	(b)	27.	(c)	28.	(a)
29.	(d)	30.	(d)	31.	(b)	32.	(a)

33.	(b)	34.	(c)	35.	(c)	36.	(a)
37.	(c)	38.	(d)	39.	(c)	40.	(b)
41.	(d)	42.	(b)	43.	(c)	44.	(c)
45.	(b)	46.	(c)	47.	(b)	48.	(b)
49.	(c)	50.	(a)	51.	(a)	52.	(b)
53.	(a)	54.	(b)	55.	(a)	56.	(c)
57.	(c)	58.	(c)	59.	(c)	60.	(c)
61.	(d)	62.	(d)	63.	(d)	64.	(b)
65.	(c)	66.	(a)	67.	(d)	68.	(c)
69.	(d)	70.	(b)	71.	(b)	72.	(d)
73.	(d)	74.	(b)	75.	(a)	76.	(a)
77.	(b)	78.	(c)	79.	(d)	80.	(a)
81.	(d)	82.	(a)	83.	(b)	84.	(d)
85.	(c)	86.	(c)	87.	(c)	88.	(c)
89.	(d)	90.	(a)	91.	(b)	92.	(d)
93.	(c)	94.	(b)	95.	(a)	96.	(a)
97.	(c)	98.	(d)	99.	(c)	100.	(c)
101.	(c)	102.	(b)	103.	(a)	104.	(c)
105.	(b)	106.	(d)	107.	(b)	108.	(d)

3
GLIMPSES OF ANCIENT SOCIETY

1. Besides the caste system the two most important aspects affected by constant social change in ancient India were
   (a) Position of women and institution of marriage
   (b) Food and drinks and fashion
   (c) Social morality and position of woman
   (d) Urban life and amusements.

2. Our main sources of information on the social structure in ancient India are
   (a) Secular and religious literature
   (b) Foreign accounts
   (c) Both (a) and (b) above
   (d) Epigraphic sources and the Puranas.

3. Detailed social rules and regulations were laid down in the
   (a) Smritis
   (b) Grihya-Sutras
   (c) Both (a) and (b) above
   (d) Puranas Niti literature.

4. The varnas came to be transformed into the hereditary castes during the
   (a) Later Vedic period
   (b) Gupta period
   (c) Post-Gupta period
   (d) Mediaeval period.

(5) The gotra signified the
(a) common ancestor of each subcaste
(b) Professional subcastes
(c) Common residence of subcastes
(d) Region to which the particular caste belonged.

6. Form conception to cremation the number of samskaras each individual was supposed to perform was
(a) 16 (b) 12
(c) 10 (d) 8.

7. The three-fold objectives of purusharthas of life were respectively
(a) Religion, livelihood and sex
(b) Moral, material and sensual needs of man
(c) Spiritual, material and moral ideals
(d) Morality, wealth and luxury.

8. The term varna was used in the Vedic period to donate
(a) Professional groups
(b) Distinctions between the Aryans and the non-Aryans
(c) Both (a) and (b) above
(d) The four castes.

9. The smritis permit a man to marry a girl
(a) Form his own varna
(b) Form any of the varna lower than his own
(c) Both (a) and (b) above
(d) Form a varna higher than his own.

10. Punarbhu was a
(a) Mixed caste
(b) Remarried widow
(c) Child born of a widow
(d) Divorced woman.

11. Out of the eight forms of marriages prevalent in ancient India, the most ideal form of marriage was
(a) Brahma (b) Daiva
(c) Arsha (d) Gandharva.

12. The term dvija i.e. twice-born was given to the
    (a) Brahmins
    (b) Brahmins and Kshatriyas
    (c) To the members of first three varnas
    (d) Learned Brahmins.

13. Which of the following Sanskaras or Sacraments was forbidden for women and Shudras?
    (a) Chuda-Karma
    (b) Upanayana
    (c) Nishkramana
    (d) Nama-dheya.

14. The term Dvija was used for those who could
    (a) Interdine together
    (b) Intermarry together
    (c) Wear sacred thread after upanayana
    (d) Perform all sacraments and sacrifies.

15. The Buddhist and Jain works refer to the rich Vaishya Capitalist class as
    (a) Dhanika (b) Grihapatis
    (c) Sresthi (d) Vanika.

16. The lowest place among the Shudras was assigned to
    (a) Butchers (b) Fisherman
    (c) Chandalas (d) Antyajas.

17. The categories of persons temporarily enslaved were
    (a) Enslavement by way of punishment
    (b) Prisoners of war
    (c) Enslavement of debtors
    (d) All of the above.

18. The Yavanas, Shakas, and other foreigners were absorbed in the Indian Society as
    (a) Mlechhas (b) Shudras
    (c) Sat-Shudas (d) Kshatriyas.

19. A widow could inherit the property of her deceased husband if
    (a) She had no sons
    (b) She had no male members in the family
    (c) She had been divorced before the death of her husband.
    (d) The deceased husband had a will to this effect.

20. The detailed account of the Nagarakas in Vatsayayana's Kamasutra is of the
    (a) Nouveau-riche of the urban areas
    (b) City-bred wealthy man of fashion
    (c) Urban people of loose morals
    (d) Rich Urban people.

21. The Ganikas or courtesans were given respectable status in society because
    (a) They were highly cultured and educated women.
    (b) They were well-versed in dance, music and etiquettes of the day.
    (c) Both (a) and (b) above
    (d) They merely entertained the people.

22. According to Manu and Yajanavalkya marriages could be performed
    (a) In the same varna, but not in the same Gotra
    (b) Among the men and women of the first three varnas
    (c) Both (a) and (b) above
    (d) Between a man of a higher varna and woman of a lower varna.

23. The term sapinda referred to
    (a) Blood relations on the mother's side
    (b) Persons of the same Gotra on the father's side
    (c) Both (a) and (b) above
    (d) Persons of the same varna.

24. The food or drink which was completely prohibited for the Brahmins was
    (a) Liquer
    (b) Meat
    (c) Both (a) and (b) above
    (d) Food offered by the shudras.

25. The ministers and royal counsellors were employed/ appointed from amongst the
    (a) Kashatriyas
    (b) Brahmins
    (b) Vaishyas
    (d) Antyajas.

26. Megasthenes divides Indian Society into Seven classes of which the second class was that of
    (a) Merchants
    (b) Farmers
    (b) Warriors
    (d) Philosophers and Teachers.

27. In the Mauryan Government women could be employed as
    (a) Royal bodyguards
    (b) Superintendents of weaving establishments
    (c) Intelligence agents and spies
    (d) All of the above.

28. The famous woman ruler of the Gupta period was
    (a) Kuber-naga
    (b) Prabhavati-Gupta
    (c) Rajyashri
    (d) Kumaradevi.

29. According to the Chinese traveller Huentsang a group of people who stayed outside the city limits and had to play a wooden clapper when they entered the city so that people could move away from them were
    (a) Butchers
    (b) Hunters
    (c) Shudras
    (d) Chandalas.

30. The proliferation of the Kshatriya class took place because of the
    (a) Prevalance of polygamy amongst them
    (b) Assimilation of foreigners as second class Kshatriyas
    (c) Need to create a large warrior class
    (d) All of the above.

31. The number and variety of Shudra castes greatly increased on account of the
    (a) Conquest of the backward and tribal people
    (b) Assimilation of aboriginals into the Hindu Society
    (c) Both (a) and (b) above
    (d) Assimilation of foreigners into the Hindu society.

32. The first epigraphic reference of committing Sati has been found from
    (a) Eran (M.P.) (b) Prayaga (U.P.)
    (c) Bhitari (U.P.) (d) Vidisha (M.P.).

33. The varna distinctions became pronounced in various spheres of life. In which of the following fields were these distinctions less rigid than earlier times?
    (a) Commensality (b) Craft-exclusiveness
    (c) financial matters (d) Judicial matters.

34. Lending money by a Brahmin at interest was disapproved of which of the following law-givers, however, allowed him to lend at low interest to "wicked people"?
    (a) Apastambha (b) Patanjali
    (c) Manu (d) Brihaspati.

35. The term dvija which originally stood for the three higher classes, began increasingly to be used during the Gupta period only for:
    (a) Brahmins and Kshatriyas
    (b) Brahmins and Vaishyas
    (c) Brahmins
    (d) Brahmins and Rajputs.

36. The status of which of the following could be said to have same what improved during the Mouryan period?
(a) Kshatriyas (b) Vaishyas
(c) Shudras (d) Untouchables.

37. Which of the following was not one of the factors responisble for professional as castes
(a) Tribal affiliations
(b) Emergence of professional associations
(c) Development of new crafts
(d) The desire of the law-givers to maintain social purity.

38. What was the primary social significance of the caste system?
(a) It helped in organising the economic activity of the community
(b) It provided social security
(c) It helped in the maintenance of racial purity
(d) It controlled social tensions.

39. Which of the following correctly indicates the dominant class composition of the south Indian society?
(a) Brahmins, Kshatriyas and Shudras
(b) Kshatriyas, Vaishyas and Untouchables
(c) Brahmins, Shudras and Untouchables
(d) Brahmins, Vaishyas and Shudras.

40. The assimilation of foreigners into a caste based society was a problem for the social theorists. What was the status assigned to the earlier foreign immigrants by Manu?
(a) Kshatriyas (b) Fallen Kshyatriyas
(b) Shudras (d) Mlechhas.

41. With which of the following are the later foreign immigrants, who came after the fall of the imperial Guptas identified?
(a) Kshatriyas (b) Fallen Kshatriyas
(b) Rajputs (d) Mlechhas.

42. Why did the institution of slavery tend to become weak?
    (a) There were numerous kinds of slaves
    (b) They were not engaged in productive activities
    (c) They were treated humanely on account of the Smriti laws
    (d) They were regarded as a part of the household.

43. The text books enumerate eight types of marriage only the first four of which were generally approved and were permissible to Brahmins which of the following was not generally approved?
    (a) Brahma (b) Gandharva
    (c) Daiva (d) Arsa.

44. To which of the following traditional categories did the svayamvara form of marriage, which later become popular among Kshatriyas belong?
    (a) Brahma (b) Gandharva
    (c) Daiva (d) Arsa.

45. What was the status assigned to a person born of an anuloma marriage?
    (a) Same as that of the father
    (b) Same as that of the mother
    (c) In between that of the two parents
    (d) Lower than that of either parent.

46. The caste assigned to a cross between a Brahmin male and a Shudra female was
    (a) Kshatriya (b) Vaishya
    (c) Shudra (d) Nishada.

47. Illegitimate offspring of a Brahmin couple were counted as
    (a) Brahmins (b) Kastriyas
    (c) Vaishyas (d) Shudras.

48. Which of the following sects gave woman an important place in their cult and instituted orders of female ascetics?
    (a) Jains (b) Buddhists
    (c) Ajivikas (d) Tantric Sects.

49. The life of elite and sophisticated urbanites as described by Vatsyayana indicates
    (a) The emergence of cities as centres of fashions
    (b) The rise of rich merchants
    (c) The rise of fashion consciouness
    (d) The emergence of rich and sophisticated urban moneyed class.

50. Stridhana was the personal property of a woman in the form of her
    (a) Jewellery and clothes
    (b) Dowery received from her father
    (c) Property inherited from her mother
    (d) All of the above.

ANSWERS

1.	(a)	2.	(c)	3.	(c)	4.	(a)
5.	(a)	6.	(a)	7.	(b)	8.	(b)
9.	(c)	10.	(b)	11.	(a)	12.	(c)
13.	(b)	14.	(c)	15.	(b)	16.	(c)
17.	(d)	18.	(d)	19.	(a)	20.	(b)
21.	(c)	22.	(c)	23.	(c)	24.	(a)
25.	(b)	26.	(b)	27.	(d)	28.	(b)
29.	(d)	30.	(b)	31.	(c)	32.	(a)
33.	(b)	34.	(b)	35.	(c)	36.	(c)
37.	(d)	38.	(b)	39.	(c)	40.	(b)
41.	(c)	42.	(b)	43.	(b)	44.	(c)
45.	(c)	46.	(d)	47.	(d)	48.	(d)
49.	(d)	50.	(c)				

4
THE MAURYAN EMPIRE

1. Who of the following dedicated the caves in Nagarjuni Hills to the Ajivikas?
   (a) Kunala (b) Dasharatha
   (c) Samprati (d) Indrapalit.

2. Who of the following was the last of the Mauryas, assassinated by his commander in chief Pushyamitra, the founder of the Shunga dynasty?
   (a) Samprati
   (b) Devavarman
   (c) Shatadhanvah
   (c) Brihadratha.

3. How long did the entire Mauryan dynasty last according to the Puranas?
   (a) 218 years (b) 137 years
   (b) 85 years (c) 152 years.

4. Which of the following supposed causes of decline and disintegration of the Mauryan empire is the least likely?
   (a) Succession of weak kings after Asoka and the partition of the empire after Asoka
   (b) Military inactivity on account of Asoka's pacifist policies
   (c) Brahmanical revolt against the pro-Buddhist policy of Asoka
   (d) Absence of national consciousness and representative institutions.

5. Which of the following was not one of the reason for gradual weakening of the Mauryan finances?
   (a) Need for vast revenues to maintain a huge but inactive army
   (b) Need for finance to maintain a very large bureaucracy
   (c) Unfavourable balance of trade with foreign countries
   (d) The strain on the exchequer of Asoka's charitable public works.

6. Which of the following was a measure adopted by the later Mauryas to meet the needs of a depleted treasury?
   (a) Increase in taxes
   (b) Imposition of new taxes
   (c) Debasement of currency
   (d) Increase of exports.

7. Pushyamitra Sunga, who killed the last Mauryan ruler Brihadratha and founded the Sunga dynasty, was a
   (a) Prime Minister of the Maurya
   (b) General of the Mauryas
   (c) Both (a) and (b) above
   (d) Feudatory ruler.

8. The Mauryan government was
   (a) An autocracy
   (b) An absolute monarchy
   (c) A benevolent despotism
   (d) A centralized despotism.

9. Which of the following statements about the Mauryan kings is not correct?
   (a) They had extensive powers encompassing administrative, judicial, and legislative functions
   (b) They laid claim to divinity
   (c) Appointments to the most important offices were made by the ruler him-self
   (d) The kings often laid down codes of regulation for the guidence of their officers and the people.

10. Which of the following was not one of the checks on the powers of the Mauryan Kings?
    (a) Customs of the land
    (b) Guilds
    (c) Brahmins
    (d) Mantri-parishad.

11. Which of the following would be the most accurate description of the Mauryan monarchy under Asoka?
    (a) Enlightened despotism
    (b) Centralized autocracy
    (c) Paternal despotism
    (d) Guided democracy.

12. Which of the following statements about the legislative process during this period is not correct?
    (a) Legislation was largely a matter of confirming social usage
    (b) The king had a fairly free hand intaking decisions
    (c) Certain matters concerning professional ethics were regulated by the guilds
    (d) The king was expected to consult his ministers but the final decision lay with him alone.

13. Which of the following statements about the Mauryan Council of Minister is not correct?
    (a) The members of the council were personally selected by the king
    (b) The number of members of the council was fixed and it consisted of three councillors and a Chief Minister
    (c) It was specially consuited in times of emergency
    (d) It may have acted as a political check on the king.

14. The largest number of officers of the central administration were associated with the duties of
    (a) Social welfare
    (b) Administration of Justice
    (c) Public works
    (d) Revenue administration.

15. The officer of the Central Government, who was in charge of collection of revenue was
    (a) Adhyaksha or Superintendent of Departments
    (b) Sannidhata or High Treasurer
    (c) Samaharta or Collector General
    (d) Karmika or Clerk.

16. Which of the following authorities describes the offices of the superintedents of various departments and their duties?
    (a) Kautilya (b) Megasthenes
    (c) Arrian (d) Strabo.

17. Which of the following was not one of the departments administered by the superintendents?
    (a) Store-house
    (b) Fisheries
    (c) Passport and prostitutes
    (d) Weights and measures.

18. Who of the following was responsible for collection of taxes at the intermediate level of administration, between the district and the village?
    (a) Gopa (b) Rajuka
    (c) Sthanika (d) Pativedakas.

19. The officers, who were special reporters and had district access to the king were
    (a) Pulisani (b) Pativedakas
    (c) Lipikara (d) Tirthas.

20. The most important duty of the city superintendent or nagaraka was
    (a) Law and order (b) Cleanliness
    (c) Fire precautions (d) Famine relief.

21. In describing city administration, Megasthenes mentions six committees. Indian sources do not directly mention the existence of these committees but their functions are relatable to the duties of
    (a) Mahamattas (b) Nagaraka
    (c) Adhyakshas (d) Yuktas.

22. Which of the following categories of troops listed by Kautilya constituted the standing army of the king?
    (a) Hired troops
    (b) Soldiers belonging to corporations
    (c) Hereditary troops
    (d) Feudatory troops.

23. Which of the following did not form part of the traditional four arms of the Indian army?
    (a) Navy
    (b) Elephants
    (c) Cavalry
    (d) Chariots.

24. Innovations introduced by the Mauryas in the military organisation were the establishment of
    (a) Navy
    (b) Transport and Comissioariat
    (c) Both (a) and (b) above
    (d) The Army Medical and Nursing corps.

25. Why, during the Mauryan period, was the registration of birth and deaths compulsory and also annual census of population conducted?
    (a) To know the demographic pattern
    (b) For law and order purposes
    (c) For the purpose of taxation
    (d) Both (b) and (c) above.

26. Which of the following public health measures was not punishable under the Mauryan public health laws?
    (a) Throwing dirt, mud or dead bodies on public thoroughfares
    (b) Polluting the water tanks or sources of water
    (c) Taking the dead bodies for cremation or burial along paths not meant for the purpose
    (d) Treating patients and selling herbs and drugs without securing registration.

27. Which of the following wings was not part of the espionage system described by Kautilya?
    (a) Crime Branch
    (b) Special Branch
    (b) Political Branch
    (d) Foreign Intelligence.

28. Which of the following was not the function of the special intelligence branch?
    (a) V.I.P. security
    (b) Political intelligence
    (c) Counter intelligence
    (d) Revenue intelligence.

29. Which of the Judicial reforms was not introduced by Asoka ?
    (a) Grant of three days' reprieve to the condemned prisoners
    (b) Introduction of uniformity injudicial procedure and punishment
    (c) Ensuring judicial impartiality and fairness
    (d) Liberalising the rigorous punishments.

30. According to the Junagarh Rock Inscription of Rudradaman during the reign of one of the following rulers a dam was built on the Sudarshan lake to facilitate water supply to the neighbouring countryside in Saurashtra. The ruler who got the said dam built was
    (a) Chandragupta Maurya
    (b) Bindusara
    (c) Asoka
    (d) Dasharatha.

31. Megasthenes states that Indian society was divided into seven classes, namely, philosophers, farmers, herdsmen, artisans, soldiers, overseers and councillars. On what consideration does this division appear to have been based?
    (a) Social (b) Economic
    (c) Political (d) Religious.

32. The first class mentioned by Megasthenes, namely, the philosophers, is believed to represent
(a) Brahmins (b) Kshatriyas
(c) Vaisyas (d) None of the above.

33. Which of the following was one of the most significant privileges of the Brahmins?
(a) Exemption from capital punishment
(d) Exemption from taxation
(c) Freedom from all regulation of the state
(d) Permission to own land.

34. Which of the following gives the correct order of the first three varnas according to their importance during the Mauryan period?
(a) Brahmins, Kshtriyas, Vaisyas
(b) Vaisyas, Brahmins, Kshatriyas
(c) Kshtriyas, Brahmins, Vaisyas
(d) Kshatriyas, Vaisyas, Brahmins.

35. Which of the following was not one of the symptoms which showed that the caste system did not work smoothly during the period?
(a) The support of the vaisyas for such heterodox sects as Buddhism and Jainism
(b) Organisation of artisans into guilds
(c) Indulgence of sudras in criminal activities
(d) Belief in the Kshatriyas as ideal rulers.

36. To which of the following varnas did the cultivators mostly belong?
(a) Brahmins (b) Kshatriya
(c) Vaisya (d) Sudra.

37. Kautilya classified the spies into
(a) Sansthah stationary spies
(b) Sancharah wandering spies
(c) Both (a) and (b) above
(d) Gudha purusha-secret agents.

38. According to the indigenous sources including Asokan epigraphs slavery existed in India during the Mauryan period, but Megasthenes said "all Indians are free and not one of them is a slave" on what grounds did he infer so?
    (a) Their status was not much different from hired labourers
    (b) They could own property and also earn for themselves
    (c) In some cases they could also buy back their freedom
    (d) Both (a) and (b) above.

39. The most common occupation of slaves during the Mauryan period was to work as
    (a) Agricultural labour
    (b) Domestic servants
    (c) Industrial labour
    (d) Labourers in the army.

40. What did the term vishti stands for during the Mauryan Period?
    (a) Province (b) District
    (c) Forced labour (d) Seasonal conditions

41. Why did Megasthenes divide Indian Society into seven classes instead of the usual four?
    (a) Because there was proliferation of castes
    (b) Megasthenes included outcastes
    (c) Megasthenes was confused between castes and classes of men engaged in various occupations
    (d) He divided society into main occupational groups.

42. During the Mauryan times royal houses were nastly built of
    (a) Baked bricks (b) Wood
    (c) Mud and Lime (d) Stones.

43. In the Mauryan period tax evasion was punished with
    (a) Death
    (b) Confiscation of goods
    (b) Flogging
    (d) Imprisonment.

44. In the Mauryan empire 10 per cent valorem excise duties were levied on
   (a) Liquor
   (b) Imported goods
   (b) Manufactured goods
   (d) All the above.

45. Which of the following was not a state monopoly during the Mauryan Period?
   (a) Mines and forests
   (b) Pearl fisheries
   (c) Ferries and bridges
   (d) Slaughter houses and gambling houses.

46. Which of the following modern methods of administration was not prevalent during the Mauryan Peirod?
   (a) Registration of foreigners
   (b) Issue of licences to merchants
   (c) Regulating weights and measures
   (d) Supply of safe drinking water in towns and cities.

47. Which of the following Asokan inscriptions makes a specific reference to taxation?
   (a) Rummindei Inscription
   (b) Nigalisagar Inscription
   (c) Kandahar Inscription
   (d) Barabar Cave Inscription.

48. The most famous centre of learning during the Mauryan period was
   (a) Taxila (b) Ujjain
   (c) Nalanda (d) Vallabhi.

49. Guilds were an intermediate step between
   (a) A family and a society
   (b) A society and a community
   (c) A tribe and a caste
   (d) A tribe and a society.

50. The masterpieces of Mauryan art were the
   (a) Stupas
   (b) Ashokan Pillars
   (c) Sculpture
   (d) Both (b) and (c) above.

51. The lowest order in the social scale of Mauryan society was not a slave but the outcaste. Which of the following statements about the outcastes is not correct?
   (a) Their caste names referred directly to their profession or work
   (b) They accepted the position of social obstractism
   (c) They lived together with their families outside the towns
   (d) They were not allowed to perform any rituals.

52. During the Mauryan period which of the following rights of the king implied his ownership of the land?
   (a) His right to collect rent for the land
   (b) His right to collect tax on the produce of the land
   (c) His right to demand a compulsory second crop in times of heed
   (d) The classification of the crown lands.

53. Which building of the Mauryan period was appreciated by Megasthenes as more magnificent than the palaces of Susa and Ecbatana?
   (a) The Mauryan Palace at Pataliputra
   (b) The Relic Tower at Taxila
   (c) The Mauryan Court at Pataliputra
   (d) The Mauryan gardens at Rajagriha and Pataliputra.

54. Which of the following was not one of the items of expenditure under public works?
   (a) Roads and buildings
   (b) Irrigation works and wells
   (c) Construction of temples
   (d) Construction of rest-houses and hospitals.

55. The expansion of village settlements during the Mauryan Period was accompanied by the growth of trade which of the following was not one of the reason which helped in this process?
(a) Development of internal communications
(b) Peaceful relations with foreign countries
(c) Technological breakthroughs achieved in various trade crafts
(d) Political unification of the country.

56. What was the main advantage of the guild system from the point of view of the state?
(a) It ensured a steady production and supply of goods.
(b) It regulated employment and payment of fair wages.
(c) It facilitated the collection of taxes.
(d) It ensured the quality of goods production.

57. The use of currency became a fairly common feature of the Mauryan Period which of the following was not one of the main purposes for which money was used?
(a) Trade
(b) Payment of salaries to officers
(c) Taxes
(d) Banking.

58. The metals, mainly used for mounting coins during the Mauryan Period, were:
(a) Gold and Silver
(b) Silver and Copper
(c) Copper and Bronze
(d) Lead and Bronze.

59. One of the caves built by Asoka and dedicated to the Ajivika sect is:
(a) Nagarjuna Cave
(b) Jarasandha Cave at Rajagriha
(c) Sudama Cave at Barabara hills
(d) Bhartihari Cave at Ujjain.

60. The Asokan Pillar found at which of the following sites is considered to be the most grateful of all Asokan Pillar?
   (a) Laurya-Nandangarh (b) Rampurva
   (c) Barnath (d) Sarnath.

61. Which of the following is not one of the animals carved on the Sarnath Pillars?
   (a) Humped Bull (b) Deer
   (c) Elephant (d) Horse.

62. Which of the following is the most striking feature of the Asokan Pillars?
   (a) Monolithic structure (b) Carving
   (c) Polish (d) Quality of stone.

63. The red sand stones for Asokan Pillars were mainly quarried from
   (a) Taxila (b) Chunar
   (c) Aravali Hills (d) Both (b) and (c) above.

64. It has been suggested that the pillar capitals were all sculpted by craftsmen from the same region. What is the basis for this hypothesis?
   (a) Closeness in style to Persian craftsmanship.
   (b) Uniformity of workmanship.
   (c) Reference in one of Asoka's edicts to his harming imported Persian craftsman.
   (d) Remains of unfinished Pillar capitals from Taxila.

65. The Mauryan empire had brisk foreign trade with
   (a) West Asia
   (b) Hellenistic West
   (c) Both (a) and (b) above
   (d) South-east Asia.

66. The historian, who strongly argued that the Mauryan empire declined as a result of Brahmanical revolt against anti-Brahmanical and pro-Buddhist policies of Asoka was
   (a) H.C. Ray Choudhuri (b) H.P. Sastri
   (c) R.K. Mukerjee (d) D.R. Bhandarkar.

67. Which of the following is the least important as a source material for the Mauryan history?
    (a) Numismatic evidence
    (b) Literary sources
    (c) Epigraphic sources
    (d) Foreign accounts.

68. The Asokan inscriptions and their Brahmi script were first deciphered by
    (a) Alexander Cunningham
    (b) Max Muller
    (c) James Princep
    (d) Mortimer Wheeler.

69. One of the edicts discovered in 1951, which gave the name of its as King Asoka, Priyadarsi, is
    (a) Mansehra Edict
    (b) Girnar Edict
    (c) Maski Edict
    (d) Sarnath Inscription.

70. The latest inscriptions of Asoka were discovered from
    (a) Kandahar bi-lingual Inscriptions
    (b) Sannatai Inscriptions
    (c) Maski Inscription
    (d) Bhabru Edict.

71. Which of the following is not one of the edicts and inscriptions issued by Asoka?
    (a) Junagadh Rock Inscription
    (b) Bhabru Edict
    (c) Kalinga Edict
    (d) Delhi-Topara Pillar Inscription.

72. Which of the following inscriptions of Asoka was discovered on the outskrits of New Delhi in 1966?
    (a) Ahraura Inscription (b) Kandahar Inscription
    (c) Bhapur Inscription (d) Bairat Inscription.

73. Which of the following is not correctly matched?
    (a) Asoka's mother-Subhadrangi or Dharma
    (b) Asoka's wife-Mahadevi of Vidisha
    (c) Asoka's son-in-law-Agnibrahma
    (d) Asoka's younger brother-Kunala.

74. The script used in the two northern major rock edicts of Asoka at Mansehra and Shahbazgarhi is
    (a) Aramaic (b) Greek
    (c) Kharosthi (d) Both (b) and (c) above.

75. The Kandahar inscriptions were written in—script
    (a) Kharosthi (b) Greek
    (c) Aramaic (d) Both (b) and (c) above.

76. Which of the following Buddhist literary sources does not provide information about the Mauryas?
    (a) Mahaparibbanasutta (b) Dipavamsa
    (c) Maharamsa (d) Asokavadan.

77. One of the following secular literature on the period which of the most important single sources?
    (a) Purans
    (b) Mudrarakshasa of Visa Khadtta
    (c) Arthashastra of Kautilya
    (d) Indika of Megasthenes.

78. A Mauryan King, who in his old age abdicated the throne and followed the Jain saint Bhadrabahu to the south, was?
    (a) Chandragupta Maurya
    (b) Bindusara
    (c) Dasharatha
    (d) Samprati.

79. Who has stated that Chandragupta Maurya as a young man had met Alexandra face to face in the Punjab?
    (a) Plutarch (b) Justin
    (c) Megasthenes (d) Arrian.

80. Unfortunately, the original document of Megasthenes, Indika has not survived and what remain are only quotations from it in various classical texts. Which of the following was not one of the letter Greek writers to qute from Megasthenes?
(a) Pliny (b) Strabo
(c) Diodorus (d) Arrian.

81. Which of the following post-Asokan inscriptions does not help us in understanding certain aspects of the Mauryan history?
(a) Priyadarsi Inscription at Taxila
(b) Sohgaura copper-plate Inscription
(c) Nagar juni Hill Cave Inscriptions of Dasharatha
(d) Meharatha.

82. One of the non-Indian Buddhist texts built around the personality of Asoka, is—
(a) Maharamsa (b) Dipavamsa
(c) Divyaradan (d) Asokavadan.

83. Asoka's Pillar inscriptions, which were shifted from the original sites to Delhi, were:
(a) Meerut and Topara Pillars
(b) Sanchi and Saranath Pillars
(c) Lumbini and Rampurwa Pillars
(d) Kusambi and Lauriyanandangrah Pillars.

84. The chronology of the Mauryas hinges round the date of:
(a) Alexander's invasion
(b) Death of Mahavira
(c) Death of Buddha
(d) Year of Asoka's coronation.

85. The Greek sources mention Chandragupta Maurya as:
(a) Sandro Cottus
(b) Andro Cottus
(c) Both (a) and (b) above
(d) Chandro Kottus.

86. Chandragupta Maurya launched his victorious career by first over throwing the:-
   (a) Greek's from the north-west frontier
   (b) Nandas from Magadha
   (c) Both (a) and (b) above
   (d) Himalayan Chief Parvataka.

87. For the early life of Chandragupta Maurya we have to depend on the
   (a) Puranas
   (b) Buddhist sources
   (c) Jain sources
   (d) Greek accounts.

88. How many years after the Buddha's death did Asoka come to the throne according to the Sri Lankan chronicles?
   (a) 218 (b) 155
   (c) 275 (d) 278.

89. The Buddhist regard Chandragupta Maurya to be
   (a) A son of the Chief of peacock-tamers
   (b) A kshatriya of the Moriya clan
   (c) A son of Mura, one of the wives of the Nanda King
   (d) A son of the Chief of Moriyanagar.

90 Who was popularly known as Vishnugupta
   (a) Vikramaditya (b) Bindusar
   (c) Harshavardhan (d) Chanakya.

91. Which of the following is considered to be a controversial part of the treaty of 303 B.C. between Chandragupta and Seleucus?
   (a) Seleucus surrendered his large territories to Chandragupta
   (b) Chandragupta made a gift of 500 elephants to Seleucus
   (c) Seleucus gave his daughter in marriage to Chandragupta
   (d) A Greek envoy (Megasthenes) was accredited to the Mauryan Court at Pataliputra.

92. Which of the following inscriptions proves Chandragupta Maurya's conquest of Western India?
(a) Junagarh Rock Edict of Rudradaman
(b) Girnar Rock Edict of Asoka
(c) Sopra Rock Edict of Asoka
(d) Separate (Kalinga) Rock Edict.

93. Which of the following literary works furnishes the details of the revolution by which Chandragupta Maurya, with the help of Kautilya overthrow the Nandas?
(a) Mudrarakshasa of Vishakhadatta
(b) Bana's Harsa Charita
(c) Devi Chandragupta of Vishakhadatta
(d) Parisishtaparvan.

94. Who was the envoy of the Egyptian King Ptolemy Philadelphos in the Mauryan Court?
(a) Dionysius (b) Deimac Hos
(c) Megasthenes (d) Diodarus.

95. The Mauryan King Bindusara requested the son and successor of Seleucus Nikator named to send him some figs, raisin wine and a Greek philosopher:
(a) Ptolemy Philadelphos
(b) King Antiochus of Syria
(c) King Antiochus Theos of Syria
(d) Alexander of Epirus.

96. The Jain text which describes that Chandragupta embraced Jainism towards the end of his life, is:
(a) Ratnamalika (b) Jayadhavala
(c) Parishisthaparvan (d) Dravya-Samgraha.

97. In which of the following regions of his kingdom did Bindusara have to face two revolts, one of which was quelled by Asoka?
(a) Saurashtra (b) Taxila
(c) The Deccan (d) Ujjaini.

98. Who replaced Megasthenes as the ambassador of Syrian King in the court of Bindusara?
   (a) Dionysius (b) Deimachos
   (c) Ptolemy Philadelphos (d) Diodorus.

99. In which of the following sects Bindusara interested?
   (a) Buddhism (b) Jainism
   (c) Ajivikas (d) Lokayata.

100. At which of the following places was Asoka stationed as Viceroy at the time of Bindusara's death?
   (a) Taxila (b) Ujjain
   (c) Saurashtra (d) Tosali.

101. In which of the following edicts does Asoka use the term "Priyadarsi King of Magadha."
   (a) Minor Edict at Kausambi
   (b) Maski Edict
   (c) Bhabru Edict
   (d) Sarnath Pillar Edict.

102. The first major event of the reign of Asoka was the Kalinga war and conquest of Kalinga. Which of the following was the actual cause of Kalinga war?
   (a) Kalinga was a thorn in the body-politic of the empire.
   (b) "Asoka wished to control both the land and sea routes to South India"
   (c) Kalinga had grown very powerful during the reign of Bindusara and was posing a danger to the Mauryan empire
   (d) Independent Kalinga posed a threat to the Mauryan possessions in Andhra and Bengal.

103. Which of the following was not the result of the Kalinga war?
   (a) The number of casualties of combatants and non-combatants is stated to have been around four lakhs.
   (b) The cruel consequences of war revolutionised the personality and public policies of Asoka
   (c) He waged no wars after the Kalinga war
   (d) The strength of the Mauryan army was curtailed.

104. Which of the following does not constitute the doctrinal aspects of Asoka's dhamma?
(a) Non-injury (b) Restraint in behaviour
(c) Equal treatment to all (d) Fear of sin

105. Which of the following has not been enumerated as a sin in the Asokan edicts?
(a) Rage or fury (b) Cruelty and anger
(c) Pride and chug (d) Greed and Passions.

ANSWERS

1.	(b)	2.	(d)	3.	(b)	4.	(d)
5.	(c)	6.	(c)	7.	(b)	8.	(c)
9.	(b)	10.	(c)	11.	(c)	12.	(c)
13.	(b)	14.	(d)	15.	(c)	16.	(a)
17.	(b)	18.	(c)	19.	(b)	20.	(a)
21.	(c)	22.	(c)	23.	(a)	24.	(c)
25.	(d)	26.	(d)	27.	(c)	28.	(d)
29.	(d)	30.	(a)	31.	(b)	32.	(a)
33.	(b)	34.	(a)	35.	(b)	36.	(d)
37.	(c)	38.	(d)	39.	(b)	40.	(c)
41.	(c)	42.	(b)	43.	(a)	44.	(d)
45.	(d)	46.	(d)	47.	(a)	48.	(a)
49.	(c)	50.	(a)	51.	(d)	52.	(c)
53.	(a)	54.	(c)	55.	(c)	56.	(c)
57.	(c)	58.	(b)	59.	(c)	60.	(a)
61.	(b)	62.	(c)	63.	(d)	64.	(b)
65.	(c)	66.	(b)	67.	(a)	68.	(b)
69.	(c)	70.	(b)	71.	(a)	72.	(d)
73.	(d)	74.	(c)	75.	(d)	76.	(d)
77.	(c)	78.	(a)	79.	(b)	80.	(a)
81.	(d)	82.	(c)	83.	(a)	84.	(c)
85.	(c)	86.	(a)	87.	(b)	88.	(a)
89.	(b)	90.	(d)	91.	(c)	92.	(a)
93.	(a)	94.	(a)	95.	(b)	96.	(c)
97.	(b)	98.	(b)	99.	(c)	100.	(b)
101.	(c)	102.	(a)	103.	(d)	104.	(d)
105.	(d)						

5
SANGAM LITERATURE

1. The last anthology or group of Sangam Literature known as Ten idylls', is:
   (a) Tolkappiyam (b) Karal
   (c) Manimekalai (d) Pattupattu.
2. The centre of Sangam Literature and the patrons of Sangam poets were:
   (a) The Cheras of Vanji
   (b) The Cholas of Vraiyur
   (c) The Pandyas of Madurai
   (d) All the above.
3. Which of the following is not a great epic of the Sangam literature:
   (a) Silappadikaram (b) Manimekalai
   (c) Pattupattu (d) Ettutoggai.
4. The Greco-Roman merchants visiting South India during the Sangam Age were referred to in the Tamil literature as:
   (a) Yavanas (b) Pahalvas
   (c) Yauvanas (d) Ayyavanas.
5. Which of the following was not one of the royal dynasties of the Tamil country during the Sangam Age?
   (a) Pandya (b) Pallava
   (c) Chera (d) Chola.

6. To which of the following dynasties did Karikala, the famous king of this period, belong?
   (a) Chera (b) Chola
   (c) Pandya (d) Pallava.

7. Which of the following dynasties were constantly at war with the Cheras during the later Sangam Age?
   (a) Chola
   (b) Pandya
   (c) Ikshvaku
   (d) Pallava.

8. Which of the following was not one of the conventional checks on a king's power?
   (a) Customs
   (b) Maxims of the wise
   (c) Occasional intercessions of the ministers
   (d) Dictates of the priests.

9. The correct Tamil designation of the ministers during the Sangam Age was:
   (a) Amaichchon or Amaichchar
   (b) Mantri
   (c) Amatya
   (d) Surram.

10. The spies during the Sangam Age were known as:
    (a) Spasas (b) Dutas
    (c) Orrars (d) Sanjayans.

11. Small village assemblies during the Sangam Age were known as:
    (a) Manaram (b) Ambalan
    (c) Avai (d) Podiyil.

12. The Provinces during the Sangam age were known as mandalams and mandalams were further subdivided into:
    (a) Nadu (b) Kurram
    (c) Kottam (d) UR.

13. Which of the following statement was not one of the better known agricultural product of the Sangam Age?
(a) wheat (b) rice
(c) sugarcane (d) turmeric.

14. The richest and biggest land-owning class during the Sangam Age were:
(a) Brahmins (b) Velas
(c) Nayaks (d) Ulavar.

15. The *INDIAN* bird or animal most widely exported to the Roman world was:
(a) Monkey (b) Peacocks
(c) Tiger (d) Deer.

16. The chief centre or meeting point of the Indo-Roman trade was:
(a) Arikamedu
(b) Alexandria
(c) Madurai
(d) Muziris.

17. A good contemporary account of the trade between the Tamil state of the Sangam Age and Greece and Rome has been given in:
(a) Das Wurfelspiel in *alten Indien*
(b) The Sangam work Pattinapalai
(c) Periplus of the erythrean sea
(d) Ptolemy's Geography.

18. A Tamil King who is said to have sent the earliest embassy to August at Athens about 20 B.C. was a .... king.
(a) Pandyan (b) Chola
(c) Chera (d) Pallava.

19. Which of the following was not one of the important articles of export?
(a) Spice and perfumes (b) Jewels
(c) Fine Textiles (d) Sugar.

20. Which of the following was the main article of import?
(a) Gold and silver (b) Pottery and glassware
(c) Wine and slave girl (d) Horses.

21. After the death of which one of the following Roman king was the trade conducted more by barter than by coins on account of the financial difficulties of the Roman empire?
(a) Augustus (b) Claudius
(c) Pius (d) Nero.

22. Which of the following was a great centre of cotton trade?
(a) Uraiyur (b) Korkai
(c) Tondi (d) Musiri of Muzuris.

23. The Chera king who is said to have gone to North *INDIA* to get a Himalayan stone to make the image of Goddess *KANNAGI* was:
(a) Imayavaramban (b) Senaguttuvan
(c) Kuttvancheral (d) Nedumcheral Adan.

24. Which of the following was not one of the methods of disposal of the dead practised in the Sangam Age?
(a) Cremation
(b) Simple burial
(c) Urn burial
(d) Giving watery grave to the dead.

25. The most favourite god of the Tamils during the Sangam Age was:
(a) Indra (b) Murugan
(c) Tirumal (d) Varuna.

26. Which of the following was not one of the popular deities of the Sangam Age?
(a) Indra and Murugan
(b) Siva and Vishnu
(c) Krishna and Balaram
(d) Ganesh.

27. At Puhar or Kaveripumpattinam a great festival described Vividly by the Sangam Epics was held in honour of Lord:
    (a) Venkateswara (b) Murugan
    (c) Indra (d) Svamimalai.

28. In which of the following respects did the Romans not profoundly influenced *INDIAN* life and culture?
    (a) Coinage (b) Art
    (c) Astronomy (d) Fashions.

29. The Goddess Kannagi, whose many temples were erected during the Sangam Age, was the goddess of
    (a) Wisdom (b) Learning
    (c) Chastity (d) Prowess.

30. Which of the following Sangam works tries to expound the excellence of Buddhism?
    (a) Manimekalia
    (b) Silappadikaram
    (c) Kurla
    (d) Tolkappiyam.

31. The basis on which the chronology of the Sangam Literature is fixed between the first to third century A.D., was—
    (a) King Gajabalree I of Sri Lanka was contemporary of the Chera monarch Senaguttuvan.
    (b) Stri king similarity between the Sangam poems and Greco-Roman accounts on trade.
    (c) Both (a) and (b)
    (d) Reference to the 'Chola-Chera-Pandya' kingdoms in Asokan edicts.

32. Which of the following was not one of the ideas of Sanskrit literature incorporated into Sangam Literature?
    (a) Worship of Indra as the principal deity
    (b) Arundhati as the ideal of chastity
    (c) The concept of three-foeld debt of man
    (d) Uttar-karu as a land of perpetual enjoyment.

33. Which of the following does not testify to the impact of Aryan culture on the Sangam age?
    (a) Incorporation of Sanskrit ideas into Sangam Literature.
    (b) The anxiety to connect the local dynasties with the events of Mahabharata.
    (c) The worship of the forest tree and animal deities.
    (d) The concept of marriage as a sacrament attended with rituals.

34. Which of the following statement about the institution of kingship during this period is not correct?
    (a) The form of government was hereditary monarchy
    (b) The king, whose conquering expedition was led by a mysterious wheel of gold and gem, was called Chakravartin
    (c) The crown prince was called Komahan
    (d) In the Sangam Literature we come across numerous instances of woman rulers.

35. Which of the following statements about the army of the king is not correct?
    (a) The army traditionally had four arms, namely, chariots drawn by oxen, elephants, cavalry and infantry
    (b) The captains of the army were invested with the title of enadi
    (c) The soldires wounded in battle were well attended
    (d) Death on the battlefield was considered to lead to heaven.

36. Which of the following statements about the Manaram, the sabha of this period, is not correct?
    (a) It was the common meeting place in the village
    (b) It was the highest court of justice
    (c) It also served the purpose of a political gathering
    (d) It was a general assembly dealing with all affairs.

37. During the Sangam Age a tutelary tree called kadimaram or kavalmaram was planted by the rules at a central place in the town and they took great care to protect the tree because—
    (a) It was belived that the tree had power to protect the town
    (b) The destruction of the tree was symbolic of the defeat of the ruler
    (c) Both (a) and (b)
    (d) The tree was symbolic dynastic growth.

38. During the Sangam Age war was usually declcared or provoked by—
    (a) Cutting the tutelary tree of the enemy
    (b) Lifting the cattle of the enemy
    (c) Besieging the enemy's fort
    (d) Curshing the crops of the enemy's territory under the feet of elephants.

39. Which of the following works provide a beautiful account of Madurai during the Sangam Age—
    (a) Manimekalai
    (b) Silappadikaram
    (c) Kural
    (d) Pattupattu.

40. Which of the following was not a source of income to the state?
    (a) Escheats and treasure troves.
    (b) State trading
    (c) Custom and tolls
    (d) Stamp duties on civil suits.

41. Karikala, the Chola king made a grand auction of the Kaveri water of which now a days drawn off though a new channel called Vennar Which of the following regions of Tamilnadu does it irrigate?
    (a) West Madurai (b) South Arcat
    (c) South Thanjavur (d) Chinglepet.

42. Writing about the volume of Indo-Roman trade who bitterly remarked "not a year passed without the empire paying out 100 million restores to India to the Chera land and Arbian"?

(a) Ptolemy (b) Pliny
(c) Author of Periplus (d) Caldwell.

43. Which of the following was the wonderful discovery made by Hippalus in A.D. 45 leading to increase of trade with Rome?

(a) Fitting of sails to the ships
(b) Propelling of ship with mechanical aid.
(c) The existence of the monsoon winds blowing across the Indian Ocean
(d) A shorter route from Rome to the eastern cost of India.

44. Which of the following was not one of the reasons why India had favourable balance of trade with the west?

(a) Great demand for Indian luxury goods.
(b) Import of gold by India in return for her exports.
(c) Import of coins by India.
(d) Better business sense of Indian traders.

45. Which of the following was a great customs port with an artificial harbour?

(a) Musiri (b) Tondi
(c) Puhar (d) Uraiyur.

46. Which of the following institutions did not exist during the Sangam Age?

(a) Slavery (b) Sati
(c) Ritualistic marriage (d) Courtesans.

47. Which of the following was not one of the popular beliefs and customs prevalent during the Sangam Age?

(a) There was much faith in omens and astrology.
(b) A woman with dishevelled hair was a bad omen.
(c) Rites were performed to avert the mischief of demons.
(d) Eclipse were believed to be the result of Rahu and Ketu eating up the Sun and the Moon.

48. A righteous government to the Sangam Tamils meant over which—
(a) Promoted agriculture and trade.
(b) Maintained social solidarity.
(c) Provided correct, quick and straight justice.
(d) Pursued social and ethical values.

49. One of the religious beliefs of the Sangam people, which was deities of the Sangam Age?
(a) Indra and Murugan (b) Siva and Vishnu
(c) Krishna and Balaram (d) Ganesh.

50. One of the religious beliefs of the Sangam people which was primitive in nature, was:-
(a) Worship of totemic symbols
(b) Ancestor worship
(c) Worship of stars and planets
(d) Worship of the Gods and goddess of the hill-side.

ANSWERS

1.	(d)	2.	(c)	3.	(c)	4.	(a)
5.	(b)	6.	(b)	7.	(b)	8.	(d)
9.	(a)	10.	(c)	11.	(c)	12.	(c)
13.	(a)	14.	(b)	15.	(b)	16.	(b)
17.	(c)	18.	(a)	19.	(d)	20.	(a)
21.	(d)	22.	(a)	23.	(b)	24.	(d)
25.	(b)	26.	(d)	27.	(c)	28.	(d)
29.	(c)	30.	(a)	31.	(c)	32.	(a)
33.	(c)	34.	(d)	35.	(c)	36.	(c)
37.	(c)	38.	(b)	39.	(a)	40.	(d)
41.	(c)	42.	(b)	43.	(c)	44.	(d)
45.	(c)	46.	(a)	47.	(d)	48.	(c)
49.	(d)	50.	(a)				

6

FACTS ON RELIGIOUS MOVEMENTS

1. One of the sects born in the sixth century B.C., which discarded the Theory of Karma and argued that 'man is subject to the laws of nature, was:

   (a) Bhagavata (b) Shunyavadin
   (c) Ajivika (d) Pashupata.

2. Who was the propounder of the Ajivika sect?

   (a) Purana Kassapa (b) Pakudha Kaccayana
   (c) Makkali Gosala (d) Ajita Keshakambdin.

3. The followers of which of the following sects worshipped the Asoka tree as God and carried in their hands a bunch of peacock feathers?

   (a) Shakta (b) Pashupata
   (c) Ajivika (d) Digambar Jain.

4. In which of the following years was the 2500th anniversary of the Buddha's mahapairinirvana celebrated?

   (a) 1944 (b) 1952
   (c) 1956 (d) 1958.

5. Which of the following events of the Buddha's life did not take place on the full moon of Vaishakha month?

   (a) Birth
   (b) Renunciation
   (c) Enlightenment
   (d) Mahaparinirvana.

6. Lord Buddha was born in ______ B.C.:
   (a) 623 (b) 543
   (c) 563 (d) 507.

7. Which of the following probable years of the Buddha's death is linked with Asoka's consecration and the 'dotted record' at Canton?
   (a) 544 B.C. (b) 487 B.C.
   (c) 483 B.C. (d) 485 B.C..

8. Which of the following was the real name of the Buddha?
   (a) Siddhartha (b) Tathagata
   (c) Gautama (d) Boudhayana.

9. Which of the following Buddhist symbols does not stand for the great events of the Buddha's life?
   (a) Lotus and Bull (b) Horse
   (c) His footprints (d) The Stupa.

10. Which of the following is the most popularly known name of Lord Buddha's wife?
   (a) Yashodhara (b) Gopa
   (c) Bimba (d) Sujata.

11. From the point of view of places of Buddhist pilgrimage interest, which of the following is the latest archaeological discovery?
   (a) Discovery of the Buddha's tooth relic at Bharhut in M.P.
   (b) Discovery of a Pillar indicating the actual birth place of the Buddha, at Lumbini
   (c) Sanghol—a Kushana Buddhist site
   (d) None of these.

12. What, according to the chain of Dependent Origination, is the original cause of human suffering?
   (a) Desire (b) Ignorance
   (c) Consciousness (d) Attachment.

13. Which of the following steps of the Eight-fold Path relates to the attention paid to the activities and weaknesses of ones body and mind?
    (a) Right thought
    (b) Right endeavour
    (c) Right recollection
    (d) Right meditation.

14. Which of the following is not one of the Four Noble sentiments that a person aspiring for nirvana should cultivate?
    (a) Metta or universal love
    (b) Karuna or compassion
    (c) Mudita or sympathetic joy
    (d) Upekkha or equanimity.

15. In which of the following contemporary Brahmanic beliefs did the Buddha show absolute faith?
    (a) God
    (b) Doctrine of Karma
    (c) Transmigration of the soul
    (d) None of these.

16. The first council was held immediately after the Buddha's death. How many years after the Buddha's death was the second Council held?
    (a) 100 (b) 200
    (c) 300 (d) 400.

17. Which of the following is not a representative of Buddhist art?
    (a) Stupa (b) Chaitya
    (c) Vihara (d) Relic towers.

18. Under the aegis of which of the following kings was the third Buddhist council held?
    (a) Asoka (b) Kanishka
    (c) Menander (d) Harsha.

19. The third Buddhist council made a new classification of the Buddhist canonical texts, by adding a third Pitaka to the existing two Pitakas . The new Pitaka was
    (a) Vinaya Pitaka
    (b) Abhidhamma
    (c) Dhamma Pitaka
    (d) Sutta Pitaka.

20. The _______ council made Sanskrit the vehicle of Buddhist scriptures:.
    (a) First (b) Second
    (c) Third (d) Fourth.

21. Which of the following was added to the Buddhist canonical texts by the Fourth Buddhist council?
    (a) Dhammapada
    (b) Jatakas
    (c) Vibhashas or commentaries
    (d) None of these.

22. Which of the following is considered the oldest orthodox Buddhist sect?
    (a) Mahayanism
    (b) Sthaviravadhins or Theravadins
    (c) Vatisputriyas
    (d) Prajnaptivadins.

23. During the reign of which of the following kings did Mahayanism formally come into existence?
    (a) Ajatashatru (b) Dharmapala
    (c) Asoka (d) Kanishka.

24. Which of the following is not a Mahayanist sect of Buddhism?
    (a) Madhyamika (b) Yogachara
    (c) Vijnangvadins (d) Sthaviravadins.

25. The famous Dhammapada —the discourages of the Buddha is a part of:
    (a) Sutta Pitaka (b) Vinaya Pitaka
    (c) Abhidhamma Pitaka (d) Digha Nikaya.

26. Which of the following Palicanons of the sthaviravadins consists of metaphysical disquisitions?
   (a) Sutta Pitaka (b) Vinaya Pitaka
   (c) Abhidhamma Pitaka (d) Dhamma Pada.

27. Which of the following is not one of the Mahayana texts?
   (a) Lalitavistara (b) Sutta Vibhanga
   (c) Saddharma-Pundarika (d) None of these.

28. Which of the following is not a biography of Lord Buddha:
   (a) Lalitavistara (b) Mahavasta
   (c) Nidankatha (d) Mahavamsa.

29. Which of the following works, included in Vaipulgasutras, is a typical Mahayana work containing all the characteristic features of that school?
   (a) Saddharmapundarika (b) Lalitavistara
   (c) Lankavatara (d) Suvarnaprabhasa.

30. Which of the following is considered the most important philosophical works of the Mahayana School?
   (a) Praijnaparamita
   (b) Avadankalpalata of Kshemendra
   (c) Lalitavistara
   (d) Lankavatara.

31. The famous Jataka stories, dealing with the previous births of Gautama Buddha are included in _______ Nikaya:
   (a) Samgutta (b) Khuddaka
   (c) Digha (d) Anguttara.

32. Who was the greatest Buddhist commentator of the Buddhist canonical literature?
   (a) Ashvaghosha (b) Buddhaghosha
   (c) Vasumitra (d) Nagarjuna.

33. Which of the following is not of the three Jewels of Buddhism?
   (a) Buddha (b) Sangha
   (c) Dhamma (d) Nirvana.

34. Which of the following was not the symbols of the Buddha used for his remembrance before the introduction of his images?
(a) Bodhi trees (b) Footprints
(c) Four Lions (d) None of these.

35. Who of the following Pali authors is believed to have written Millinda-Panho (Questions of King Milinda)?
(a) Nagasena (b) Buddhadatta
(c) Buddhaghosa (d) Dhammapala.

36. The famous Buddhist Scholar Ashvaghosha was a contemporary of:
(a) Asoka (b) Menander
(c) Kanishka (d) Harsha.

37. Nagarjuna was a friend and contemporary of the Satavahana King:
(a) Gautamiputra Sri Satakarni
(b) Vasishthiputra or Pulumaji II
(c) Pulumayi IV
(d) Yajnashri Gautamiputra Orsiri-yajna.

38. Which of the following Mahayanist Buddhist writers is regarded as the Kant of India by Dr. Stcherbatsky?
(a) Dharmakirti (b) Dingnaga
(c) Vasubandhu (d) Asanga.

39. Which of the following writers was the founder of Buddhist logic and has been called the father of Medialval Nyaya?
(a) Dharmakirti (b) Dingnaga
(c) Bhavaviveka (d) None of these.

40. Which of the following ways not one of the Buddhist scholars from China that visited India?
(a) Fa-hien
(b) Hiuen-tsang
(c) T' ai-tsung
(d) None of these.

41. The most important Buddhist mission, sent by Asoka outside India, was to:
(a) Sir Lanka (b) Burma
(c) Combodia (d) Land of the Yavanas.

42. A royal patron of Buddhism, who like Asoka tried to bring the Buddhist Sangha into strict discipline, was:
(a) Kanishka (b) Mesander
(c) Harsha (d) Dharmapala.

43. The disciple of the Buddha, who was with him at Kusinara at the time of his death, was:
(a) Sariputra (b) Ananda
(c) Nagasena (d) Ambapali.

44. Buddhism was introduced in China in the
(a) Third century B.C. (b) First century B.C.
(c) Third century A.D. (d) First century A.D..

45. The Tibetan monarch credited with introduction of Buddhism in Tibet in the seventh century A.D. is:
(a) Sron-btsan-sgam-po (b) Opal-hkhov-btsan
(c) Mu-nu-btsan-po (d) None of these.

46. The Buddhist Stupa of Borobadur, the largest and the only stupa of its type in the world, was build by the Shailendra kings in:
(a) Central Java, Indonesia (b) Angkorvat, Cambodia
(c) Rangoon, Burma (d) None of these.

47. An Indian Buddhist monk, who went to China in the first century A.D. and translated the Buddhist works in the Chinese language was:
(a) Dharmakirti (b) Asanga
(c) Kashyap Matanga (d) Nagarjuna.

48. At which of the following places has the earliest example of the Buddhist Stupa architecture been found?
(a) Sanchi (b) Sankasya
(c) Sarnath (d) Lumbini.

49. To which of the following schools of art do the earliest images of the Buddha in human form belong?
(a) Gandhara (b) Mathura
(c) Pala (d) Gupta.

50. The most beautiful images of the Buddha were curved out in the ______ school of Art.
(a) Kushana (b) Shunga
(c) Gupta (d) Pala.

51. Which of the following was not one of the common features of the non-Brahmanical and non-Vedic sects of the sixth century B.C.?
(a) Rejection of fatalism of orthodox brahmanism.
(b) Opposition to social discriminations based on caste.
(c) Stress on certain ethical principles.
(d) Emphasis on the cyclic law of the universe.

52. From which of the following is the Vaisheshika school of philosophy believed to have originated?
(a) Anuvad (b) Materialism
(c) Scepticism (d) Akriyavad.

53. On the basis of which of the following traditional records have the dates of Lord Buddha's birth and death been fixed?
(a) Chinese tradition—Cantonese records
(b) Simhalese tradition—Mahavamsa and Dipavamsa
(c) Indian Buddhist texts—Asokavadan and Divyavadan
(d) None of these.

54. Which of the following is not considered a great event in Lord Buddha's life?
(a) Marriage and birth of a son
(b) First sermon
(c) Enlightenment
(d) Nirvana or death.

55. The Buddha was born in ______.
(a) Kapilavastu (b) Lumbini
(c) Urubela (d) Rajagriha.

56. Who were the first teachers of the Buddha, after his great renunciation?
    (a) Alar and Udraka
    (b) Ananda and Ashvaghosha
    (c) Sariputra and Maudagalyayona
    (d) None of these.

57. Of the following Four Noble Truths taught by the Buddha, the basic truth was:
    (a) Existence of sorrow
    (b) Sorrow causation
    (c) Cessation of sorrow is possible by elimination of desire
    (d) None of these.

58. The Buddha called the Eight-fold Path preached by him as the Middle Path, because it was a:
    (a) Middle path preached by all religions
    (b) Eternal truth of all religions
    (c) Balanced view of life
    (d) None of these.

59. Which of the following is not a practical aspect of the Buddha's teachings?
    (a) Man is the arbiter of his own testing, not any God or Gods.
    (b) Every pleasure is illusory.
    (c) Life is nothing but a cycle of sorrows
    (d) None of these.

60. The Buddhist council were called four times to:
    (a) Compile the canonical texts
    (b) Resolve the religious disputes
    (c) Maintain unity in the sangha
    (d) All the above.

61. _________ presided over the proceedings of the first council:
    (a) Thera Yasha (b) Mahakassapa
    (c) Moggaliputta Tissa (d) Vasumitra.

62. What was the occasion for the second Buddhist council?
    (a) To prepare a complete and authentic collection of the teachings of Lord Buddha
    (b) To settle the controversy arising from the adoption of certain practices by the Vajjian monks of Vaishali
    (c) To establish the purity of the canon which had been imperilled by the rise of different sects
    (d) None of these.

63. The despatch of missionaries to the different countries of the world for the first time for the propagation of Buddhism was the result of the ______ council:
    (a) First (b) Second
    (c) Third (d) Fourth.

64. Which of the following was not one of the common beliefs of both Jainism and Buddhism?
    (a) Belief in the Law of Karma.
    (b) Belief in Atheism
    (c) Belief in Vigorous asceticism
    (d) None of these.

65. The Sarvastivadin school of Buddhism mainly flourished in:
    (a) Bengal (b) Magadha
    (c) The Punjab and NWFP (d) Maharashtra

66. Which of the following was not a disqualification for entry to the Buddhist Sangha?
    (a) Being below the age of fifteen
    (b) Suffering from infectious disease
    (c) One who had to pay debts
    (d) One who had been convicted.

67. According to the Buddha, the cause of all human sorrows is trishna which means:
    (a) Desire for worldly things
    (b) Desire for material enjoyments and worldly things
    (c) Worldly attachments
    (d) Hyperactivity of the mind.

68. The site of the Buddha's birth is marked by which of the following?
(a) Rampurwa pillar of Asoka
(b) Rummindesi pillar of Asoka
(c) Sarnath pillar of Asoka
(d) Ghositaramma monastery at Piparhawa.

69. The child Siddhartha was brought up by his aunt and stepmother:
(a) Prajapati Gautami (b) Sujata
(c) Amrapali (d) Mahamaya.

70. Which of the following is considered the most important vehicle of Buddhist ethical teachings?
(a) Jataka Stories (b) Sutta-Vibhanga
(c) Vinaya Pitaka (d) Mahavagga.

71. A Buddhist scholar, who has been described as "poet, musician, preacher, moralist, philosopher, playwright, tale-teller........., an inventor in all these arts........ he recalls Milton, Goethe, Kant and Voltarire", was:
(a) Asanga or Aryasanga (b) Nagarjuna
(c) Asvaghosha (d) Vasubandhu.

72. One the Buddhist scholars, who enjoyed great celebrity all over the Buddhist world as grammarian, philosopher and poet, was:
(a) Chandragomin (b) Santideva
(c) Vasumitra (d) Nagarjuna.

73. The Mahaparinibbna-sutta, which is a detailed account of the last days of the Buddha, is included in the ________ Nikaya of Sutta Pitaka.
(a) Majjhima (b) Digha
(c) Samyutta (d) Khuddaka.

74. How many stories are included in the Jatakas?
(a) 500 (b) 550
(c) 750 (d) 860.

75. Which of the following is the most famous non-canonical work of Buddhism, providing invaluable information on the history of India and Sri Lanka?
(a) Mahavamsa (b) Dipavamsa
(c) Harivamsa (d) Attha Katha.

76. One of the Buddhist works, which is a source of many Jataka stories and similar other narratives, is:
(a) Mahavastu (b) Kathavatthu
(c) Mahavamsa (d) Lalitavistara.

77. At which of the following places did a Buddhist university not evolve from the nucleus of an existing monastery?
(a) Nalanda (b) Valabhi
(c) Vaishali (d) Vikramshila.

78. Which of the following works of Buddhaghosa is veritably a small encyclopaedia on early Buddhism?
(a) Samanta-pasadika (b) Visuddhimagga
(c) Sumangalavilasini (d) Manarathapurani.

79. Who of the following Mahayanist Sanskrit authors was at first a Hinayanist Buddhist?
(a) Ashvaghosha (b) Nagarjuna
(c) Asanga (d) Vasubandhu.

80. Which of the following works of Ashvaghosha is considered to be the oldest dramatic work extant in Sanskrit literature?
(a) Buddhacharita
(b) Saundarananda
(c) Shariputraprakarana
(d) Gandistotragatha.

81. Nagarjuna is known as the Einstein of India because:
(a) Like Einstein he had a rare insight into the nature of the universe.
(b) He was one of the greatest physicists of all time.
(c) He propounded the theory of Shonyavada similar to Einstein's theory of relativity.
(d) `He was a great dialectician.

82. Which of the following was not one of the Buddhist scholars to go from India to Tibet?
   (a) Acharya Dipankara
   (b) Acharya Jitbari
   (c) Acharya Shantavakshita
   (d) None of these.

83. Which of the following was the most renowned Buddhist scholar of Indian origin to propagate Madhyamika Buddhism in China?
   (a) Kumarajiva (b) Paramartha
   (c) Bodhidharma (d) Bodhivuci.

84. Which of the following was the first great royal patron of Buddhism?
   (a) Ajatashatru (b) Udayayan
   (c) Asoka (d) Kanishka.

85. The greatest royal patron of the University of Nalanda was were:
   (a) King Harsha of Kanauj
   (b) King Balaputradeva of Sumatra
   (c) Pala King's Dharmapala and Devapala
   (d) None of these.

86. The so-called university of Nalanda, Vikramshila, etc., were actually:
   (a) Buddhist monasteries
   (b) Apex bodies of Buddhist monasteries
   (c) Learning centres of Buddhist monks
   (d) None of these.

87. Buddhism experienced a great revival in eastern India under the patronage of the Palas of Bihar, which of the following was not one of the great monasteries founded by them?
   (a) Vikramshila (b) Nalanda
   (c) Odantapuri (d) Somapuri.

88. The earliest stronghold of Buddhism in Central Asia was:
    (a) Yarkand (b) Khotan
    (c) Kashgar (d) Tashkent.

89. The monks of which of the following places took a leading part in the propagation of Buddhism in China?
    (a) Kashmir (b) Kuchi
    (c) Khotan (d) Tibet.

90. The school of Indian art which is known as the Greco-Roman-Buddhist Art, is the _______ school:
    (a) Mauryan (b) Shunga
    (c) Gandhara (d) Gupta.

91. At which of the following places has a Stupa of the Kushana period been recently discovered?
    (a) Sanghol (b) Besnagar
    (c) Amravati (d) Lumbini.

92. Which of the following was the construction of the stupas in the earliest period invariably associated?
    (a) The concept of the universe
    (b) The life of the Buddha
    (c) The relics of the Buddha
    (d) None of these.

93. The Buddhists who believed in strict monastic life and rigid disciplinary laws were known as:
    (a) Thera or sthavira-vadins
    (b) Mahasanghikas
    (c) Vajrayayins
    (d) Sunyauadins.

94. The Vibhashas are three large commentaries of:
    (a) Abhidhamma Pitaka
    (b) Vinaya Pitaka
    (c) All the three Pitakas
    (d) None of these.

95. The Buddhist Law or Doctrine of Karma meant
(a) A man reaps what he sows
(b) Every individual is the maker of his own destiny.
(c) Prayers to a God or gods alone cannot change the destiny of man.
(d) All the above.

96. In which of the following countries of South-East Asia was Mahayana Buddhism not the dominant school?
(a) Burma
(b) The Malaya Peninsula
(c) Champa
(d) Tibet.

97. Which of the following Buddhist philosopher is said to have visited Nepal in the fourth century A.D. in order to propagate his own doctrine?
(a) Acharya Atisha
(b) Acharya Kamalashila
(c) Acharya Shantarakshita
(d) Acharya Vasubandhu.

98. Zen Buddhism, introduced in the twelfth century A.D., found its adherents mainly among the warriors and influenced Japanese culture considerably. The key to enlightenment, according to Zen Buddhism, is:
(a) Recollection (b) Virtuous life
(c) Meditation (d) Piety.

99. Which of the following did for Buddhism in Japan, what king Asoka had done for it in India?
(a) Prince Shotoku (b) Empress Suiko
(c) Heina (d) Kamakura.

100. Buddhism was first introduced in Japan in the ______ century A.D.:
(a) First (b) Third
(c) Seventh (d) Eighth.

101. The foreigners particularly Greeks, were most attracted to Bhagavatism because:
   (a) it opened its portals of bhakti to all.
   (b) its appeal was catholic and universal.
   (c) it was truly a democratic religion.
   (d) All the above.

102. The concept of Trimoorti—the Supreme God manifested in the form of Brahma, Vishnu, and Siva _______ was the expression of:
   (a) The spirit of reconciliation and harmony between orthodox and sectarian forms.
   (b) Adoption of Vedic and non-Vedic deities into a unified deity
   (c) Both (a) and (b) above.
   (d) None of these.

103. In the Tamil country Durga was identified with the Tamil goddess Korravai, who was a Tamil goddess of:
   (a) Motherhood
   (b) Nature and productivity
   (c) War and victory
   (d) Earth.

104. Saktism centred around the worship of
   (a) Durga in one of her nine forms
   (b) Harappan mother goddess
   (c) The Vedic Parvati
   (d) The Virgin Goddess, enshrined at Kanyakumari.

105. Saivism spread to various Hindu states of South-East Asia, from:
   (a) Kashmir (b) Punjab
   (c) North India (d) South India.

106. Which of the following was not one of the Siva sects?
   (a) Lakula (b) Pasupata
   (c) Maheshwara (d) Saktism.

107. The non-Aryan god Siva was identified with the Vedic god:

(a) Indra (b) Maruta
(c) Rudra (d) Prajapati.

108. Which of the following non-Vedic sects, which later on merged into Brahmanism, was the earliest?

(a) Bhagavatism (b) Saivism
(c) Vaishnavism (d) Saktism.

109. Which of the following does not prove that Siva was a non-Vedic or non-Aryan deity?

(a) Siva as a deity was unknown to Vedic Aryans
(b) Worship of linga, the chief emblem of Saivism was condemned in the Rigveda
(c) The worship of linga was prevalent in the Harappan period
(d) The characteristics of Siva are of a folk deity.

110. The earlist exposition of Saiva system was established by:

(a) Basava (b) Lakula
(c) Bijjala (d) Sankaracharya.

111. The beginning of Saivism can be traced to the ______ period:

(a) Harappan (b) Later Vedic
(c) Mauryan (d) Kushana.

112. Which of the following was common to both Bhagavatism and Jainism?

(a) Austerity as the essential means of Salavation
(b) Belief in eternal individual souls
(c) The concept of Salvation as final independence of the soul
(d) Respect for animal life.

113. Which of the following heterodox assertions of Bhagavatism was not supported by Buddhism?

(a) An open denial of the efficacy of sacrifices and austerities.
(b) Denunciation of the slaughter of animals.

(c) Stressing the element of Bhakti in place of abstract knowledge
(d) One's caste or occupation was no hindrance to spiritual progress.

114. Which of the following was not one of the features which Bhagavatism shared in common with Buddhism and Jainism?

(a) All the three constituted a revolt against the accepted religious creeds of the day
(b) All of them originated in the free atmosphere of independent republican clans
(c) The founders of all the three were from royal families
(d) All the three believed in the concept of ahimsa.

115. Which of the following paved the way for reconciliation between Bhagavatism and Brahmanism?

(a) Replacement of Shraddha by bhakti.
(b) Growth of image worship and construction of temples
(c) Identification of Vasudeva Krishna with Vishnu.
(d) Philosophy of Advaita.

116. One of the concepts of Brahmanism which is not accepted by Bhagavatism is:

(a) Doctrine of Samsara
(b) Doctrine of Karma
(c) Elaborate sacrificial rituals
(d) Varnashrana dharma.

117. After the rise of the heterodox sects like Jainism and Buddhism, which of the following rulers was the first staunch supporter of orthodox Brahmanical faith and who is alleged to have persecuted Buddhists?

(a) Agnimitra (b) Bhulinimitra
(c) Pushyamitra Sunga (d) Pushyagupta.

118. The practice of image worship started among the followers of Brahmanism with the emergence of:

(a) Ajavaka Sect (b) Bhagavatism
(c) Vaishnavism (d) Saivism.

119. Panchratrikas were those who worshipped:
    (a) Vasudeva in his four-fold vyuha form
    (b) The deified sage Narain
    (c) Both (a) and (b) above
    (d) None of these.

120. Bhagavatism came to be known and merged with the Vaishnavism when:
    (a) Vasudeva Krishna was identified with Vedic deity Vishnu
    (b) The Vedic social rituals were adopted by Bhagavatism
    (c) The cosmic gods, such as Nara and Narain, were adopted in Bhagavatism
    (d) Bhagavatism adopted the concept of Varnashrama dharma.

121. Which of the following was the most important aspect of Brahmanism?
    (a) The concept of mantra
    (b) Sacrificial rituals
    (c) The practice of tapas
    (d) Attaining spiritual bliss through knowledge.

122. Which of the following schools of philosophy was the main offshoot of Bhagavatism?
    (a) Sankhya (b) Vaisheshika
    (c) Advaita (d) Vishishta dvaita.

123. Which of the following means of achieving Salvation is open to all according to Bhagavatism?
    (a) The knowledge of the self
    (b) Religious observances
    (c) Devotional worship
    (d) Total self-surrender to him.

124. How does devotion bring about liberation according to Bhagavatism?
    (a) It releases the soul from the bondage of action.
    (b) It destroys illusions by obtaining the grace of God

(c) It purges the soul of egoism

(d) Complete self-surrender arouses the compassion of God.

125. Bhagavatism has been regarded as a completely democratic religion because:

(a) It opened the portals of Salvation to all irrespective of caste, creed or sex

(b) It preached a simple religion in the language of the masses

(c) It was a totally non-ritualistic religion emphasising only individual's devotion

(d) It was free from high sounding philosophical speculations.

126. According to Bhagavatism the cause of all human sins is:

(a) Lobha (greed) (b) Asatya

(c) Avidya (d) .Maya.

127. The Bhagavata religion does not preach the cult of inactivism or quietism. Which of the following statements about Bhagavatism's attitude towards action is not correct?

(a) We should not give up action, but we should do our duty without any attachment

(b) We should surrender the fruits of action to God

(c) We should live an active life completely dedicated to God

(d) Actions for the preservation of life are irrelevant.

128. Bhagavatism considers bhakti as the best means of salvation, better than, karma and yoga because:

(a) Unlike knowledge and action, devotion is within the reach of everyone

(b) Unlike devotion, knowledge and actions are motivated by egoism and pride, and cannot activate God's compassion or grace

(c) No one is deare: to God than his devotee

(d) It could be pursued through individual efforts.

129. Which of the following statements correctly describes the concept of preman in Bhagavatism?
(a) It is love in the physical sense
(b) It is attachment to worldly objects of pleasure
(c) It is another name of bhakti
(d) It is the completion and perfection of devotion.

130. Which of the following texts is not one of the sources of Bhagavatism?
(a) Mahabharta
(b) Narada and Shandilya Sutras
(c) Bhagavata Purana
(d) Vishnu Dharmottar Purana.

131. Which of the following kinds of devotion is 'primary devotion' according to Bhagavatism?
(a) Devotion of total detachment
(b) Devotion of the inquisitive
(c) Devotion of the distressed
(d) Unmotivated and selfless devotion.

132. According to Bhagavata texts a definition of bhakti includes:
(a) Intense love for God
(b) Most perfect attachment to God
(c) Observance of one's duties
(d) All the above.

133. Which of the following means for achieving bhakti is the most important?
(a) Giving up egoism, pride and other passions
(b) Renunciation of all objects of enjoyment
(c) Praying incessantly to God
(d) Companionship of devotees.

134. One obtains the grace of God through:
(a) Bhakti
(b) Preman

(c) Complete self surrender to God
(d) Observance of social obligations.

135. According to Bhagavatism, salvation primarily depends on:
(a) Bhakti (b) Prasad
(c) Prapatti (d) Preman.

136. Which of the following moral virtues is not a part of Bhagavatism?
(a) Dana (b) Arjava
(c) Ahimsa (d) Samyaka ajiva.

137. When did Bhagavatism first come into prominence and spread to western and central India and the Deccan?
(a) Sixth century B.C.
(b) Second century B.C.
(c) First century A.D.
(d) Third century A.D..

138. From whose account do we know that Bhagavatism first grew up along the Yamuna in Mathura district?
(a) Herodotus (b) Arrian
(c) Megasthenes (d) Strabo.

139. Which of the following was not the principal deity of the Bhagavatas and Panchratras?
(a) Krishna (b) Narayan-Vishnu
(c) Balarama (d) Rama.

140. In which of the following books concerning Bhagavatism is the most authoritative exposition of its principles to be found?
(a) Chhandogya Upanishad
(b) Bhagavadgita
(c) Bhagavatapurana
(d) Narada-sutra.

141. In which of the following are the traces of the Bhagavata cult not to be found?
(a) Brahmanas (b) Epics
(c) Upanishads (d) Puranas.

142. On what basis is it said that Bhagavatism is as old as Buddhism and Jainism?
(a) References to Vasudeva Krishna in the Chhandogya Upanishad
(b) References in the Jain literature that Vasudeva Krishna was a scion of Jain Tirthankara Neminath
(c) Bhagavatism adopted the cult of non-violence from Jainism and Buddhism
(d) The ethical and social concepts of.

143. The main Bhagavata deity Vasudeva Krishna was identified with the Vedic deity/deities:
(a) Vishnu
(b) Narayan or Hari
(c) Both (a) and (b) above
(d) Varuna and Indra.

144. In which of the following texts was the first mention of sage Krishna, son of Devaki, made?
(a) Bhagavata Purana
(b) Mahabharta
(c) Chhandogya Upnishad
(d) Atharvaveda.

145. The main Bhagavata deity Vasudeva Krishna was a:
(a) Warrior God
(b) Philosopher and preacher
(c) Protector of cattle world
(d) All the above.

146. Who of the following was the earliest known Greek follower of Bhagavatism?
(a) Megasthenes (b) Antialkidas
(c) Heliodorus (d) Demetrius.

147. The Panchratra and Bhagavata sects both ultimately merged into:
(a) Vaishnavism (b) Saivism
(c) Saktism (d) Tantrism

148. Which one of the following are the main Bhagavata texts?
(a) The Smritis (b) The Puranas
(c) The Upanishads (d) The Brahmanas.

149. The Panchratras were basically the worshippers of:
(a) Narain-Vishnu
(b) Five Vrishni heroes
(c) Vasudeva Krishna and his brother Balarama
(d) Trimoorti.

150. The term Bhagavastism basically stands for a sect:
(a) Related to the worship of Vasudev Krishna
(b) Related to the worship of non-Vedic deity of the cowherds
(c) Which believed in the Upanishadic philosophy of Advaita
(d) All the above.

151. The mercantile community was most attracted to Jainism because:
(a) It could follow the religion without any hindrance to its economic activities
(b) The Vedic rituals and sacrifices were hindrances to its vocation
(c) The peace and non-violence of Jainism was conductive to the development of trade and commerce
(d) The doctrine of Karma or Jainism greatly impressed the merchants and traders.

152. Which of the following are known as the 'Four Great Signs'?
(a) The Four sights of old age, disease, death and a mendicant, which affected the life of the young Siddhartha
(b) The Four Noble Truths which provide the clue to human suffering and its cessation
(c) The Four Noble sentiments which are considered a must for a spiritual aspirant
(d) The Four Heavenly sights which accompanied the birth of the Buddha and proclaimed his future greatness.

153. Which of the following is known as the turning of the wheel of law?
   (a) The first sermon preached by the Buddha at the Deer Park at Sarnath
   (b) The practice of setting the wheel in motion everyday in the morning in the Sanghas
   (c) The extinction of Karma leading to the achievement of nirvana
   (d) The continuous existence of human beings like the wheel of causes and effects.

154. Which of the following was not one of the special injunctions which the Buddha prescribed for the Buddhist Sangha?
   (a) Not to kill and tell lies
   (b) Not to use intoxicants
   (c) Not to sing or dance
   (d) Not to eat at odd hours.

155. The doctrine of Karma in Buddhism means:
   (a) Predestination
   (b) The justification for social and economic inequalities in life
   (c) The deeds of a person determine the state of his life
   (d) Doing one's duty without bothering about the result.

156. The Buddha did not talk of spiritual aspects such as God, soul, life after death etc., because
   (a) He was only concerned with the ethical aspects of life
   (b) He wanted to resolve the practical problems of life
   (c) He considered such speculation unnecessary
   (d) He did not intend to establish a formal religion.

157. Which of the following was the most scientific belief of Jainism?
   (a) Physical endurance as a mental phenomenon
   (b) Life in all animate and inanimate things
   (c) All sins originate in one's mind
   (d) The cycle of nature.

158. The admission of which of the following to the sangha, at the instance of Ananda, marked the beginning of an order of nuns in India?
   (a) Yashodhara, the wife of the Buddha
   (b) Gautami, the widowed step-mother of the Buddha
   (c) Sujata, the merchant's daughter who offeared a bowl of milk to the Buddha after he had decided to give up austerities
   (d) Mahamaya, the Buddha's mother.

159. The basis on which it is said that the Indo-Greek king Menander or Menandros was a great patron and suppoter of Buddhism, is/are:
   (a) He is the hero of a work Milind-Panho, in which the Buddhist monk Nagasena answers his questions
   (b) His coins bear the Buddhist emblem Dharmachakra
   (c) He helped in the propagation of Buddhism in the region between Hindu Kush and Sindh
   (d) All the above

160. The reign of the Kushana monarch Kanishka was a turning point in the history of Buddhism, because:
   (a) It witnessed the rise of Mahayanism
   (b) Buddhism was introduced in China and Central Asia in his time
   (c) Both (a) and (b) above
   (d) The images of Buddha and Bodhisattvas began to be carved out during this period.

161. Which of the following was not one of the reasons for the popularity of Buddhism in China?
   (a) There were no rival religions at the time of introduction of Buddhism in China
   (b) The writing of such people as Mou-tseu created confidence in the minds of the educated Chinese
   (c) The life of purity followed by the immigrant Indian Buddhists and their Chinese disciples attracted the Chinese to Buddhism
   (d) The patronage of the reigning dynasties in China helped the cause of Buddhism.

162. Which of the following did not produce an impact on the Chinese life and though as a result of the influence of Buddhism?
 (a) Doctrine of rebirth
 (b) Belief in reward and retribution
 (c) The idea of causality
 (d) Faith in Ahimsa.

163. Which of the following constitutes the chief significance of Korean Buddhism?
 (a) The preservation of Mahayana Buddhism in its purest form
 (b) The role it played of an intermediary between China and Japan
 (c) The unique synthesis of the orthodox and the Tantric schools of Buddhism
 (d) None of these.

164. Which of the following was not one of the great events in the early history of Buddhism in Sri Lanka which left a deep impression and still evoke pious enthusiasm among millions of its votaries?
 (a) The visit of Mahendra and Sanghamitra
 (b) The transplantation of a branch of the Bodhi tree under which Gautama attained Buddhahood
 (c) The bringing of the Buddha's foot relic from India
 (d) Introduction of sacred Buddhist scriptures and architecture in Sri Lanka.

165. What is the greatest debt owed by the Buddhist world to Sri Lanka?
 (a) The preservation of Buddha's relics and Sacred Bodhi tree
 (b) The preservation of the Pali canon in its entirety
 (c) The development of Buddhism through Simhalese commentaries of Buddhist texts
 (d) The propagation of Buddhism in South-East Asian countries.

166. Which of the following pairs indicating the contents of the sacred Buddhist Pitakas is not correctly matched?
   (a) Vinaya Pitaka (b) Abhidhamma Pitaka
   (c) Sutta Pitaka (d) Dhammapada.

167. What was the purpose of the chaityas during the early phase of Buddhism?
   (a) They served the purpose of temples
   (b) They were meditation halls
   (c) They were used for religious assemblies and prayers
   (d) They were used for holding social function.

168. Which of the following statements correctly describe the difference between a chaitya and a stupa?
   (a) Chaitya is a religious term, while stupa is an architectural term for a mound containing a relic of the Buddha and later on of leading Buddhist Saints
   (b) Chaitya is a place of prayers/worship, while, stupa is a funeral monument
   (c) Chaityas were constructed by the monasteries while stupas were constructed by the kings and the rich merchants
   (d) Chaitya represent Mahayanism and stupas Hinayanism.

169. The richest source of the well-known smooth images of the Buddha in black slate and an extensive series of Buddhist bronzes is:
   (a) Kurkihar (b) Nalanda
   (c) Tanjore (d) Amravati.

170. The finest specimens of Buddhist paintings are found in the caves at Bagh and Ajanta. How do the Buddhist paintings at Bagh differ from those found at Ajanta?
   (a) They are mostly depictions of Jataka stories
   (b) They contain representations of scenes from the Buddha's life from conception to the attainment of Nirvana
   (c) They are basically secular in character, and significantly reflect contemporary life
   (d) The style of the paintings reveals great delicacy and depth of feeling.

171. The Prajnaparamita is the Buddhist deity of:
(a) Learning (b) Prosperity
(c) Mind (d) Compassion.

172. Bamiyan, a great centre of Buddhism and Buddhist art from the first to the fourth centuries A.D., is located in:
(a) Kashmir
(b) South-Central Asia
(c) NWF Province of Pakistan
(d) Afghanistan.

173. The greatest centres of Buddhism in the Deccan were:
(a) Ajanta and Ellora
(b) Nasik and Karle
(c) Amravati and Nagarjunikonda
(d) Kanchi and Nagapatam.

174. Which of the following places is not connected with the four important events in the Buddha's life?
(a) Rummindei (b) Kasia
(c) Deer Park at Isipatana (d) Sankasya.

175. Which of the following was not the scene of miracles connected with the Buddha's life?
(a) Sanchi (b) Shravasti
(c) Sankasya (d) Rajagriha.

176. Which of the following can be called the birth place of Buddhism?
(a) Lumbini (b) Sarnath
(c) Rajagriha (d) Kushinagar.

177. During the reign of which of the following rulers did most of the holy places of Buddhism acquire celebrity?
(a) Chandragupta Maurya
(b) Ajatashatru
(c) Asoka
(d) Kanishka.

178. Which of the following is not one of the common points of significance of both Rajagriha and Vaishali?
   (a) Both places are associated with the miracles performed by the Buddha
   (b) At both places one of the Buddhist councils was held
   (c) At both places a stupa was built with the mortal remains of the Buddha enshrined in them
   (d) Both places were important centres of Buddhist art.

179. The last great royal patrons of Buddhism were:
   (a) The Palas of Bengal and Bihar
   (b) Harshavardhana of Kannauj
   (c) The Chalukyas of Gujarat
   (d) The Paramaras of Malwa.

180. Which of the following places can be regarded as the largest monastic establishment in Western India?
   (a) Karle (b) Ajanta
   (c) Junnair (d) Kanheri.

181. The stupa constructed at which of the following places in southern India is not only the earliest but also a mahastupa enshrining the mortal remains of the Buddha?
   (a) Amravati (b) Jaggayyapeta
   (c) Bhattiprolu (d) Nagarjuni Konda.

182. The stupa at which of the following places in Southern India is larger than the one at Sanchi and would well vie in artistic beauty and grandeur with the Sanchi and Bharhut stupas in the North?
   (a) Amravati (b) Nagarjuni Konda
   (c) Bhattiprolu (d) Ghantashala.

183. Which of the following is considered to be the actual founder of Jainism?
   (a) Risabhanath
   (b) Parsvanath
   (c) Neminath
   (d) Vardhaman Mahavira.

184. Which of the following lived with Mahavira during his mendicancy but subsequently left him and became the leader of another Shramana sect?
(a) Makkhali Gosala (b) Ajita Keshakambalin
(c) Purana Kassapa (d) Pakudha Kaccayana.

185. On the authority of which of the following is Mahavira's year of death placed as 468 B.C.?
(a) Taranath (b) Siddhasena
(c) Haribhadra (d) Hemachandra.

186. What was the original name of the sect lead by Mahavira which later came to be popularly known as Jains?
(a) Jina (b) Kevalin
(c) Nirgranthas (d) Tirthankaras.

187. What was the name of the village where Mahavira attained the highest spiritual knowledge?
(a) Kundapura or Kundagrama
(b) Vaishali
(c) Gaya
(d) Trimbhikagrama.

188. At which of the following place did Mahavira's death take place?
(a) Kusinara (b) Vaishali
(c) Rajagriha (d) Pava.

189. Which of the following vows was added by Mahavira to the four great vows enjoined by the twenty-third Thirthankara Parsvanath?
(a) Non-Injury
(b) Continence or chastity
(c) Truthfulness
(d) Non-attachment.

190. During his lifetime, Mahavira's teachings were confined to the Ganga valley. But in later centuries they spread to many regions, which of the following was not such region?
(a) Gujarat (b) Rajasthan
(c) Karnataka (d) West Bengal.

191. Which of the following were not one of the royal patrons of Jainism?
(a) Satvahanas
(b) Gangos
(c) Chalukyas of Gujarat
(d) Rashtrakutas.

192. What was the name of the Jain monk under whose leadership, a large Jain community migrated from Magadha to Shravanabelagola in Karnataka in the fourth century B.C.?
(a) Nagarjuna (b) Samghadasa
(c) Haribhadra (d) Bhadrabahu.

193. Where was the first Jain Council held around the third century B.C.?
(a) Vallabhi (b) Pataliputra
(c) Vaishali (d) Trimbhikagrama.

194. When was the second and the last Jain council held at Vallabhi which made a final collection of the scriptures and reduced them to writing?
(a) Third century B.C.
(b) First century A.D.
(c) Fifth or sixth century A.D.
(d) Seventh or Eighth century A.D.

195. When did the final compilation of Mahavira teachings take place?
(a) Sixth century B.C.
(b) Third century B.C.
(c) Fifth or Sixth century A.D.
(d) Eleventh century A.D.

196. Which of the following are considered to be the oldest texts containing Mahavira's teachings received by Sthulabhadra at the feet of his guru Bhadrabahu?
(a) Angas (b) Fourteen Purvas
(c) Prakirnas (d) Four Mulasutras.

197. Which of the following Jain texts were compiled at the first Jain council held at Pataliputra in the third century B.C?
(a) Purvas
(b) Twelve angas
(c) Ten Prakirnas
(d) Six Chheda sutras.

198. Which of the following is considered to be the greatest of Jain Scholars?
(a) Bhadrabahu (b) Sthulabhadra
(c) Amoghavarsha (d) Hemachandra.

199. The greatest Jain scholar Hemchandra was a court Pandit and analyst at the court of
(a) Rashtrakuta Amoghavarsa
(b) Chalukya Kumarapala
(c) Chalukya Jayasimha Siddaraja
(d) Chandel Vidyadhara.

200. The eleven Gandharvas in Jainism were
(a) Close disciples or apostles of Mahavira
(b) Heads of the school of Jainism
(c) Great angels of Jainism
(d) Future pontiffs of Jainism.

201. A Jain Tirthankara who is supposed to have been the Kinsman of Lord Krishna was:
(a) Risabha (b) Neminatha
(c) Parsvanath (d) Mahavira.

202. Which of the following is not one of the languages to the development of which the Jain have made important contributions?
(a) Ardha Magadhi
(b) Apabhramsha
(c) Gujarati and Marathi
(d) Malayalam.

203. Which of the following is not one of the examples of Jain art and architecture?
(a) Huge statues of Bahubali
(b) Tiger Cave at Udayagiri
(c) Indra Sabha at Ellora
(d) Painting of Lord Mahavira at Ajanta and Bagh.

204. Which of the following is not one of the Jain cave dwellings?
(a) Tiger Cave at Udayagiri
(b) Indra Sabha at Ellora
(c) Ghantai and Adinath temples at Khajuraho
(d) Sittannavasala Cave at Padukottai.

205. Jainism had derived its metaphysical thought from
(a) Buddism (b) Ajivakas
(c) Samkhya Philosophy (d) Bhagavatas.

206. Jainism was propagated in South India by
(a) Gautama (b) Indrabhuti
(c) Sudharman (d) Bhadrabahu.

207. A great contemporary of the Jain Saint Bhadrabahu, who is said to have retired to Karnataka and died there, was
(a) Nagarjuna
(b) Chandragupta Maurya
(c) Gautamiputra Satkarni
(d) Rudradaman.

208. Mahavira attained intuitive knowledge or enlightenment near
(a) Vallabhi (b) Vaishali
(c) Parsvanath hills (d) Pava.

209. The great pontiff or saint of Jainism after Mahavira was/were
(a) Sumbhutavijaya (b) Bhadrabahu
(c) Sthulabhadra (d) Hemachandra.

ANSWERSS

1. (c)	2. (c)	3. (c)	4. (c)
5. (b)	6. (c)	7. (b)	8. (a)
9. (c)	10. (a)	11. (c)	12. (b)
13. (c)	14. (d)	15. (b)	16. (a)
17. (d)	18. (a)	19. (b)	20. (d)
21. (c)	22. (b)	23. (d)	24. (d)
25. (a)	26. (c)	27. (b)	28. (b)
29. (a)	30. (a)	31. (b)	32. (b)
33. (d)	34. (c)	35. (a)	36. (c)
37. (d)	38. (a)	39 (b)	40. (c)
41. (a)	42. (c)	43 (b)	44 (d)
45. (a)	46 (a)	47. (d)	48. (c)
49 (a)	50. (c)	51 (d)	52 (a)
53. (a)	54. (a)	55. (b)	56. (a)
57. (a)	58. (c)	59. (c)	60. (d)
61 (b)	62 (b)	63 (c)	64 (c)
65 (c)	66 (d)	67 (b)	68 (b)
69 (a)	70 (a)	71 (c)	72. (a)
73 (b)	74 (a)	75 (a)	76 (b)
77 (c)	78 (b)	79 (c)	80 (c)
81 (c)	82 (b)	83 (a)	84 (c)
85 (c)	86 (a)	87 (b)	88. (b)
89 (b)	90 (c)	91 (a)	92 (c)
93 (a)	94 (c)	95 (d)	96 (a)
97 (d)	98 (c)	99 (a)	100. (c)
101 (d)	102. (c)	103. (a)	104. (d)
105. (d)	106. (d)	107. (b)	108. (b)
109. (d)	110. (b)	111. (a)	112. (d)
113. (c)	114. (c)	115. (c)	116. (c)
117. (c)	118. (b)	119. (c)	120. (a)
121. (b)	122. (d)	123. (c)	124. (c)
125. (a)	126. (c)	127. (d)	128. (b)
129. (d)	130. (c)	131. (d)	132. (d)
133. (d)	134. (a)	135. (b)	136. (d)
137. (b)	138. (c)	139. (d)	140. (b)
141. (a)	142. (a)	143. (c)	144. (c)
145. (d)	146. (c)	147. (a)	148. (b)
149. (a)	150. (d)	151. (c)	152. (a)
153. (a)	154. (c)	155. (c)	156. (d)

157.	(b)	158.	(b)	159.	(d)	160.	(c)
161.	(a)	162.	(d)	163.	(b)	164.	(d)
165.	(d)	166.	(d)	167.	(c)	168.	(a)
169.	(b)	170.	(c)	171.	(c)	172.	(d)
173.	(c)	174.	(d)	175.	(a)	176.	(b)
177.	(c)	178.	(d)	179.	(a)	180.	(c)
181.	(c)	182.	(a)	183.	(b)	184.	(a)
185.	(d)	186.	(c)	187.	(d)	188.	(d)
189.	(b)	190.	(d)	191.	(a)	192.	(d)
193.	(b)	194.	(c)	195.	(c)	196.	(b)
197.	(b)	198.	(d)	199.	(c)	200.	(a)
201.	(b)	202.	(d)	203.	(d)	204.	(c)
205.	(c)	206.	(d)	207.	(b)	208.	(c)
209.	(a)						

7
ANCIENT RELIGIOUS SOCIETY

1. In Ancient India the state promoted trade through
   (a) Foundation of market towns
   (b) The making and maintenance of roads
   (c) Ensuring security on trade roads
   (d) All of the above.

2. The socio-economic significance of the trade and craft guilds was that
   (a) They maintained the business occupational monopoly of particular varnnas
   (b) They turned into castes
   (c) They enforced a social discipline
   (d) They provided economic support and organisation to trade and crafts.

3. In the promotion and expansion of trade and commerce the greatest contribution was made by the
   (a) Mauryas
   (b) Indo-Greeks, Sakas, Kushanas, etc.
   (c) Sungas
   (d) Imperial Guptas.

4. Kautilya's Arthashastra's chapter on Kantakasadhana is mostly devoted to
   (a) Regulation of profits, wages and prices
   (b) Regulations against adulteration of goods
   (c) Strict control of artisans and traders by the state
   (d) Measures for the protection of merchants and artisans by the state.

5. In early Ancient India, the largest urban centre was
   (a) Kausambi (b) Champa
   (c) Pataliputra (d) Taxila.

6. The industries in early Ancient India were concentrated in the areas where :
   (a) Raw materials and markets were available
   (b) The craftsmen were concentrated
   (c) The foreign merchants could easily arrive
   (d) The state presumed the policy of free trade.

7. The great increase in the number of crafts resulted in
   (a) Mass production of goods
   (b) Greater specialisation in production techniques
   (c) Both (a) and (b)
   (d) Stiff competition among craftsman.

8. The history of Ancient India trade rightly begins from the------period.
   (a) Harappan (b) Later Vedic
   (c) Buddhist (d) Mauryan.

9. The main land route between India and Western Asia passed through
   (a) The pass of Khyber and Valley of Kabul
   (b) The passes of Khyber and Balan
   (c) Taxila, Peshawar and Kabul
   (d) Kabul and Bamiyan.

10. In the Mauryan and post-Mauryan periods the most important emporium of trade in Western India was
   (a) Bharukachchha (b) Superaka
   (c) Kalyana (d) Chaul.

11. The great Royal Road mentioned by Megasthanes ran from ----- to------.
   (a) The Indus to Pataliputra
   (b) Pataliputra to Prayaga
   (c) Prayaga to Ujjaini
   (d) Pataliputra to Taxila.

12. Sind Sauvira was famous in Ancient India as the home of
    (a) Fine Swords and daggers
    (b) Horses and asses
    (c) Woollen textiles
    (d) Leather goods.

13. According to Patanajali, Mathura was specially famous for its textile industries which of the following varieties of textile was the speciality of Mathura?
    (a) Dukula (b) Sataka
    (c) Kshauma (d) Chinasunka.

14. Which of the following had the monopoly of iron deposits?
    (a) Kalinga (b) Kashi
    (c) Magadha (d) Vatsa.

15. Which of the following was not the main product of South India?
    (a) Musks and Saffron
    (b) Spices
    (c) Sandalwood
    (d) Gold and Precious stones.

16. Which of the following categories of crafts were regarded as lower in status?
    (a) Those which used perishable commodities for raw material
    (b) Those associated with destruction of life
    (c) Those producing goods meant for poor people
    (d) Those employing untouchable as hired labourers.

17. Which of the following was not responsible for the thriving trade between India and the Western world in this period?
    (a) Discovery of the monsoon winds by the Greek Saloar Hippalus in the first century A.D
    (b) Foreign invasions and external contacts
    (c) Decline in production of fashion goods in the western world
    (d) emergence of the Roman empire as paramount and most prosperous in the western world.

18. Which of the following was not one of the countries/regions with which India had trade relations during the early centuries of the Christian era?
    (a) Roman Empire
    (b) Japan and Korea
    (c) Malay Peninsula
    (d) North east Africa.

19. The first to establish trade contacts with Roman empire were
    (a) Kushanas
    (b) Tamil and Chera kingdoms
    (c) Western Sakas
    (d) Vakatakas.

20. The main items of export from India to the Roman empire were
    (a) Agricultural commodities
    (b) Raw materials for industries
    (c) Luxury goods
    (d) Capital goods.

21. Which of the following was not one of the luxury and fashions goods of export to the Roman empire?
    (a) Perfumes and spices
    (b) Jewels and Precious stones
    (c) Fine textiles
    (d) Hair dyes, wigs, ivory combs etc..

22. In return for her exports, which of the following was not one of the items imported by India from the Roman Empire?
    (a) Wine (b) Tin and lead
    (c) Iron (d) Linen.

23. On account of the use of which of the following items imported from India did the Roman ladies became a menace to the city's morals?
    (a) Pearls (b) Muslin
    (c) Silk (d) Perfumes.

24. The balance of trade was very un favourable to the west and resulted in a serious drain of gold from the Roman Empire which of the following lamented the degenerate habits of the Romans of his day, which resulted in this drain?

(a) Pliny (b) Ptolemy
(c) Nero (d) Strabo.

25. What was the reason for India becoming an intermediary in the silk trade between China and West?

(a) The Chinese were *persona non grata* in the western countries
(b) After the building of the Great Wall by Shijuanga Ti, the relations between the Chinese and the Roman Empire were estranged
(c) On account of Roman conflict with Parthia the latter prevented Chinese merchandise from reaching the west directly
(d) India had the best expertise in silk weaving.

26. There are records of several embassies from Indian kings to the caesars. To which of the following was an Indian embassy not sent?

(a) Augustus (b) Nero
(c) Antonius (d) Pius.

27. The most interesting thing about the punch marked coins in that they

(a) Remained in circulation for about five centuries
(b) Were in circulation in the North and South both
(c) Have various religious symbols on them
(d) Do not bear the name of any ruler.

28. The primary reason for the extension of India's trade with South East Asia was

(a) The Roman need for spices could not be met entirely by local supply, and this led Indian merchants to venture as middlemen in to South East Asia
(b) The merchants of South East Asian countries wanted to develop trade relations with the Roman Empire through India

(c) The Spirit of adventure of the Indian People and the religious zeal of the Buddhist monks combined to take them to South East Asian countries
(d) India had direct land and maritime routes of South East Asia.

29. Exchange of merchandise led inevitably to an exchange of ideas which of the following was not the result of this interaction with the west?
(a) The borrowing of wards largely of technical kind, on both sides
(b) Conversion of foreigners of Hinduism and of Indians to Christianity
(c) The emergence of the hybrid Indo-Greek style of Gandhara art
(d) Adoption of Indian folk tales and fables in European literature.

30. Which of the following works does not help us in tracing Ancient India's trade contacts with the Western world?
(a) The book of Duarte Barbosa
(b) Strabo's Geography
(c) Pliny of the Elder's Natural History
(d) Ptolemy's Geography.

31. Which of the following is said to have introduced Indian Culture in Combodia?
(a) Kharevela (b) Kaundinya
(c) Kshemeshvara (d) Kumaragupta.

32. Who constructed the Royal Highway from Pataliputra to Taxila the most widely used highway?
(a) Mauryas (b) Kushanas
(c) Sakas (d) Guptas.

33. Which of the following towns did not lie on the Royal Highway?
(a) Varanasi (b) Kausambi
(c) Vidisha (d) Mathura.

34. From which point on the Royal Highway did a branch take off for the part of Bharukachchha?
    (a) Kausambi (b) Varanasi
    (c) Mathura (d) Taxila.
35. From the branch road connecting Kausambi and Bharukachchha, the main route to the south took off from Ujjaini, which of the following did not lie on this route to the south?
    (a) Vidisha
    (b) Pratishthana
    (c) Matupalti
    (d) Madurai.
36. From which point in the north west did roads go in different directions to countries outside India?
    (a) Taxila (b) Shakala
    (c) Kabul (d) Kandahar.
37. Which of the following did not lie on the same route taking off from Kabul?
    (a) Kandahar (b) Bacteria
    (c) Herat (d) Ecbatana.
38. Which of the following towns was not connected by land route from India?
    (a) Persepolis (b) Susa
    (c) Seleucia (d) Alexandria.
39. Through Central Asia passed Silk Route which connected China with the west Asian provinces of the Roman Empire through Central Asia, which of the following controlled the Silk Route?
    (a) Sakas (b) Kushanas
    (c) Parthians (d) Guptas.
40. At which of the following places was a trading station not set up in Central Asia by Indian merchants missionaries?
    (a) Yharkand (b) Kabul
    (c) Miran (d) Kashgarh.

41. Which of the following parts was on the Indus Delta?
   (a) Tamralipti (b) Kabul
   (c) Barbaricum (d) Kashgarh.

42. The part known to the author of Periplus Moris Erthreae as Pudduke was
   (a) Arikamedu (b) Tamralipti
   (c) Karkai (d) Barbaricum.

43. The oldest and the largest entrepot on the western cost of India which handled the bulk of trade with western Asia was
   (a) Barbaricum (b) Bariygaza
   (c) Suparaka (d) Patala.

44. At which of the following parts have a sizable Roman settlement and a Roman factory been discovered?
   (a) Tamralipti (b) Muziris
   (c) Kaveripattanam (d) Arikamedu.

45. Arikamedu was the most important Indo Roman trading station because
   (a) Its coast was ideal for the anchorage of Roman ships
   (b) It produced fine muslins and other fashion goods according to the Roman taste and specifications
   (c) Both (a) and (b)
   (d) It was the first part of call for the Roman ships.

46. About which of the following south Indian cities are there descriptions in early Tamil literature to the effect that the yavana ships used to arrive with their cargoes and that the yavana section of the city overload with prosperity?
   (a) Arikamedu (b) Kaveripattanam
   (c) Mamallapuram (d) Muziris.

47. An early Ancient Indian city which was a nodal point trade routes East to West and from north to south was
   (a) Mathura (b) Vidisha
   (c) Ujjaini (d) Pratishthana.

48. Which of the following was not one of the reasons for the vast majority of artisans joining the guilds?
    (a) The membership of a guild provided social status
    (b) It offered a degree of general security
    (c) It was difficult for them to compete as individuals against the guilds
    (d) Without the membership of a guild the craftsmen were not eligible for various concessions offered by the state.

49. Which of the following was not one of the leading guilds of the period?
    (a) Potters
    (b) Stone workers
    (c) Metal workers
    (d) Carpenters.

50. Which of the following rules were not fixed by the guilds?
    (a) Social conduct
    (b) Quality of goods
    (c) Prices of commodities
    (d) Sale of commodities.

51. Which of the following statements about the organisation of the guilds is not correct?
    (a) The guild was headed by a chief usually called the Elder.
    (b) The Elder was assisted by a small council of senior members
    (c) The office of the Elder was usually elective
    (d) The guilds had a corporate life systembalised by the banners of each guilds.

52. The behaviour of the guild members was controlled through
    (a) The Elder
    (b) Members of the Council
    (c) Guild Court
    (d) Conduct Committee.

53. The merchant groups of which of the following towns did not issue coins?
(a) Taxila (b) Prayaga
(c) Kausambi (d) Vidisha.

54. The great meeting ground of the Indian and Western Merchants during the early centuries of the Christian era was
(a) Dedesiya (b) Alexandria
(c) Taxila (d) Palmya.

55. The donation made by which of the following guilds is recorded in a famous inscription?
(a) Mandasor silk weavers
(b) Vidisha ivory workers
(c) Nasik weavers
(d) Corn dealers.

56. What was the possible reason for the guilds to employ hired labour in addition to artisans?
(a) Increasing prosperity
(b) To meet greater demand
(c) The desire for greater freedom
(d) Directives of the state.

57. Artisans and Craftsmen were largely drawn from
(a) Vaisyas (b) Surdas
(c) Venas (d) Rathakaras.

58. Which of the following was not one of the important centres of guilds of artisans according to available inscriptions?
(a) Mathura region in the North
(b) Magadha in the East
(c) Govardhana in the western Deccan
(d) Mandasor in Central India.

59. Before the establishment of Indo-Greek rule in India, the coins were issued by the
(a) Rulers

(b) Individual Merchants
(c) Merchant Corporations
(d) All of the above.

60. The most commonly used coin during the Mauryan period was
(a) Nishka (b) Suvarna
(c) Karshapana (d) Kakini.

61. The metal in which the Karshapana coins were minted was
(a) Gold and Silver (b) Copper
(c) Lead (d) Silver or Copper.

62. Which of the following coins was issued in Silver?
(a) Nishka (b) Pala
(c) Shatamana (d) Kakini.

63. Imported coins were mostly used as
(a) Items of jewellery (b) Legal tender
(c) Bullion (d) Foreign Exchange.

64. The most unusual item of export from India to the Roman world was/were
(a) Singing and talking birds
(b) Wild and pet animals, such as monkeys
(c) Both (a) and (b)
(d) Mineral water and Himalayan herbs.

65. Which of the following was not one of the terms used to describe professions bankers and moneylenders?
(a) Srenis (b) Chattis
(c) Chettiyars (d) Sresthins.

66. Which of the following institution did not act as bankers?
(a) Trade guilds (b) Royal treasury
(c) Larger temples (d) Village assemblies.

67. The largest number of Roman coins have been found from
(a) Kerala (b) Tamil Nadu
(c) Both (a) and (b) (d) West Bengal.

68. Seaborne trade between India and Rome received great impetus during the reign of Roman Emperor
    (a) Cladius (b) Augustus
    (c) Trajan (d) Nero.

69. Which of the following banking functions was not performed by the trade guilds of the period?
    (a) Accepting money as fixed deposit
    (b) Granting loans to the members of the guild
    (c) Accepting safe deposits
    (d) Issuing demand drafts and promissory notes.

70. The most widely exported metal from India was
    (a) Gold
    (b) Iron and Steel
    (c) Copper
    (d) Brass.

71. The gold standard was introduced in Ancient India on account of
    (a) Increase in the price of commodities
    (b) Decline in the value of gold vis-a-vis silver
    (c) India's favourable balance of trade
    (d) Global scarcity of silver.

72. Which of the following towns as not an important commercial centre in early Ancient India.
    (a) Bharukchchha in the West
    (b) Patala in the Indus delta
    (c) Pushkalavti in the North West
    (d) Malainamdalam in South India.

73. Which of the following Indian commodities was not exported to Rome?
    (a) Spices
    (b) Indian parrots, exotic birds, lions and tigers
    (c) Ivory articles perfumes and costly timber
    (d) Indian sculptures.

74. The first Indian rulers to issue gold coins on the Rome pattern were
(a) Sungas (b) Indo-Greeks
(c) Kushanas (d) Guptas.

75. Which of the following was perhaps the most advanced industry of the period?
(a) Textile (b) Pottery
(c) Jewellery (d) Metal work.

76. Which of the following was not one of the varieties of textiles produced during the period?
(a) Silk (b) Cotton
(c) Velvet (d) Calico.

77. Which of the following cities of North India was regarded as the best producer of silk?
(a) Taxila (b) Pataliputra
(c) Kausambi (d) Varanasi.

78. The rulers of an Ancient Indian ruling dynasty, who issued the coins representing as many as thirty five deities worshipped by different peoples living in their kingdom were the
(a) Mauryas (b) Sakas
(c) Kushans (d) Guptas.

79. India maintained connection with Egypt through the
(a) Red Sea route
(b) Persian Gulf route
(c) Indian ocean route
(d) Mediterranean sea route.

80. The term akshayanivi signifies
(a) A permanent endowment with a guild or a banker
(b) The guild spent the profits or interest on the deposits according to the forms stated by the depositors
(c) Both (a) and (b)
(d) The fixed deposits of the people with the banker or guild.

81. For which of the following purposes was hired labour not used?
   (a) Agriculture
   (b) Industry and trade
   (c) Protection of kings person
   (d) Animal rearing.

82. Which of the following acted as bankers and moneylenders?
   (a) Sarthavahas
   (b) Sresthis
   (c) Nagar Sresthins
   (d) Nagarakas.

83. Which of the following was not one of the important item of export during this period?
   (a) Rice
   (b) Pepper, spices and herbs
   (c) Sandalwood and indigo
   (d) Pearls and precious stones.

84. Which of the following, metals was extensively imported from Sri Lanka and Afghanistan?
   (a) Iron (b) Lead
   (c) Copper (d) Silver.

85. Apart from Chinese silk, other important items of import were ivory and horses. From where was ivory imported?
   (a) China (b) Arabia
   (c) Ethopia (d) South East Asia.

86. Which of the following countries was the centre of East-West trade during this period?
   (a) India (b) Burma
   (c) Sri Lanka (d) North Africa.

87. Which of the following seem to have monopolised trade in silk?
   (a) Chinese (b) Arabs
   (c) Persians (d) Sinhalese.

88. Among trade routes which of the following was added to the existing ones during the Gupta period?
    (a) Overland route to China
    (b) Overseas route to Alexandria
    (c) Overseas route to South Africa
    (d) Overland route to North Russia.

89. Which of the following parts on the east coast was the part of call for voyagers from China, Indonesia and Sri Lanka?
    (a) Kangoda (b) Kadura
    (c) Tamralipti (d) Satagaon.

90. Which of the following was the greatest emporium of trade on the eastern coast?
    (a) Tamralipti (b) Calicut
    (c) Bharukachchha (d) Kalyana.

91. There is a mention in the records of five market towns on the coast of a particular region of India, which was that region?
    (a) Kalinga (b) Sindhu Delta
    (c) Malabar (d) Pandyan Country.

92. Which of the following cities lost its prominence during the post Gupta period?
    (a) Kannauj (b) Pataliputra
    (c) Mathura (d) Varanasi.

93. The silver coins of the Gupta period were known as
    (a) Dinar (b) Rubyaka
    (c) Satamana (d) Karshapana.

94. The Suvarnabhuni was a generic name for
    (a) Burma
    (b) Malay Peninsula
    (c) Neighbouring Indonesian Islands
    (d) All of the above.

95. The fine textiles known as deikula were made of
    (a) Cotton (b) Silk
    (c) Artificial silk (d) Fibres of a plant.

96. The term puga stood for a
    (a) Guild of artisans
    (b) Group of merchants
    (c) Group of inhabitants of the same town
    (d) Cartel of bankers.

97. The term naigama stood for a
    (a) Cartel of financiers
    (b) Group of merchants
    (c) Group of inhabitants of the same town
    (d) Corporation of guilds.

98. In the Gupta period the largest number of coins were issued in
    (a) Gold (b) Silver
    (c) Copper (d) Iron.

99. Which of the following was the common medium of exchange, according to Fa-hien?
    (a) Nishka (b) Karshapana
    (c) Kakini (d) Cowries.

100. Certain scholars interpret the decline in the many economy in the post Gupta period as indicative of
    (a) Emergence of feudalism
    (b) Localisation of economy
    (c) Decline in per capita income
    (d) Decline in the value of gold and silver.

101. Which at the following statement about the corganisation of the guilds is not correct?
    (a) The guild was headed by chief usually called the Elder
    (b) The Elder was assisted by a small council of senior members
    (c) The office of the Elder was usually elective.
    (d) The guilds had a corporate life symbolised by the banners of each guild.

102. The behaviour of the guild member was controlled through
   (a) The Eler
   (b) Members of the council
   (c) Guild court
   (d) Conduct committee

103. The rate of interest in ancient India varied according to the venture and also perhaps according to the caste of the borrower. For which of the following was the rate of interest the highest?
   (a) Unsecured loan taken by sudras
   (b) Loans taken by overland caravan traders
   (c) Loans taken by sea faring merchants
   (d) Short-term loans for commercial ventures.

104. From the first century A.D. India's foreign trade was mainly carried on by sea, because of
   (a) Disruption of land route on account of foreign invasion
   (b) Obstacles to India's trade by the Arab merchants
   (c) Increase of India's trade with the eastern Roman empire
   (d) Discovery of monsoon winds.

105. Ship plying in mid ocean took Grown with them for
   (a) Keeping them alert about attack by pirates
   (b) Helping the navigators in locating the right direction
   (c) Sending messageors to homeland
   (d) Protecting the ship from being overturned by whales and sharks.

106. Which of the following was not one of the urban centres which gradually declined during the Gupta period and after?
   (a) Mathura
   (b) Modern Patna
   (c) Gaya district
   (d) Gorkahpur district.

107. The most important imports to India from the Western world were
   (a) Wine, medicines and herbs
   (b) Horses, chemicals and nuts
   (c) Fine, textiles, woollens and lead
   (d) Gold, silver, glass vessels and chemicals.

108. The issue of a large number of gold coins during the Gupta period indicates
   (a) Discovery of new gold mines
   (b) Higher inflation rates
   (c) Large inflow of Gold due to growth in foreign trade
   (d) Import of gold by the Gupta kings.

109. The issue of a large number of Gold coins during the Gupta period indicates
   (a) Discovery of new gold mines
   (b) Higher inflation rates
   (c) Large inflow of gold due to growth in foreign trade
   (d) Import of gold by the Gupta kings.

110. Chandragupta II Vikramaditya was the first Gupta king to issue silver coins. He issued his silver on the model of silver coins of
   (a) Sakas of western and central India
   (b) Punch marked coins
   (c) King Vikrama of Ujjaini
   (d) Indo-Greek kings.

111. Which of the following was common to the Tantra, Bhakti and Lingayat movements?
   (a) Rejection of austerities
   (b) Opposition of Orthodox Brahmanism
   (c) Disregard of caste inequalities
   (d) Personal relationship with God.

112. Which of the following statements about Nayanars and Alvars of South India is not correct?
   (a) They believed in austerities

(b) They looked upon religion as a living bond based on love between the god and the worshipper
(c) They spoke and wrote the language which everyone could understand
(d) They disregarded the inequalities of caste.

113. The Lingayats are worshippers of
(a) Vishnu (b) Shiva
(c) Ganesha (d) Sun God.

114. Jainism was ousted from Mysore by
(a) Shankaracharya (b) Lingayats
(c) Nayanars (d) Alvars.

115. The support of the Pala kings sustained Buddhism in eastern India for some time and royal patronage kept it flickering in Orissa, Kashmir and part of north-western India. Which of the following dealt the final blow leading to its disappearance?
(a) Bhakti movement
(b) Induction of Tantric cult
(c) Coming of Islam to India
(d) Revival of Hinduism.

116. Which of the following were not influenced by Tantrism?
(a) Jains
(b) Buddhists
(c) Worshippers of Shakti
(d) North-Panthis.

117. Which of the following statements about the ebb and flow of religious movements during this period is not correct?
(a) Jainism had become especially connected with the merchants and traders
(b) Tantrism also gained in popularity and become a prominent feature of religious life
(c) The orthodox Saivism had become largely associated with the ruling aristocracy
(d) All theological conflicts were connected with the possession and exploitation of land.

118. The only category of commercial professionals whose prosperity increased during this period were the
    (a) Makers of agricultural implements
    (b) Arms manufacturers
    (c) Weavers
    (d) Moneylenders.

119. Which of the following was not one of the consequences of the general decline in trade during this period?
    (a) Decline of towns
    (b) Trade guilds lost their former importance
    (c) Emergence of the powerful land owning community
    (d) Paucity of gold coins.

120. In the East trade with south-éast Asia and China was in operation. The main participants in this trade were
    (a) Palas (b) Senas
    (c) Pallavas (d) All of the above.

121. The followers of the religious sects who were considered as untouchable were
    (a) Materialists
    (b) Kapalikas
    (c) Atheists
    (d) Digambar Jains.

122. The most important mixed caste of the period was that of
    (a) Kayasthas (b) Vaidya
    (c) Jats (d) Gurjars.

123. The most valuable contribution of the period to technical literature was
    (a) Commentaries on medical texts of dharaka and Sushruba
    (b) Writings concerning astronomy and astrology
    (c) Discussions on problems of Algebra
    (d) Commentaries on law and legal institutions.

124. The legal and scientific works of the period were mostly in the nature of

(a) Plagiarisms from earlier writings
(b) Commentaries on earlier works and treatises on occult sciences
(c) Borrowings from foreign sources
(d) Original writings of great merit.

125. The Rajputs who were the ruling class of the period originated from the

(a) Firepit of sacrifice held at Mount Abu
(b) Assimilation of foreign tribes in Indian Society
(c) Assimilation of certain aboriginal tribes
(d) Both (b) and (c) above.

126. The most famous seat of learning during the period was

(a) The University of Vikramsila
(b) The University of Nalanda
(c) Valabhi
(d) The University of Jagadalla.

127. In the eleventh century the greatest centre of Sanskrit learning and scholarship in Central India was

(a) Dahara (b) Ujjaini
(c) Vidisha (d) Mandasor.

128. Which of the following scientific subjects was not taught at the University of Nalanda?

(a) Medicine at the University of Nalanda
(b) Astronomy
(c) Metallurgy
(d) Life Sciences.

129. Most large villages had schools attached to the

(a) Mathas
(b) Guilds
(c) Viharas
(d) Local Temples.

130. Which of the following was the most marked change in the institution of marriage?
   (a) Vigorous attempts to discourage all intercaste marriages
   (b) The progeny of the pratiloma marriages were regarded as shudras
   (c) Though monogamy was the normal rule, polygamy was widely practised by the aristocracy
   (d) Marriage of widows and divorcees was prohibited.

131. The remarriage of a widow was allowed when the
   (a) Husband died childless
   (b) Husband had deserted
   (c) Husband was impotent
   (d) Husband suffered from a contagious and incurable disease.

132. A large number of mixed castes were born out of mainly
   (a) Promiscuous marriages
   (b) Deserting and profession of one's caste
   (c) Prohibited marriages
   (d) Fallen women.

133. Which of the following was not one of the well-known mixed caste of the period?
   (a) Ambastha (b) Magadha
   (c) Modaka (d) Kayasthas.

134. The antyajas were those castes which were
   (a) Outside the purview of the four fold castes
   (b) Lowest and degraded out castes
   (c) Practitioners of certain or professions
   (d) All of the above.

135. Why has Alberuni written that there was little difference between the Vaishyas and Shudras?
   (a) Vaishyas joined the fold of agriculturists
   (b) With the decline of trade and commerce, the Vaishyas lost their economic status

(c) Both (a) and (b) above
(d) Vaishyas came to marry freely with the Shudra castes.

136. There was a very large proliferation of castes during the early mediaeval period due to
(a) Transformation of crafts and occupations into castes
(b) Emergence of a large number of mixed castes
(c) Both (a) and (b) above
(d) Localisation of castes.

137. The determinates of caste was/were
(a) Varna
(b) Occupation or profession
(c) Place of residence
(d) All of the above.

138. Which of the following was not one of the effects of the growth of a feudal society in India
(a) It weakened the position of the ruler
(b) The law and order situation uniformly deteriorated
(c) The growing social gaps between the upper and the lower social structure
(d) Growing rigidity regarding marriage, touch taboos and food taboos.

139. The surplus wealth of feudatories and the king was user for?
(a) Investments in craft production or trade
(b) Construction of temples and monuments
(c) Creation of works of pubic utility
(d) Conspiaicuous consumption and waging of wars.

140. During this period the political and economic power was concentrated in the hands of?
(a) Landed intermediaries
(b) Royal family
(c) Feudal lords
(d) All the above.

141. Which of the following was not one of the main factors responsible for reducing the mobility of the peasant population during this period?
(a) The localisation of economy
(b) The general poverty of the people
(c) The loss of social mobility due to the feudal system
(d) Decline of trade and commerce and urban life.

142. The name of the Chandella kingdom Jeja Kabhukti was derived from the name of Chandella king?
(a) Jayashakti (b) Vijayashakti
(c) Nannuka (d) Harsha.

143. The Chalukyas of Gujarat were out thrown by
(a) Baghelas or Solankis (b) Eastern Chalukya
(c) Gujaras (d) Kachhapaghatas.

144. What was the advantage of the feudal system from a purely administrative point of view?
(a) It led to better administration
(b) It made the administration more efficient
(c) It obviated the need for a centrally administered bureaucracy
(d) It made the administration more responsive to the needs of the people.

145. Which of the following was not one of the rights of feudatories?
(a) Collection of land revenue
(b) Right of awarding punishments and exacting fines
(c) Right of concluding treaties with other kings
(d) Right of treasure troves and mines on their lands.

146. The feudal relationship which gradually gained importance during this period was?
(a) Payment of tribute to overlord
(b) Payment of share of taxes to the king
(c) Hierarchy among the feudatories
(d) Military services.

147. Which of the following titles was not used by the feudatories of the period?
(a) Panchamahasabda (b) Mahamandalesvara
(c) Mandalika (d) Mahasmanta.

148. The feudataries were largely drawn from?
(a) Government officers and military chiefs
(b) Local hereditary chief and landed aristocracy
(c) Tribal or clan leaders
(d) All of the above.

149. In India feudalism the relationship of the vassal of the king was?
(a) Very close
(b) Of equals
(c) Close but subordinate
(d) Distant but equal.

150. The feudal process in India was intensified owing to?
(a) Turko Afghan attacks from the north-western region
(b) Lack of powerful central authority
(c) Granting off and
(d) The rise of the Rajputs.

151. Medhatithi was the famous commentator on?
(a) Manusmriti (b) Kamandakantisara
(c) Trihyasutras (d) Naradasmriti.

152. Which of the following was the greatest royal patron of Jainism in the 7th century?
(a) Kumarapala, Chalukya
(b) Jayasimha Siddharaja, Chalukya
(c) Gangeyadeva, Kalachuri
(d) Vidyadhara, Chandella.

153. A Buddhist monk who went to Tibet in the eleventh century to propagate Buddhism was?
(a) Dipankara Srijnana (b) Nagarjuna
(c) Pujyapada (d) Vasubandhu.

154. The temple of Somnath which was destroyed by Mahmud Ghazni was a temple dedicated to Lord?

(a) Vishnu (b) Shiva
(c) Surya (d) Krishna.

155. A ruler of Assam who was Prachi Pradip or the light of the East was

(a) Barahmapal (b) Indrapala
(c) Vidyanath (d) Vallabhadeava.

156. The Chandella king who in old age is said to have sacrificed his life at the Sangam in Prayaga was?

(a) Dhanga (b) Vidyadhara
(c) Harsha (d) Yasovarman.

157. The famous image of Vagdevi, which is the insignia of Jnanpith Award is associated with king

(a) Bhoja, Paramara
(b) Vigraharaja IV, Chauhan
(c) Kumarapala, Chaluka
(d) Vidyadhara, Chandella.

158. A Pala king who has been immortalised in popular Bengali traditions, folk songs and ballads as

(a) Dharmapala (b) Devapala
(c) Gopala (d) Mahipala I.

159. An Arab Astronomer who all the way went to Varanasi and studied Sanskrit language and astronomy therefore a decade was

(a) Alberuni (b) Amir Khusrau
(c) Al M, ashar (d) Al, Bidari.

160. The Arab traveller to India whose work is called the "mirror of the eleventh century India" was

(a) Al M ashar (b) Al Beruni
(c) Al Hajjaj (d) Almansur.

ANSWERS

1	(d)	2	(a)	3	(b)	4.	(c)
5	(c)	6	(a)	7	(c)	8	(a)
9	(a)	10	(a)	11	(a)	12	(b)
13	(b)	14	(c)	15	(a)	16	(b)
17	(c)	18	(b)	19	(b)	20	(c)
21	(d)	22	(c)	23	(b)	24	(a)
25	(c)	26	(b)	27	(d)	28	(a)
29	(b)	30	(a)	31	(b)	32	(a)
33	(c)	34	(a)	35	(a)	36	(c)
37	(b)	38	(b)	39	(b)	40	(b)
41	(c)	42	(a)	43	(b)	44	(d)
45	(b)	46	(b)	47	(b)	48	(b)
49	(b)	50	(d)	51	(c)	52	(b)
53	(b)	54	(a)	55	(b)	56	(b)
57	(b)	58	(d)	59	(c)	60	(d)
61	(c)	62	(c)	63	(a)	64	(a)
65	(b)	66	(b)	67	(a)	68	(b)
69	(b)	70	(c)	71	(d)	72	(d)
73	(c)	74	(a)	75	(c)	76	(d)
77	(c)	78	(a)	79	(c)	80	(c)
81	(c)	82	(a)	83	(d)	84	(c)
85	(c)	86	(c)	87	(a)	88	(a)
89	(a)	90	(c)	91	(b)	92	(b)
93	(b)	94	(d)	95	(b)	96	(c)
97	(a)	98	(d)	99	(d)	100	(a)
101	(c)	102	(c)	103	(c)	104	(d)
105	(b)	106	(a)	107	(a)	108	(c)
109	(a)	110	(a)	111	(c)	112	(a)
113	(b)	114	(b)	115	(c)	116	(a)
117	(d)	118	(d)	119	(d)	120	(d)
121	(d)	122	(a)	123	(c)	124	(b)
125	(d)	126	(b)	127	(a)	128	(d)
129	(d)	130	(a)	131	(d)	132	(a)
133	(c)	134	(d)	135	(c)	136	(c)
137	(d)	138	(b)	139	(d)	140	(d)
141	(b)	142	(a)	143	(a)	144	(c)
145	(c)	146	(d)	147	(a)	148	(d)
149	(c)	150	(c)	151	(a)	152	(a)
153	(a)	154	(b)	155	(b)	156	(a)
157	(a)	158	(c)	159	(c)	160	(b)

8
AGRICULTURAL SET UP : POST GUPTA PERIOD

1. The term 'Vishti' stands for
   (a) Landless labourers
   (b) Forced labour
   (c) Payment of rent for land partially in the form of free labour
   (d) Both (b) and (c) above.

2. The beginning of the practice of land grants with fiscal and administrative immunities to Brahmins and Buddhists monks was made by the
   (a) Mauryas (b) Satavahanas
   (c) Kushanas (d) Guptas.

3. The most important privilege, enjoyed by the persons who received those grants was/were
   (a) Right to impose taxes
   (b) Exemption from payment of taxes
   (c) Managing the administration of the donated area
   (d) All the above.

4. The most solemnification result of the surrender of administrative rights to the donors of lands was
   (a) Gift villages acquired semi-independent status
   (b) The pace of colonisation of land was accelerated
   (c) It enfeebled royal control over the country side
   (d) It created intermediaries between the king and the people.

5. The underlying ideas of donating land was
   (a) To appease the Brahmins
   (b) To earn spiritual merit
   (c) Receiving the grant of land was socially more prestigious and economically more productive
   (d) To reduce the burden on the exchequer.

6. The secular land grants were given
   (a) In lieu of salary to officers
   (b) As reward or pension to warriors and others
   (c) As a gift on festive occasions
   (d) All the above.

7. The whole village granted to the Brahmins was known as
   (a) Agrahara (b) Purchitagrama
   (c) Brahmagrama (d) Brahmadeya.

8. In what way did this land grant to officials not have the regular feudal character?
   (a) It did not stipulate provision of troops or revenue for the state
   (b) It did not contain the provision for resumption of land by the king in certain circumstances
   (c) It did not permit construction of forts
   (d) It could not be sub-infeudated.

9. The person who received the grant of land enjoyed the privilege of
   (a) Imposing the rent and taxes on tenants
   (b) Realising the rent in cash, kind, or even in the form of free labour
   (c) Both (a) and (b) above
   (d) Evicting the existing tenants.

10. The significance of the transfer of royal rights over mining and manufacture of salt to the donors was that it
    (a) Ensured regular income
    (b) Ensured loyalty from the donors
    (c) Amounted to transfer of sovereignty
    (d) Resulted in explanation of the miners.

11. In which of the following parts of India did the land grants empower the recipients of grants to punish the criminals?
    (a) North (b) South
    (c) West (d) North-east.

12. In which of the following was not one of the result of the vesting of magisterial and police powers together with fiscal rights on the donors of land grants?
    (a) It led to increase in administrative control
    (b) It put the owners for out of reach of the control of the central authority
    (c) It weakened the authority of the king
    (d) It led to the oppression of the inhabitants.

13. In south India the biggest beneficiaries of land grants were the
    (a) Brahmins
    (b) Temples
    (c) Both (a) and (b) above
    (d) Warriors and officials.

14. In the south, crown lands were rented out to
    (a) Tenant farmers (b) Tenants in chief
    (c) Tenants at will (d) Permanent tenants.

15. The natural resources which were donated by the king were
    (a) Water resources (b) Mines
    (c) Forest lands (d) All the above.

16. The royal writs of land grants during the post Gupta period were known as
    (a) Sasanapatra (b) Jayapatra
    (c) Ajnapatra (d) Prasadpatra.

17. Which of the following literary sources is not relevant for the agrarian condition of the post-Gupta period?
    (a) Kethana's Rajatarangini
    (b) Jimutavahan's Dayabhaga
    (c) Medathiti's commentary and Manusamriti
    (d) Bana's Harshacharita.

18. In the post-Gupta period royal deeds of lands were known as Samsanas and private persons deeds were called
    (a) Lankikalekha
    (b) Karyalekha
    (c) Both (a) and (b) above
    (d) Adhikarlekha.

19. That during the post-Gupta period of king was not the absolute owner of the land is proved by
    (a) Kings buying the lands from individuals for purposes of royal donations
    (b) Records of private land transactions
    (c) Individuals measuring and demarcating their lands
    (d) All the above.

20. When the law books of the period referred to the king as the lord of the whole earth, it only meant
    (a) His right of taking taxes
    (b) His right over the treasure troves
    (c) Both (a) and (b) above
    (d) A sovereign authority.

21. The practice of escheating the property of a person dying issueless, to the royal treasury was abolished by king
    (a) Kumarapala of Gujarat
    (b) Boja Paramara of Malwa
    (c) Mihirbhoja of Kannauj
    (d) Vallalsena of Bengal.

22. The term Satka Kautumbika Khetra was used for land which was
    (a) Community land
    (b) Joint land owned by a large family
    (c) Given to the cultivator or superior for the services rendered by him
    (d) Crown land.

23. Which of the following was not one of the causes for the hard lot of the peasants during this period?
    (a) Heavy taxation
    (b) Forced labour
    (c) High rate of interest on agricultural loans
    (d) Growth of landed intermediaries.

24. How did the practice of land grants reduce a large number of peasants of serfdom
    (a) It aggravated their poverty forcing them to the position of slaves
    (b) They were often required to work on the land even when it had been granted to others
    (c) The exploitation of private landlords was greater than that of king
    (d) Due to absentee landlordism.

25. Vishti, a kind of tax which was to be given in the form of physical labour, was mainly forced on
    (a) Artisans, craftsman and the sudras
    (b) Sudra and Vaisya peasant cultivators
    (c) The whole village population irrespective of caste or profession
    (d) Only the sudras and slaves.

26. The king's share of the produce was normally known as
    (a) Bhaga
    (b) Chauth
    (c) Kara
    (d) Hiranya.

27. Which of the following was not one of the services to be performed by the villagers, when royal troops and officials halted at or passed through the village
    (a) Vacate house for them
    (b) Contribute money and gifts
    (c) Contribute provisions
    (d) Provide cattle for transport.

28. Peasant women were forced to perform unpaid work of various kinds which of the following was not one of them
   (a) Filling the granaries of the village headman
   (b) Taking things in and out of the house
   (c) Acting as body guards
   (d) Working in the fields.

29. Which of the following was not one of the reasons for groups of peasants sometimes emigrating into the jungle to form new settlements
   (a) Over population and consequent pressure on land
   (b) To escape the attentions of extrotionate tax collectors
   (c) To colonise the virgin lands for higher production
   (d) To gain the status of free peasants.

30. The labourers were paid wages in cash or as a share of the produce. What was their share of the produce, if accompanied by food
   (a) One third (b) One fourth
   (c) One fifth (d) One sixth.

31. Udranga Uparikara, found mentioned in several post-Gupta epigraphs had been interpreted as a tax
   (a) Levied for the maintenance of police
   (b) On fish and other water products
   (c) On cultivators not having proprietary rights
   (d) All the above.

32. The burden of taxation during this period was generally
   (a) Average
   (b) Heavy and discriminatory
   (c) Oppressive
   (d) Extortionote.

33. The most popular industry, relating to agriculture products was
   (a) Sugar manufacturing (b) Oil milling
   (c) Cotton ginning (d) Diary products.

34. The king's share of the produce was normally
    (a) One sixth to one forth
    (b) One tenth to one twentieth
    (c) One tenth to one fifteenth
    (d) One third to one fourth.

35. Besides collecting the share of the produce, the state also collected tax/taxes on
    (a) Cattle (b) Irrigation works
    (c) Forest resources (d) All the above.

36. The body of officials entrusted with the job of collection of taxes was known as
    (a) Kutumbin (b) Panchkula
    (c) Kshetrakara (d) Saulkika.

37. According to the sacred law, certain persons were exempted from taxation, which of the following was/were not one of them?
    (a) Learned Brahmins (b) Women and destitute
    (c) Students (d) Slaves.

38. During the post-Gupta period, the taxation system was most oppressive in
    (a) Gujarat (b) Bengal and Bihar
    (c) Kashmir (d) Malwa.

39. The most interesting details on land and land use are available in
    (a) The land grant charters
    (b) Kalhana's Rajatarangini
    (c) Medhatithi's commentary of Manusmriti
    (d) Gurjara-Pratihara epigraphs.

0. Lands, during the post-Gupta period, were classified on the basis of
    (a) Being cultivated and uncultivated
    (b) Being irrigated and unirrigated
    (c) Gaps being grown on the lands
    (d) All the above.

41. Among the food grains, the most widely cultivated crops was

(a) Wheat (b) Rice
(c) Millets (d) Pulses.

42. The most important change in the agrarian life of the post-Gupta period was that

(a) Large scale transfer of land and land revenue to both secular and religious elements
(b) A vigorous process of subinfatuation
(c) Creation of social hierarchy based on ownership of land
(d) Degradation of agriculture as an honoured occupation.

43. The mobility of the peasantry during the post-Gupta period was last due to

(a) Peasants being tied to lands due to land grants
(b) The social structure including the castes were localised
(c) The whole economy become localised
(d) All the above.

44. The pressures on the agrarian economy increased during the post-Gupta period because

(a) Due to the decline of trade and commerce, urban artisans and craftsmen shifted to rural areas
(b) The largest share of agricultural surplus went towards payment of revenue and rent
(c) Total burden of the state and landed intermediaries fell on the agrarian classes
(d) All the above.

45. In several land grants the share croppers and peasants were specifically asked to remain attached to the soil in order to

(a) Remove all ambiguities in the relationship between the peasants and donors
(b) Keep the interests of the donors intact
(c) Both (a) and (b) above
(d) Keep the composition of the village population intact.

46. The feudal structure of the society is evident from the
    (a) Social structure based on the control and possession of land
    (b) Social and political prestige dependent on ownership of land
    (c) Both (a) and (b) above
    (d) Divisions of the society between landed intermediaries and peasant cultivators.

47. The Vaisyas came to Join the fold of the peasantry on account of
    (a) Restrictions of free trade
    (b) Localisation of economy
    (c) Decline of trade and commerce
    (d) Decline of money economy.

48. The lowest stratum of the dependent peasantry was represented by the
    (a) Share croppers
    (b) Dependent peasants
    (c) Ploughmen and field labourers
    (d) Both (b) and (c) above.

49. A religious sect, born out of agrarian protest against the existing system, was
    (a) Lingayat
    (b) Tantric
    (c) Sakta
    (d) Virasaivite.

50. The theory of the emergence of feudalism in the post-Gupta period is disputed on the ground that
    (a) All the lands were not given in land grants
    (b) Private ownership also existed and the status of peasants was not that of serfs
    (c) Both (a) and (b) above
    (d) There is no nexus between the Brahmins and the ruling class.

ANSWERS

1.	(d)	2.	(b)	3.	(b)	4.	(c)
5.	(c)	6.	(d)	7.	(c)	8.	(a)
9.	(c)	10.	(c)	11.	(a)	12.	(a)
13.	(c)	14.	(c)	15.	(d)	16.	(a)
17.	(d)	18.	(c)	19.	(d)	20.	(c)
21.	(a)	22.	(c)	23.	(c)	24.	(b)
25.	(b)	26.	(a)	27.	(a)	28.	(c)
29.	(c)	30.	(c)	31.	(d)	32.	(b)
33.	(b)	34.	(a)	35.	(d)	36.	(b)
37.	(d)	38.	(c)	39.	(a)	40.	(d)
41.	(b)	42.	(a)	43.	(d)	44.	(d)
45.	(c)	46.	(c)	47.	(c)	48.	(c)
49.	(a)	50.	(c)				

9
DRAVIDIAN HISTORY [DURING 800-1200 AD]

1. The glory of the Rashtrakuta art and architecture is/are
   (a) The Elephanta caves
   (b) Dasavatara temple, Ellora
   (c) Kalash temple, Ellora
   (d) Ravana-ki-Khai, Ellora.

2. What was the purpose of the embassies sent by the Chola kings to China?
   (a) To build up a common front against the kingdom of Sarivijaya
   (b) To establish cultural relations
   (c) To promote trade with China
   (d) To pay homage to the mighty Chinese emperors.

3. Which of the following was not one of the usual types of tenancy in the Chola system?
   (a) Feudal ownership
   (b) Communal ownership
   (c) Peasant proprietorship
   (d) Joint and service tenures.

4. To what purpose did Chola rulers carry out an elaborate survey of land?
   (a) To determine ownership right
   (b) For estimation of crop yields
   (c) To fix governments share of the land revenue
   (d) To demarcate the ayacut of the irrigation sources.

5. What portion of the produce was generally collected as land tax?
   (a) Half (b) One-third
   (c) One fourth (d) One sixth.

6. The largest single source of income to the Chola state was?
   (a) Land tax
   (b) Toll on trade
   (c) Taxes on professions, mines and forests
   (d) Plunder of neighbouring territories.

7. Which of the following was not one of the categories of non-taxable land?
   (a) Residential plots
   (b) Donated land
   (c) Temples and Cremation grounds
   (d) Tanks and irrigation channels.

8. The Chola kings spent a lot of money on public works, which of the following received special attention from them?
   (a) Roads
   (b) Hospitals
   (c) Rest House
   (d) Irrigation system.

9. The tenures which were meant for educational purpose were?
   (a) Brahimadeya (b) Devadana
   (c) Salabhoga (d) Sarvamanya.

10. The reason for a marked increase in the use of coins during the Chola period as compared to earlier dynasties of the region was
    (a) Increase in trade with foreign countries
    (b) Roman influence
    (c) Growth of Urban centres
    (d) Convenience of exchange.

11. The basis of exchange for commonplace articles in rural areas was:
    (a) Money (b) Cow
    (c) Paddy (d) Gold ornaments.

12. Overseas trade was the strength of the Chola Merchants. Which of the following was not one of the important Port towns of the Cholas?
    (a) Mahabalipuram (b) Masula
    (c) Kaveripttinam (d) Korkai.

13. What was importance of Sirafun Chola trade with Persia and Arabia?
    (a) It was the main market for purchases of horses
    (b) It had the maximum demand for Indian goods
    (c) It was the first halt for ships going to Persia and Arabia
    (d) It was a meeting point of the sailors and merchants of the entire Indian Oceans.

14. Which of the follwoing was not one of the important items of export to China and the West?
    (a) Superior quality textiles
    (b) Perfumes and spices
    (c) Precious stones
    (d) Jewellery.

15. The single most important item of imports to the Chola empire was :
    (a) Dyestuff (b) Horses
    (c) Precious stone (d) Metalware.

16. The consequence of trade with China reaching an unprecedented volume during the period was
    (a) It made for general prosperity of the people
    (b) It led to Indian merchants taking interest in Chinese politics
    (c) Trade with India became a state monopoly in China
    (d) The Chinese government saw in it a threat to its independence and hurried to curb it.

17. Which of the following was not one of the categories of gigantic merchant guilds of the Chola country?
    (a) Nagaram (b) Manigramam
    (c) Valanjiyar (d) Nanadesis.

18. A Rashtrakuta monarch who to avert the calamities being faced by his kingdom, cut off the fingers left hand as a sacrifice to the Goddess Mahalakshmi and Kolhapur was
    (a) Krishna (b) Dhruva IV
    (c) Amoghavarsha (d) Govinda III.

19. The most important factor on the economic life of the Chola empire was
    (a) First systematic survey of land
    (b) Assessment of land revenue on the basis of actual survey of land
    (c) Trade and craft guilds emerged very large and powerful
    (d) The division of the industrial workers into right and left handers.

20. Inspite of being well organised and heaving immense economic resources at their command the merchant guilds of the period did not aspire for any political power because
    (a) The Chola merchant on their own took keen interest to protect the interest of guilds
    (b) The Chola merchants took a great deal of military and diplomatic measures to promote trade
    (c) Both (a) and (b) above
    (d) Merchants had been granted many tax exemptions.

21. Besides the artistic merit, the other significance of the Chola temple was/were
    (a) Temples emerged as very large establishment
    (b) Temples were one of the biggest owners of land
    (c) Temples became centres of economic, social and cultural activities
    (d) All of the above.

22. The broad division of society was into Brahmins and non-Brahmins. Among the non-Brahmins the most prominent were
    (a) Kshatriyas (b) Vaishyas
    (c) Shudras (d) Out castes.

23. The secular functions performed by the temple of the Chola period were
    (a) Employment of Musicians and dancers
    (b) Provision of education and Medical treatment
    (c) Acting as bankers and granting loans to weavers
    (d) All of the above.

24. What the growth of trade, commerce and industries, there was a rise in the position of the industrial classes and some of these industrial classes, to improve their social status, tried to gain privileges which led to social tensions, who were right and left handers?
    (a) They were a special category
    (b) They were palace guards of officials
    (c) They were two groups of rival industrial classes
    (d) They were royalists the republicans.

25. The right and left handers (Valangai and idangi) classes struggled between themselves for
    (a) Secuarring special social privileges
    (b) Maintaining their exclusive residential areas
    (c) Securing political rights
    (d) All of above.

26. The Devadasi system became quite prevelent from the Chola period because of the
    (a) Feudal character of polity and society
    (b) Decline in the position of women
    (c) Temples became large complexes which required a large number of permanent women workers
    (d) All of the above.

27. The Chola monarchs were patrons of
    (a) Shaivism
    (b) Vaishnavism
    (c) Shaktism
    (d) Buddhism.

28. The most famous and beautiful Chola bronzes were those of
    (a) Nataraza
    (b) Murugan
    (c) Lord Venkateshwara
    (d) Lord Vishnu.

29. The most famous Buddhist monastery in the Chola empire, to which liberal donations were made by the Chola monarch as well as by the ashailendera kings of Srivijaya, was at
    (a) Kanchi (b) Negapatame
    (c) Thanjavur (d) Sriangam.

30. What was the keynote of the esoteric cults, such as Kapalikash, Klamuklisas, Pashupatas and others?
    (a) Worship of Shakti
    (b) Strange rites
    (c) Non-conformist doctrines
    (d) Sexual orgies.

31. The main feature of this Dravida style of temple architecture was
    (a) Shikaora (b) Gopuram
    (c) Vimana (d) Mandapa.

32. The temple regarded as the first and most elaborate example of Chola architecture is
    (a) Subrahmanya temple at Thanjavur
    (b) Brihadiswara temple at Tanjavur
    (c) Temple at Kailashnath at Kanchipuram
    (d) Temple at Gangaikonda Cholapuram.

33. The art of sculpture attain a high standard in south India during this period. It was, however, in bronze sculpture that the Chola craftsmen excelled of the following types of images produced by them, which are the most famous?
    (a) Deities
    (b) Donors
    (c) Saints
    (d) Apsaras and Gandharvas.

34. Who said that "the Chola artists conceived like giants and finished like jewellers"?
    (a) Prof. K.A Niakanta (b) Percy Brown
    (c) Fergusson (d) V.V.R.Dikhitar.

35. A remarkable feature of the period was the growth of literature in the local languages of the south. Which of the following were largely responsible for this development?
    (a) The Chola
    (b) The Mathas
    (c) The Popular saints
    (d) The Temples.

36. Which of the following Tamil writers of the period wrote the Ramayana which is considered as a classic in Tamil literature?
    (a) Pugalendi (b) Kamban
    (c) Jayangondur (d) Kallandanar.

37. Which of the following kingdom of Deccan and South India achieved great prominence from the ninth century onwards?
    (a) Chalukyas of Kalyani
    (b) Kakatiyas of Warangal
    (c) Cholas of Thanjavur
    (d) Hoysalas of Dwarasamudram.

38. The Chalukya King of Kalyani who said to have established a new era in place of the old saka era was
    (a) Talia I (b) Someshvara III
    (c) Vikramaditya VI (d) Vikramaditya.

39. The bitterest enemies of the Chalukyas of Kalyani were
    (a) Cholas of Thanjavur (b) Yadavas of Devagiri
    (c) Paramaras of Malwa (d) Chalukyas of Vengi.

40. Which of the following was not one of the three Chalukyas feudatories who shared the Empire of Kalyani when it split up towards the end of the twelfth century?
    (a) Pandyas of Madurai
    (b) Yadavas of Devagiri
    (c) Kakatiyas of Warangal
    (d) Hoysalas of Dwarasamudram.

41. Which of the following established a kingdom for the Hoysala dynasty?
    (a) Vishnuvardhana (sala)
    (b) Ballala
    (c) Bhillama
    (d) Harihara.

42. The independent Yadava Kingdom of Devagiri was founded by
    (a) Prolaraja II (b) Ganapati
    (c) Bhillama (d) Singhana.

43. The Kakatiya ruler who has been mentioned in glowing terms by the Veteran traveller Marco Polo, is
    (a) Prolaraja II (b) Ganapati
    (c) Rudramma (d) Rudradeva.

44. The Pandyan rulers were chiefly engaged in battle during this period with
    (a) Cholas (b) Cheras
    (c) Pallavas (d) Hoysalas.

45. The Pandyan king who was defeated Kulottunga III and ushered into existence the glorious period of Pandyan imperialism during the thirteenth century was
    (a) Rajasimha II (b) Vargunavarman II
    (c) Vira Panday (d) Sundara Pandya.

46. The Pandyan empire was finally absorbed into the ------ kingdom.
(a) Bahmani (b) Chera
(c) Vijayanagar (d) Delhi.

47. The Chola king was subjugated the Chera ruler and destroyed his naval fleet was?
(a) Rajendra I (b) Rajaraja I
(c) Kulottunga I (d) Adhi Rajendra.

48. In which following regions did the Eastern Ganges establish their kingdom?
(a) Eastern Mysore (b) Kalinga
(c) Bihar and Bengal (d) Kamarupa.

49. The Rashtrakutas were successors of the
(a) Vikatakas
(b) Chalukayas of Kalgni
(c) Chalukyas of Badami
(d) Pallavas of Kanchi.

50. The Rashtrakuta king who conquered the Cholas, was
(a) Govinda III (b) Amoghavarsha I
(c) Indra III (d) Krishna III.

ANSWERS

1.	(c)	2.	(c)	3.	(a)	4.	(c)
5.	(b)	6.	(a)	7.	(b)	8.	(d)
9.	(c)	10.	(c)	11.	(c)	12.	(b)
13.	(d)	14.	(d)	15.	(b)	16.	(c)
17.	(a)	18.	(c)	19.	(c)	20.	(c)
21.	(c)	22.	(c)	23.	(d)	24.	(c)
25.	(a)	26.	(c)	27.	(a)	28.	(a)
29.	(b)	30.	(c)	31.	(c)	32.	(b)
33.	(a)	34.	(c)	35.	(c)	36.	(b)
37.	(c)	38.	(c)	39.	(a)	40.	(a)
41.	(a)	42.	(c)	43.	(c)	44.	(a)
45.	(d)	46.	(c)	47.	(b)	48.	(b)
49.	(a)	50.	(d)				

10
HISTORY OF NORTH-SOUTH PROVINCES

1. Bengal was frequently independent of the control of Delhi, which of the following was not one of the reason for this?
   (a) Its distance from Delhi
   (b) The composition of its population
   (c) Its communications depended upon waterways with which the Turkish rulers were unfamiliar
   (d) Its profuse wealth tempted its governors to rebel against the central authority.
2. The Ilyas Shahi Sultan who exchanged embassies with the Chinese emperor of the Ming dynasty was
   (a) Shamsuddin Ilyas Shah
   (b) Sikander Shah
   (c) Ghiyasuddin Azam Shah
   (d) Nasiruddin Mahmud Shah.
3. The Sultan of Delhi who twice made unsuccessful efforts to recover Bengal during the reign of Ilyas Shah and his son Sikander Shah was
   (a) Ghiyasuddin Balban (b) Ghiyasuddin Khalji
   (c) Allauddin Khalji (d) Firuz Tughluq.
4. During the reign of which of the following kings of Hussain Shahi dynasty did Sikander Lodi attach Bengal?
   (a) Alauddin Husain Shah
   (b) Nasiruddin Nusrat Shah
   (c) Alauddin Firuz Shah
   (d) Ghiyasuddin Mahmud Shah.

5. Slaves belonging to which of the following nationalities played an important role in the politics of Bengal in the last quarter of the fifteenth century?
   (a) Turk
   (b) Afghan
   (c) Abyssina
   (d) Arab.

6. Bengal had a number of popular rulers who promoted communal harmony and worked for the prosperity of the state. Which of the following was not one of them?
   (a) Shamsuddin Ilyas Shah
   (b) Shamsuddin Ahmad
   (c) Raja Ganesh
   (d) Alauddin Husain Shah.

7. Which of the following was not one of the contributions of Alauddin Husain Shah of Bengal?
   (a) The creative genius of the people of medialval Bengal reached its zenith
   (b) The Bengali literature made a tremendous advance
   (c) The liberally conferred high posts upon the Hindu subjects
   (d) He was a great poet of Bengali language.

8. The tribe of Ahoms, from whom formed a section of the------tribe
   (a) Bodo (b) Shan
   (c) Bhuiya (d) Kachari.

9. The Sultans of Bengal issued a rich variety of coins. The coins issued by which of the following sultans are said to carry a "refreshing air of refinement"and are regarded as "veritable gems of the art of coin striking"?
   (a) Fakhruddin Mubarak Shah
   (b) Shamsuddin Ilyas Shah
   (c) Sikander Shah
   (d) Alauddin Hussain Shah.

10. Who finally annexed Bengal and brought about the decline and fall of the dynasty of Ilyas Khan?
(a) Babur (b) Humayn
(c) Sher Shah Suri (d) Akbar.

11. Which of the following was not one of the warring kingdoms of Assam and East Bengal at the time?
(a) Kamata (b) Ahom
(c) Kamarupa (d) Vanga.

12. The founder of the Gajapati dynasty of Orissa was
(a) Narasimha I (b) Kapilendra
(c) Purushottama (d) Prataparudra.

13. The ruler of Bengal who annexed Kamata with the support of Ahoms was
(a) Shamsuddin Ilyas Shah
(b) Raja Ganesh
(c) Alauddin Husain Shah
(d) Nasiruddin Nusrat Shah.

14. During the reign of which of the following dynasties of Orissa were the temple of Jagannath at Puri and the temple of the sun god at Konarak constructed?
(a) Choda Ganga dynasty
(b) Gajapati dynasty
(c) Bhoi dynasty
(d) Ganga dynasty.

15. The rulers of which of the following provinces were the most important rivals of the rulers of Khandesh?
(a) Gujarat
(b) Malwa
(c) Berar
(d) Bahmani Kingdom.

16. Who annexed Khandesh to his empire?
(a) Sikander Lodi (b) Babu
(c) Akbar (d) Aurangzeb.

17. Who annexed Gujarat to the Delhi Sultanate?
    (a) Ghiyasuddin Balban
    (b) Alauddin Khalji
    (c) Mohammed Bin Tughluq
    (d) Firuz Tughlaq.

18. After the death of which of the following Sultans did Malik Raja Faruqi, the governor of Khandesh, declare his independence of the Delhi Sultanate?
    (a) Muhammad bin Tughluq
    (b) Firuz Tughluq
    (c) Khizr Khan
    (d) Bahlul Lodi.

19. The dynasty founded by Govinda came to be known as Bhoi dynasty because
    (a) The rulers of this dynasty belonged to the Bhoi tribe
    (b) The rulers of this dynasty originally came from Bhoi region of Orissa
    (c) Govinda, a former minister of Prataparudra, belonged to the Bhoi or witter caste
    (d) Bhoi means warrior in the Oriya language.

20. During the reign of which of the following kings was the kingdom of Orissa extended from the Ganga to the Kaveri
    (a) Narasimha I (b) Kapilendra
    (c) Prataparudra (d) Govinda.

21. The kingdom of Gujarat reached its extreme limit during the reign of
    (a) Ahmad Shah
    (b) Muhammad Shah
    (c) Qutbuddin Ahmad
    (d) Abdul Fath Khan.

22. The new town of Mustaphabad was founded by Mahmud Begarha after his victory over the part of
    (a) Champanir (b) Girnar
    (c) Chittor (d) Burhanpur.

23. Ahmad Shah built the capital city of Ahmadabad on the site of the old town of
    (a) Arawal (b) Sabarmati
    (c) Sidhpur (d) Idar.

24. Which of the following is regarded as the real founder of the independent kingdom of Gujarat?
    (a) Zafar Khan (b) Tatar Khan
    (c) Sham Khan (d) Ahmad Shah.

25. When did Zafar Khan, the governor of Gujarat, formally declare his independence?
    (a) After the death of Alauddin Khalji
    (b) During the confusion immediately after the death of Muhammad bin Tughluq
    (c) During the reign of Firuz Tughluq
    (d) After Timur's invasion of Delhi.

26. During the rule of which of the following kings did Orissa face aggression from Krishnadeva Raya of Vijayanagar as well as from the Qutb Shahi kingdom of Golcunda?
    (a) Kapilendra (b) Purushottama
    (c) Prataprudra (d) Govinda.

27. Khandesh was a province in the empire of which of the following sultans of Delhi?
    (a) Ghiyasuddin Balban
    (b) Alauddin Khalji
    (c) Muhammad bin Tughluq
    (d) Sikander Lodi.

28. The primary reason for Mahmud Begarha's attack on Dwarka was to
    (a) Loot the wealth of the temples
    (b) Destroy the temples
    (c) Suppress the pirates who preyed on the pilgrim traffic to Mecca
    (d) Check the rising power of the Portuguese in the Indian seas.

29. Which of the following was not one of the reasons why Gujarat was one of the richest provinces of the Delhi Sultanate?
    (a) Excellence of its handicraft and textiles
    (b) Its flourishing sea ports
    (c) Richness of its mineral wealth
    (d) Richness of its soil.

30. Before the coming of the Muslim rulers, Kashmir was known to be a centre of
    (a) Buddhism (b) Jainism
    (c) Vaishnavism (d) Shaivism.

31. Marwar, which was under Mewar's occupation, became independent under the leadership of
    (a) Rawal (b) Rao Jodha
    (c) Lakha (d) Mokala.

32. Rana Kumbha was not
    (a) A playwright and literary critic
    (b) A great builder
    (c) An accomplished musician
    (d) A great mathematician and astronomer.

33. Who founded the state of Mewar?
    (a) Rawal (b) Hamir
    (c) Kshitra (d) Rana Kumbha.

34. What was the occasion for Rana Kumbha's construction of the 'Tower of Victory' at Chittor?
    (a) His victory against Ahmad Shah of Gujarat
    (b) His Victory against Mahmud Khalji of Malwa
    (c) His victory against the Khan of Nagaur
    (d) His victory against Rao Jodha of Marwar.

35. What was the name of the Muslim adventurer from Swat who, having entered the service of the Hindu prince of Kashmir, seized the throne upon the latter's death?
    (a) Mirza Haider (b) Mir Jumla
    (c) Shah Mirza (d) Mirza Ghiyas Beg.

36. A ruler of Mewar who was a great expert of the art of fortifications and built thirty two forts, a number of temples, lakes, reservoirs etc. was
    (a) Rana Sanga (b) Rana Kumbha
    (c) Rana Pratap (d) Rana Amar Singh.

37. The bitterest rival of the medieaIval kingdom of Gujarat was
    (a) Khandesh (b) Malwa
    (c) Mewar (d) Marwar.

38. Mahmud Khalji, who usurped the throne of Malwa and founded the dynasty of the Khalji sultans of Malwa, was a minister of
    (a) Dilawar Khan (b) Ghazni Khan
    (c) Ghiyasuddin (d) Hushang Shah.

39. Mahmud Begarha attacked the Portuguese in alliance with the Sultan of Egypt, because
    (a) He was apprehensive of their political intentions in Gujarat
    (b) Portuguese pirates were a nuisance to his merchants and pilgrims
    (c) The Portuguese were interfering with Gujarat trade with the countries of West Asia
    (d) He was requested to do so by the Sultan of Egypt who wanted to teach the Portuguese a lesson for their arrogance.

40. Against which of the following kingdoms did the rulers of Malwa wages wars?
    (a) Gujarat (b) Mewar
    (c) Bahmani (d) All the above.

41. Who was Dalucha?
    (a) An Arab Mercenary
    (b) A Mughal leader
    (c) A Mughal governor
    (d) A Muslim minister in the court of the Hindu ruler of Kashmir.

42. The ruler of Kashmir who has been described as the Akbar of Kashmir was
   (a) Alauddin Shah
   (b) Shihabuddin Shah
   (c) Shahi Khan (Zainul Abidin)
   (d) Haider Shah.

43. Zainul Abidin was an enthusiastic builder, his greatest engineering achievement being Zaina Lanka, an artificial island in
   (a) Dal Lake (b) Woalur Lake
   (c) Mansabal Lake (d) Anachan Lake.

44. The ruler of Kashmir who earned the title of Butshikan or idol breaker was
   (a) Shamsuddin Shah
   (b) Qutbuddin Shah
   (c) Sikander Shah
   (d) Ali Shah.

45. The city of Jaunpur was founded by Firuz Tughluq to perpetuate the memory of
   (a) Ghiyasuddin Tughluq
   (b) Alaudin Khalji
   (c) Muhammad bin Tughluq
   (d) Ghiyasuddin Balban.

46. The ruler of Kashmir who, to get rid of the fanatical flights between the Shias and Sunnis and repeated rebellions and counter rebellions, sought the intervention of the Mughal Emperor Akbar was
   (a) Hussain Shah (b) Ghazi Khan
   (c) Yusuf Shah (d) Ali Shah.

47. Who annexed the Sharqi kingdom of Jaunpur to the Sultanate?
   (a) Daulat Khan Lodi (b) Bahlul Lodi
   (c) Sikander Lodi (d) Ibrahim Lodi.

48. Zainul Abidin foretested many crafts in Kashmir, which of the following did he borrow from Samarqand?
   (a) Paper making and book binding
   (b) Stone cutting and polishing
   (c) Shawal making
   (d) Musket making.

49. What was the importance of Malwa's geographical situation?
   (a) It was surrounded by the warring kingdoms of Gujarat, Khandesh and Mewar
   (b) It was on the route to the Arabian sea for the rulers of Delhi
   (c) It commanded the trunk routes from North India to Gujarat as well as South India
   (d) It was surrounded on two sides by in assessible hill ranges and by the rivers Narmada and Tapti on the remaining two sides.

50. How did the rulers of Jaunpur acquire the epithet Sharqi?
   (a) From the name of the Turkish tribe to which they belonged
   (b) From the title of Sultan-us-Sharq given to their founder Malik Sarwar
   (c) On account of the suspicious circumstances of their coming to power
   (d) From the name of the place where they originally founded their capital city.

51. Bahman Shah or Alaudin Hasan selected Gulabarga as his capital and renamed it
   (a) Hasanpur (b) Bidar
   (c) Ahsanabad (d) Bahmanabad.

52. Which of the following factors was responsible for the foundation of the Bahmani kingdom?
   (a) The break-up the kingdom of the Chalukyas of Kalyani
   (b) The chain of rebellions against the Tughluq authority in the Deccan

(c) The encouragement and military support received from the Sultanate of Delhi

(d) The rebellion of the Amiran-I. Sadahs who took advantage of the widespread rebellions and mounting discontent against Muhammad-bin-Tugluq.

53. The Bahmani Sultan who got the epithet of Zalim of the Tyrant on account of his alleged cruelties was

(a) Mujahid Shah
(b) Tajuddin Firuz Shah
(c) Humayun
(d) Mahmud Shah.

54. The Bahmani Sultan who shifted the capital from Gulabarga to Bidar was

(a) Muhammad Shah
(b) Ahmad Shah
(c) Nizam Shah
(d) Mahmud Shah.

55. The Muslim Kingdom of Golcunda grew up on the ruins of the old Hindu kingdom of

(a) Devagiri (b) Dwarasamudra
(c) Warangal (d) Kanchi.

56. The kingdom of Berar was absorbed by

(a) Bijapur (b) Ahmadnagar
(c) Golcunda (d) Bidar.

57. The Barid Shahi dynasty of Bidar arose on the ruins of the last remnants of the Bahmani kingdom. Into which of the following was the kingdom of Bidar absorbed?

(a) Bijapur (b) Ahmadnagar
(c) Golcunda (d) Berar.

58. The last Deccani state annexed to the Mughal Empire by Aurangzeb was

(a) Bijapur (b) Ahmadnagar
(c) Golcunda (d) Berar.

59. Five separate Sultanats arose in Deccan, one after another on the break-up of the Bahmani kingdom. Which of the following was the first to secede?
   (a) The Adilshahi dynasty of Bijapur
   (b) The Imadshahi dynasty of Berar
   (c) The Nizamshahi dynasty of Golcunda
   (d) The Qutbshahi dynasty of Golcunda.

60. The Afaqis in the Bahmani kingdom were :
   (a) The Muslim immigrants from Iran, Iraq, Turkey, Arabia etc.
   (b) Foreign merchants settled in the Bahmani kingdom
   (c) South Indian Muslim converts
   (d) Shia nobles of the Bahamani court.

61. The main reason for the collapse of the Bahmani kingdom was
   (a) Increased power of its traditional enemy the kingdom of Vijaynagar
   (b) The strife between the two leading groups of nobles the Deccanis and Afagans
   (c) A serious famine which led to popular revolt and consequent confusion
   (d) The powerful position of the provincial governors and their consequent rebellions after the murder of Mahmud Gawan.

62. Which of the following statements about the causes of strif between the Deccani and the Pardesi or Afaqi nobles of the Bahmani kingdom is not correct?
   (a) The pardesis were more energetic and enterprising than the Deccanis
   (b) A majority of the pardesis were Shias whereas most of the Deccanis were Sunnis
   (c) The pardesis wielded considerable influence in the politics of the country which was resented by the Deccanis
   (d) The pardesis were in favour of persecution of the Hindu population whereas the Deccanis were opposed to such a policy.

63. The Bahamanis were traditional enemies of the ruler of Vijaynagar. What was the main bone of contention between the two

(a) Telengana (b) Goa
(c) The Fort of Mudagal (d) Raichur Doab.

64. Mahmud Gawan, a pardesi, was sentenced to death as a result of a conspiracy of the Deccanis. The Sultan responsible for Mahmud Gawan's execution was

(a) Humayun
(b) Nizam Shah
(c) Muhammad Shall II
(d) Mahmud Shah.

65. A foreign traveller who visited the Bahmani kingdom during the reign of Muhammad Shah III and observed that the lot of the common people was miserable while the noble lived in luxury, was :

(a) Nicalo Conti (b) Athanasius Nikitin
(c) Nuniz (d) Abdur Razzak.

66. The Qutbshahi Kingdom of Golcunda was known all over the world for its

(a) Diamonds
(b) Textiles
(c) Both (a) and (b) above
(d) Spice.

67. To which of the following kingdoms did Chand Bibi belong?

(a) Bijapur (b) Berar
(c) Golcunda (d) Ahmadnagar.

68. The founder of the city of Hyderabad was :

(a) Ibrahim Qutb Shah
(b) Muhammad Quli Qutb Shah
(c) Muhammad Qutb Shah
(d) Jamshid Qutb Shah.

69. The Portuguese founded their kingdom at the expense of
 (a) The Adilshahi kingdom of Bijapur
 (b) The Qutbshahi kingdom of Golcunda
 (c) The Nizamshahi kingdom of Ahmadnagar
 (d) The Baridshahi kingdom of Bidar.

70. The Deccani Muslim state which declared 'Hindvi' or Dakhni Urdu as the official language of the state instead of Persian, was
 (a) Bijapur (b) Ahmadnagar
 (c) Golcunda (d) Berar.

71. The provinces of the Bahmani kingdom were known as
 (a) Taraf ar Ataraf
 (b) Subah
 (c) Subah-i-laskar
 (d) Mahamandala.

72. The Bahmani Wazir Mahmud Gawan founded a famous college at
 (a) Gulabarga (b) Daulatabad
 (c) Bidar (d) Golcunda.

73. The five Sultans of the Bahmani succession states after the decline of the Bahmani kingdom, were originally :
 (a) Ministers in the Bahmani government
 (b) Five Afaqi leaders
 (c) Governors of the Bahmani provinces
 (d) Commanders of five Bahmani regiments.

74. Shivaji's father Shahji Bhosle was initially in the service of
 (a) Ahmadnagar (b) Bijapur
 (c) Golcunda (d) Bidar.

75. Chand Bibi, the princess of Ahmadnagar was the widow of
 (a) Quli Qutb Shah of Golcunda
 (b) Fathullah Khan Imaddulmulk of Berar
 (c) Ali Barid of Bidar
 (d) Ali Adil Shah of Bijapur.

ANSWERS

1.	(b)	2.	(c)	3.	(d)	4.	(a)
5.	(c)	6.	(b)	7.	(d)	8.	(b)
9.	(a)	10.	(c)	11.	(c)	12.	(b)
13.	(c)	14.	(a)	15.	(a)	16.	(c)
17.	(b)	18.	(b)	19.	(c)	20.	(b)
21.	(d)	22.	(b)	23.	(a)	24.	(d)
25.	(d)	26.	(c)	27.	(c)	28.	(c)
29.	(c)	30.	(d)	31.	(b)	32.	(d)
33.	(b)	34.	(b)	35.	(c)	36.	(b)
37.	(b)	38.	(b)	39.	(c)	40.	(d)
41.	(b)	42.	(c)	43.	(b)	44.	(c)
45.	(c)	46.	(c)	47.	(b)	48.	(a)
49.	(c)	50.	(b)	51.	(c)	52.	(d)
53.	(c)	54.	(b)	55.	(c)	56.	(b)
57.	(a)	58.	(c)	59.	(b)	60.	(a)
61.	(b)	62.	(d)	63.	(d)	64.	(c)
65.	(b)	66.	(c)	67.	(d)	68.	(b)
69.	(a)	70.	(a)	71.	(a)	72.	(c)
73.	(c)	74.	(a)	75.	(d)		

11
VIJAYANAGAR EMPIRE

1. On the banks of which river was the city of Vijaynagar located?
   (a) Waingana (b) Kaveri
   (c) Tungbhadra (d) Krishna.

2. The Sangama king who sent embassy to China was
   (a) Harihara I (b) Bukka I
   (c) Bukka II (d) Harihara II.

3. Which of the following was primarily responsible for the extension of the Vijaynagar empire over the whole of Southern India?
   (a) Harihara II (b) Bukka II
   (c) Vira Vijaya (d) Deva Raya II.

4. The dynasty which come to the throne after the 'first usurpation' war
   (a) Tuluka (b) Saluva
   (c) Aravidu (d) None of the above.

5. Which of the following was responsible for the 'second usurpation' and laying the foundation of Tuluva dynasty?
   (a) Narasa Nayaka
   (b) Immadi Narasimha
   (c) Vira Narasimha
   (d) Krishnadeva Raya.

6. Krishnadeva Raya belonged to the
   (a) Sangama dynasty (b) Saluva dynasty
   (c) Tuluva dynasty (d) Aravidu dynasty.

7. Which of the following was not one of the fortresses captured by Krishnadeva Raya from Gajapati Prataparudra, the king of Orissa?
   (a) Udayagiri (b) Kondavidu
   (c) Khandagiri (d) Kondakilli.

8. The Sultanates of the Deccan combined in 1556 to inflict a crushing defeat on the ruler of Vijayanagar. The King of Vijaynagar at the time of this so-called battle of Talikata was
   (a) Rama Raya (b) Tirunmala
   (c) Venkata I (d) Sadashiva Raya.

9. Which of the following Deccan Sultanates did not join the allies in the battle of Rakshasa Tangadi (also called Talikota) against the Vijayanagar empire?
   (a) Berar (b) Ahmednagar
   (c) Golconda (d) Bijapur.

10. Which of the following was not one of the important officers of the state?
   (a) Custodian of the Jewels
   (b) Provider of the Haram
   (c) Prefect of the Police
   (d) Chief Treasures.

11. Which of the following constituted the greatest check on the royal authority?
   (a) The organized community
   (b) Customs and public opinion
   (c) The Royal Council
   (d) The traditional laws.

12. The president of the imperial council of the Empire of Vijayanagar was
   (a) Prime Minister
   (b) Sabhanayaka
   (c) King
   (d) Mahadandanayaka.

13. The nucleus of the administration of the empire of Vijayanagar was
    (a) Council of Ministers
    (b) Secretary
    (c) Imperial Secretariat
    (d) Imperial Revenue Department.

14. Which of the following was not one of the Provinces of the empire of Vijayanagar?
    (a) Udayagiri (b) Penukonda
    (c) Padaividu (d) Raichur.

15. The largest administrative division in the Vijayanagar empire was
    (a) Rajya (b) Mandalam
    (c) Kottam (d) Nadu.

16. The Vijayanagar empire divided for administrative purposes into several provinces. Which of the following was not one of the expressions used for provinces
    (a) Rajya (b) Mandala
    (c) Rashtra (d) Chavadi.

17. Among the following subdivision of the province in the Karnataka region in the Vijayangar empire which was the smallest?
    (a) Grama
    (b) Noduka, Valita or Vanita
    (c) Sthala, Sammat or Kampana
    (d) Sime or sema.

18. Which of the following subdivision of the provinces in Tamil region in the Vijaynagar empire was the largest?
    (a) Kottam (b) Parru
    (c) Nadu (d) Grama.

19. The Chief secretary of the Empire of Vijaynagar was designated as
    (a) Dandanayaka (b) Mahadandanayak
    (c) Sarvanayaka (d) Rayasama.

20. In the Vijaynagar administration athavane or athavana was the department of

(a) Police (b) Military
(c) Revenue (d) Intelligence.

21. The nayakar in the empire of Vijaynagar were

(a) Feudal Chiefs
(b) Hereditary military governors
(c) Military commanders
(d) Civil military officers.

22. In the Vijaynagar empire, the officer entrusted with responsibility of making the nayakar under control was

(a) Special Commissioner
(b) Special Secretary
(c) Mahadandanayka
(d) Sarvanayaka.

23. Which of the following are not one of the village assembly of the Vijaynagar period?

(a) Sabha (b) Mahasabha
(c) Mahajiana (d) Melagrama.

24. Which of the following South Indian dance traditions appeared for the first time during he Vijayanagar period?

(a) Mohiniattam (b) Yakshagana
(c) Krishnattam (d) Vyommalata.

25. Which of the following was not one of the categories into which land was classified for the purposes of assessment?

(a) Dry and wet lands (b) Orchard
(c) Rain fed (d) Reclaimed forests.

26. Besides land tax, which of the following was not one of the sources from which the income of the state was derived?

(a) Grazing tax
(b) Marriage tax
(c) Death duty
(d) Custom duties and commercial taxes.

27. A detailed land survey and assessment was conducted during the region of
    - (a) Bukka I
    - (b) Devaraya II
    - (c) Krishandeva Raya
    - (d) Achyuta Raya.
28. The Rajaguru of the great royal teacher of Krishna Deva Raya was-----
    - (a) Vyasaraja
    - (b) Vidyaranya
    - (c) Lakshmidhara
    - (d) Vamana Bhatta.
29. Which of the following crops in the Vijayanagar empire was widely exported?
    - (a) Black pepper
    - (b) Tea
    - (c) Tobacco
    - (d) Coffee.
30. Which of the following not one of the popular methods of irrigation in the Vijayanagar empire?
    - (a) Tanks
    - (b) Dams
    - (c) Canals
    - (d) Wells.
31. Which of the following was not one of the important industries of the Vijayanagar empire?
    - (a) Textile
    - (b) Mining and metallurgy
    - (c) Ivory
    - (d) Refinery.
32. The single biggest item of import to the empire of Vijayanagar was/were
    - (a) Precious stones
    - (b) Horses
    - (c) Luxury goods
    - (d) Raw silk.
33. The artisans who enjoyed a high status in the Vijayanagar society were
    - (a) Carpenters
    - (b) weavers
    - (c) Oil pressers
    - (d) Leather workers.
34. Ships were in the use for coastal and overseas trade. Where were the ships got built?
    - (a) Negapattam
    - (b) Quilon
    - (c) Calicut
    - (d) Masulipatnam.

35. The Vijayanagar king who after defeating the Sri-Lankan troops forced Sri Lanka to pay tribute to the Vijaynagar empire was
(a) Devaraya I (b) Devaraya II
(c) Harihara I (d) Krishnadeva Raya.

36. The finest specimens of the painting of the Vijayanagar period have been found from
(a) Lepaksi (b) Adikamankattal
(c) Tirupati (d) Hampi.

37. Krishnadeva Raya's Amuktamalyda is a work on
(a) His political ideas
(b) Public administration
(c) Administration of justice and foreign affairs
(d) All of the above.

38. The first Vijayanagar king who concluded treaties with the Portuguese was
(a) Devaraya II
(b) Virupaksha
(c) Saluva Narasimha
(d) Krishnadeva Raya.

39. The magnum opus in the art of temple architecture of Vijaynagar was the temple of
(a) Vittalaswami (b) Pompapati
(c) Lapakshi (d) Srirangam.

40. During which of the following festivities was the presence of the Vijayanagar king considered essential?
(a) Ramanavami (b) Mahanavami
(c) Vinayak Chaturthi (d) Janmashtami.

41. Which of the following the most popular item of luxury goods in the Vijayanagar empire?
(a) Perfumes (b) Betel leaf
(c) Ornaments (d) Chess.

42. Proficiency in which of the following games was rewarded and recognised by the state of Vijayanagar?
    (a) Wrestling (b) Animal fighter
    (c) Gymnastics (d) Chess.

43. Which of the following popular amusements of the common people was known as Kalattam in the Vijayanagar empire?
    (a) Puppet show
    (b) Dramatic performance
    (c) Stick play
    (d) Dance by Devdasis.

44. Which of the following musical instruments had acquired a prominent place in the Vijayanagar empire?
    (a) Mridangam (b) Vina
    (c) Nadaswaram (d) Cymbals.

45. The kings of Vijayanagar were said to rule on behalf of Virupaksha, who was a
    (a) Vaishanavite deity
    (b) Shaivite deity
    (c) A representativ of Vallabha
    (d) A deity popularised by Smartas.

46. Which of the following kings extended his worship of Vithoba as a concession to the growing strength of the Bhakti cult?
    (a) Krishnadeva Raya (b) Achyuta Raya
    (c) Tirumala (d) Venkata II.

47. The Vijayanagar king who totally withdrew the marriage tax was
    (a) Devaraya II (b) Krishnadeva Raya
    (c) Achyuta Raya (d) Sadashiva.

48. During the reign of which Vijayanagar king was the famous Hazura temple built?
    (a) Harihara II (b) Devaraya II
    (c) Krishnadeva Raya (d) Venkata II.

49. Which of the following important literatures of the Vijayanagar period is famous for his commentaries on the vedas?
   (a) Sayana
   (b) Peddana
   (c) Hemadri
   (d) Madhava Vidyaranga.

50. A foreign visitor to the Vijayanagar empire who was an envoy was
   (a) Ernao Nuniz (b) Dooningo Paes
   (c) Abdur Razzak (d) Micala Conti.

51. The Raichuj doab, the permanent bone of contention between the kingdoms of Vijayanagar and Bahmani, was
   (a) The Krishna-Godavari Delta
   (b) The region between the river of Kaveri and Tungabhadra
   (c) The region between the rivers Krishna and Tungabhadra
   (d) The region between the rivers Krishna and Kaveri.

52. The main cause for the defeat of the empire of Vijayanagar in the battle of Rakshasa Tangadi or Talikota was
   (a) The over confidence and houghtiness of Rama Raya, the regent to Sadashiva Raya
   (b) The interference of Rama Raya in the quarrels among the Deccani Sultanates
   (c) The common enmity of Deccani Sultanates towards Vijayanagar
   (d) Rama Raya's desire to make Vijayanagar supreme in the south.

53. The most important consideration(s) in making the administrative divisions of the Vijayanagar was
   (a) Military and police consideration
   (b) Location of the forts
   (c) Revenue consideration
   (d) Linguistic consideration.

54. Each province in the Vijayanagar empire was either under viceroy or nayaka. The nayakas were recruited from amongst the
(a) Members of the royal family
(b) Warrior class
(c) Both (a) and (b) above
(d) Old ruling family.

55. The maintenance and upkeep of which of the following wing of the army was greatest drain on the resources of the empire of Vijayanagar?
(a) Infantry (b) Cavalry
(c) Elephants (d) Artillery.

56. Which of the following professionals were exempted from the payment of profession tax by Sadashiva Raya?
(a) Musicians (b) Prostitutes
(c) Barbers (d) Goldsmith.

57. In the empire of Vijayanagar a sort of income tax on the basis of net profit was levied on
(a) Property (b) Professionals
(c) Industries (d) Trade.

58. A saint scholar whose name is associated with the foundation the empire of Vijayanagar is
(a) Madhava Vidyramya
(b) Sayana
(c) Vyasaraya
(d) Sivayya.

59. The city of Vijayanagar is now known as :
(a) Halebdu (b) Chandragiri
(c) Hamki (d) Kondavdu.

60. To secure divine favours a brutal custom which was very popular in the empire of Vijayanagar was
(a) Self immolation (b) Hook swinging
(c) Cutting of organs (d) Walking on fire.

61. Thousands of women were employed in the empire of Vijayanagar as
    (a) Accountants (b) Royal bodyguards
    (c) . Palace guards (d) All of the above.

62. The most famous state festival of the empire of Vijayanagar was
    (a) Spring (Vasant) festival
    (b) Mahanavami
    (c) Brahmatsavam
    (d) Ramanavami.

63. The position of women of the ruling classes in the Vijayanagar greatly declined on account of the wide prevalence of
    (a) Polygamy
    (b) Sati or Sahagamona
    (c) Both (a) and (b) above
    (d) Purdah.

64. Of the following, who have written about the Vijayanagar empire, who was not foreign traveller?
    (a) Ferishta (b) Nicalo Conti
    (c) Duarate Barbosa (d) Fernao Nuniz.

65. Which of the following visited India during the reign of Devaraya II?
    (a) Nicalo Conti (b) Abdur Razzak
    (c) Duarte Barbosa (d) Athanasus Nikitin.

66. Which of the following was not one of the foreign traveller to visit India during the period of the Krishnadava Raya?
    (a) Nicalo Conti (b) Fernao Nuniz
    (c) Domigo Pass (d) Duarte Barbosa.

67. Which of the following has described the fortification of the city of Vijayanagar in great detail?
    (a) Fernao Nuniz (b) Domigo Pass
    (c) Nicalo Conti (d) Abdur Razzak.

68 In which of the following languages of the period did Krishnadeva Raya write Amuktamaloda, his magnum opus?

(a) Sanskrit (b) Tamil
(c) Kannada (d) Telugu.

69. The Vijayanagar king followed a policy of religious toleration. Which of the following king allowed the Portuguese to establish churches at Vallore?

(a) Devaraya II
(b) Krishnadeva Raya
(c) Achyuta Raya
(d) Venkata II.

70. Who were sthanikar in the Vijayanagar empire?

(a) Those charged with the management of temples
(b) Officials of local bodies
(c) Village elders
(d) Those responsible for the management of mathas established by various sectors.

71. Which of the following was not one of the effects of the collapse of the Vijayanagar empire?

(a) It sounded the death-knell of Hind supremacy in the south
(b) It cleared the way for the ultimate destruction of the Deccani sultanates by the Moghuls
(c) It hampered the Portuguese trade
(d) It caused the disappearance of the Vijayangar empire.

72. Which of the following regarding the ayagar system in the Vijayanagar period is not true?

(a) The anyagaras could sell or mortgage their officers
(b) They were granted tax free lands (manyams)
(c) They were the guardians of peace within their jurisdiction
(d) These ayagaras had no hereditary rights over their offices.

73. Who proved to the worst enemy of the Vijayanagar empire in the long run?
   (a) The Deccani Sultanates
   (b) The tightness of the later rulers of the Vijayanagar empire
   (c) The Hindu feudatories (Paraigars) of the Vijayanagar empire
   (d) The incompetence of the rulers of the Aravidu dynasty.

74. Which of the following ideals of kingship prescribed by Krishnadeva Raya was not observed in practice even in the best of times?
   (a) A king should rule collecting round him people skilled in statecraft
   (b) He should levy taxes on his people moderately
   (c) He should counteract the acts of his enemies by crushing them with force
   (d) The king should always anxious to protect their subjects and redress their grievances.

75. The king was assisted in the task of administration by a council of ministers whose office was sometimes hereditary and sometimes rested on selection. From which of the following class(es) were they drawn:
   (a) Vaishyas
   (b) Brahmin and Kshatriya
   (c) Shudras
   (d) Brahmin, Kshatriya Shetti or Chetti.

76. The empire of Vijayanagar had to face certain grave social problems against which the state had to intervene and issue ordinances, such as regarding:
   (a) Caste and communal disputes
   (b) Wide prevalence of dowry
   (c) Both (a) and (b) above
   (d) Forcing unwilling widows to perform sati.

77. There were no restriction in the matter of diet in the Vijayanagar empire. Meat of all kinds excepting that of oxen

or cows, was taken. Which of the following were not necessarily vegetarians?

(a) Brahmins (b) Vaishnavas
(c) Lingayats (d) Vaishyas.

78. Which of the following statement about Kaivinaikuddi (hired labour) or kuds (farm-hands) in the Vijayanagar empire not correct?
(a) They received fixed wages
(b) This tenure indicates the well predicted condition of agricultural labour
(c) They were connected with lands as servants
(d) When land changed hands kudis went with the land.

79. What was known as varom in the Vijayanagar empire
(a) The best quality of land
(b) The system of sharing of agricultural income between the landlord and the tenant
(c) A special method of cultivation
(d) The dowry given to the bridegroom in terms of land.

80. Which of the following was not one of the defects of the nayakara system in the Vijayanagar empire?
(a) It did not help in the material advancement and development of agriculture and irrigation
(b) They engaged themselves in local wars and mutual feuds
(c) At time they even defied the central authority
(d) They exacted tributes and military services from their tenants to their advantage.

81. The nayakara in the Vijayanagar period were often called as the amaranayaka because
(a) Their position was hereditary
(b) They granted the amaram lands
(c) For their maintenance they were given revenue and tax free amaram lands
(d) Their exploit were considered immortal (amara).

82. The function of the Mahanayakacharya was to
    (a) Supervise the work of the nayakara
    (b) Exercise general supervision over village administration
    (c) Supervise observance of dharma like Asoka's dharma mathmatyas
    (d) Command nayakara troops.

83. The king of Vijayanagar empire, who appointed Muslims in his army, granted lands to them, built a mosque and kept a copy of the Koran before his throne, so that the Muslims could pay respects to it, was
    (a) Harihara (b) Devaraya I
    (c) Devaraya II (d) Krishnadeva Raya.

84. The most important reasons for the decline of the village assemblies during the Vijayanagar period was/were
    (a) The establishment of the ayagar system
    (b) The development of the nayakara system
    (c) Both (a) and (b) above
    (d) Appointment of tantriman, who controlled the working of the village assemblies.

85. Which of the following statement about the policy of taxation of Vijayanagar rulers is not correct?
    (a) Land revenue was the principal source of income
    (b) The traditional rate assessment at one-sixth of income
    (c) The incidence of taxation was heavy
    (d) Taxes were sometimes reduced or remitted.

86. Which of the following statement about the administration of justice in the Vijayanagar empire is not correct?
    (a) There were regular courts and special judicial officers for the administration of justice
    (b) Disputes were also sometimes settled by the officials with the cooperation of the local bodies
    (c) The law of the land was based on traditional regulations and customs
    (d) Punishments were only in the terms of fines or forced labour.

87. Like the Haysalas, the rulers of Vijayanagar had a carefully organised military department called Kandachara under the control of the dandanayaka. Which of the following was not one of the wing of their army?

(a) Cavalry (b) Chariots

(c) Elephants (d) Artillery.

88. Krishnadeva Raya concluded a series of treaties with the Portuguese to

(a) Secure exclusive supply of imported horses

(b) Take revenue from Bijapur, the hereditary enemy of Vijayanagar

(c) Both (a) and (b) above

(d) Oust the Arabs from the foreign trade of the Vijayanagar empire.

89. Foreign travellers have referred to numerous blood sacrifices in the Vijayanagar kingdom what was the object of an occasion for these sacrifices?

(a) Thanks giving

(b) To obtain the blessings of the deity

(c) To gain spiritual strength

(d) Superstition.

90. In the Vijayanagar empire, what was Kultagai?

(a) Lease system of cultivation

(b) Beneficiary treasurer like brahmadeva, Devodeya and Mathapura

(c) Service tenures of military or service

(d) Cervice of land to certain categories of craftsmen such as potters, goldsmiths etc.

91. Why were elephants imported from Sri Lanka and Pegu in the Vijayanagar empire.

(a) Because they were cheaper than North Indian elephants

(b) Because they were of better quality

(c) Because the Brahmans had off access North Indian elephant trade

(d) Because it was easier to transport them.

92. In the Vijayanagar empire there are many mints and a large variety of coins. Coins of which of the following metals were largely in circulation?
(a) Gold (b) Silver
(c) Copper (d) Brass

93. In the addition to the local issues, coins of foreign countries were also in circulation in the coastal area. Which of the following was not one of them?
(a) Persia (b) Portugal
(c) Italy (d) China.

94. Which of the following statement about the role played by the temples in the economic life of the people is not correct?
(a) It was the largest employer in the village
(b) It was often the biggest single landowner and consumer in an area
(c) It largely controlled rural credit
(d) It did very little encourage to rural development.

95. Which of the following was not one of the charitable activities in which temples participated?
(a) Maintenance of chatras or rest houses
(b) Maintenance of schools and libraries
(c) Maintenance of hospitals
(d) Feeding of the school children.

96. Which of the following was not one of the twelve village functionaries under the ayagar system during the Vijayanagar empire?
(a) Gouda or village headman
(b) Taliary and the tati or the watchman
(c) Neergantee or the in-charge of water distribution
(d) Karnam or accountant.

97. Who were Kaikkalas?
(a) Temple priests
(b) A community of acrobats

(c) An influential community of weavers living around temple precincts

(d) An anti religious group which entertained the people by caricaturing various godheads.

98. The Vijayanagar coins which were in circulation and were the most widely recognised currency all over the world were known as

(a) Varaha or pagada (b) Panam

(c) Huna (d) Dinar.

99. As per the latest researches, the so-called battle of the Talikota fought between the Deccani Muslim states and Vijayanagar, was actually fought at

(a) Bannihatti

(b) Between villages Rakkasi-tangadi

(c) Talikota town

(d) Raichur Doab.

100. Which of the following goes to show that the Vijayanagar state recognised prostitution?

(a) Special grants were given to prostitutes by the state if they were attached to the temples

(b) Free houses were provided to them

(c) They were taxed

(d) They were subjected to periodic medical checkups.

ANSWERS

1.	(c)	2.	(b)	3.	(a)	4.	(b)
5.	(c)	6.	(c)	7.	(c)	8.	(d)
9.	(a)	10.	(b)	11.	(b)	12.	(a)
13.	(c)	14.	(c)	15.	(b)	16.	(c)
17.	(a)	18.	(a)	19.	(c)	20.	(c)
21.	(b)	22.	(a)	23.	(d)	24.	(b)
25.	(c)	26.	(c)	27.	(c)	28.	(a)
29.	(c)	30.	(c)	31.	(b)	32.	(a)
33.	(c)	34.	(b)	35.	(a)	36.	(d)

37.	(d)	38.	(b)	39.	(b)	40.	(c)
41.	(d)	42.	(c)	43.	(b)	44.	(b)
45.	(a)	46.	(b)	47.	(c)	48.	(a)
49.	(c)	50.	(c)	51.	(c)	52.	(d)
53.	(a)	54.	(c)	55.	(b)	56.	(c)
57.	(c)	58.	(a)	59.	(c)	60.	(d)
61.	(d)	62.	(b)	63.	(c)	64.	(a)
65.	(b)	66.	(b)	67.	(d)	68.	(d)
69.	(d)	70.	(a)	71.	(d)	72.	(d)
73.	(c)	74.	(b)	75.	(b)	76.	(c)
77.	(b)	78.	(a)	79.	(b)	80.	(a)
81.	(b)	82.	(b)	83.	(c)	84.	(c)
85.	(b)	86.	(d)	87.	(b)	88.	(c)
89.	(d)	90.	(a)	91.	(c)	92.	(a)
93.	(d)	94.	(d)	95.	(d)	96.	(d)
97.	(c)	98.	(a)	99.	(b)	100.	(c)

12
EARLY MEDIAEVAL PERIOD

1. The Arab settlers in India became the cultural ambassadors of India to the Islami i.e. world and Europe through their
   (a) Trade and commerce from India
   (b) Knowledge of Indian science and literature
   (c) Both (a) and (b) above
   (d) Jihads or religious wars carried on from Sindh and Multan.

2. Wolsley Haig called the conquest of Sindh by the Arabs,"a mere episode in the history of India," because
   (a) It was a mere military incursion
   (b) It affected only a fringe of the vast country
   (c) The Arabs could not move beyond Sindh
   (d) Both (b) and (c) above.

3. Which of the following sena kings is credited with the founding of Kulinism, a system of the superiority of higher castes?
   (a) Samanta Sena (b) Vijaya Sena
   (c) Ballala Sena (d) Lakshmana Sena.

4. Bengal passed from the Palas to the control of a new dynasty, the Senas. Where did the Senas come from?
   (a) Orissa (b) Central India
   (c) Kamrupa (d) The Deccan.

5. The first early medieval dynasty to use Hindi in Devanagari script in its epigraphs was the
   (a) Chauhan (b) Gahadavala
   (c) Chandella (d) Paramara.

6. The famous romantic story of the marriage of Sanyogita, the daughter of the Gahadavala king Jaichandra, with the Chauhan King Prithviraja III is described in:
   (a) Prithviraja Vijaya (b) Prithviraja Raso
   (c) Hammir Mahakavya (d) Pavanaduta.

7. Which of the following were the bitterest natural enemies of the Chauhans?
   (a) Solankis (b) Tomaras
   (c) Gahadavalas of Kanauj (d) Chandellas.

8. The city of Dhilika was founded by the Tomaras in A.D. 736, which of the following overthrew the Tomaras and occupied Delhi in the twelfth century?
   (a) Gahadavalas (b) Chandellas
   (c) Paramaras (d) Chauhans.

9. Which of the following descriptions about the regions originally controlled by the various Rajput clans is not correct?
   (a) Pariharas of southern Rajasthan
   (b) Chauhans of eastern Rajasthan
   (c) Solankis of Kathiawar in Gujarat
   (d) Chandellas of Mewar.

10. Which of the following Rajput clans was not one of the so-called Agnikula origin?
    (a) Chandellas
    (b) Pariharas
    (c) Chanhamanas or Chauhans
    (d) Chalukyas or Solankis.

11. During the reign of which of the following dynasties of Kashmir of this period did the famous queen Didda seize the throne?
    (a) Karkota dynasty
    (b) The house of Utpala
    (c) Lohara dynasty
    (d) The line of Parva Gupta.

12. The capital of Hindu Shahiya kingdom at the time of Mahmud's invasion was
    (a) Kabul (b) Peshawar
    (c) Attok (d) Udabhanda or Und.

13. The Hindushahi ruler who burnt himself on a funeral pyre after being defeated by Mahmud of Ghazni was
    (a) Jayapala (b) Anandapala
    (c) Trilochanapala (d) Bhima.

14. The Turkish Commander was conquered Bihar and Bengal was
    (a) Mohammad of Ghur
    (b) Qutb-ud-din Aibak
    (c) Ikhiyar-ud-din Muhammad
    (d) Bakhityar Khalji.

15. Prithviraj Chauhan defeated Muhammad Ghori in the first battle of?
    (a) Panipat (b) Tarain
    (c) Chandawar (d) Thaneshwar.

16. Muhammad Ghori invaded India on account of his
    (a) Vaulting ambition for expansion of his empire
    (b) Love of conquest and power
    (c) Both (a) and (b) above
    (d) Desire to propagate Islam.

17. Muhammad Ghori directed his first invasion against
    (a) Multan (b) Sindh
    (c) Punjab (d) Anhilwara.

18. The Hindushahi king who formed a confederacy of Hindu king against Mahmud Ghazni was/were?
    (a) Gahadavalas
    (b) Karamatiyas of Multan
    (c) Hindushahiyas
    (d) Kalachuris.

19. Which of the following came to India at the instance of Sultan Mahmud?

(a) Alberuni (b) Sulaiman
(c) Al-Masudi (d) Ibn Hauqe.

20. Careful planning of the campaign by Sultan Mahmud led to the arrival of the Afghan armies in India during season?

(a) Winter (b) Summer
(c) Rainy (d) Harvest.

21. The main object of the invasions of Mahmud of Ghazni to India was

(a) Propagation of Islam
(b) To build up a large empire
(c) To acquire the wealth of India
(d) To capture Punjab and Delhi.

22. A ruler who was believed to have been author of about two dozen works on a variety of subjects, including medicine, astronomy, architecture etc. was?

(a) The Paramara King Bhoja
(b) The Ratihara King Mihirbhoja
(c) The Sena King Samantasena
(d) The Chalukya King Kumarapala.

23. Mahmud led the last expedition against India in A.D.

(a) 1025 (b) 1021-22
(c) 1027 (d) 1024.

24. Sultan Mahmud Ghazni led the first invasion against India in A.D.

(a) 1000 (b) 999
(c) 1004 (d) 1001.

25. The Sanskrit poet Padmagupta described in his work Navasahasankacharitam the exploits of

(a) Vakpati II (b) Sindhuraja
(c) Bhoja (d) Siyaka Harsha.

26. Taila II, a feudatory of Krishna III overthrew the Rashtrakutas and founded the dynasty of?
    (a) Early Western Chalukyas of Badami
    (b) Later western Chalukyas of Kalyani
    (c) Eastern Chalukyas of Vengi
    (d) Chalukyas of Arhilwad (Gujarat).

27. The Rashtrakuta king who invaded North India was/were
    (a) Dhruva (b) Govinda III
    (c) Indra III (d) All of the above.

28. The most important among the rivals of the Rashtrakutas were
    (a) Palas of Bengal and Bihar
    (b) Pratiharas of Kanauj
    (c) Eastern Chalukyas of Vengi
    (d) Pallavas of Kanchi.

29. The capital of the Rashtrakutas was
    (a) Badami (b) Kalyani
    (c) Vengi (d) Manyakhet.

30. Which of the following overthrew the Chalukays of Valapi and founded the Rashtrakuta empire?
    (a) Dhruva
    (b) Govinda III
    (c) Dantidurga
    (d) Amoghavarsha.

31. One of the last Pratihara rulers, who surrendered before Mahmud Ghazni and was finally defeated and killed by the Chandella king Vidyadhara was
    (a) Mohendrapala (b) Vijayapala
    (c) Rajyapala (d) Mahipala.

32. Which of the following arms of the Pratihara army was considered to be the best in India during their time?
    (a) Infantry (b) Cavalry
    (c) Elephants (d) Chariots.

33. The greatest ruler of the Pratihara dynasty was
(a) Dantidurga (b) Vatsaraja
(c) Bhoja (d) Nagabhata II.

34. Chachnama is a famous work on the history of
(a) Kashmir (b) Sindh
(c) Punjab (d) Gujarat.

35. The Pala supermacy in Bengal was destroyed by
(a) Rajendra Chola I (b) Dhruva IV
(c) Govinda III (d) Vijayasena.

36. A Sanskrit drama found inscribed on the stone slabs of the walls of a mosque named Adhai-din-ka-Jhopra in Ajmer is
(a) Lalitvigarharaja
(b) Harikeli Nataka
(c) Prabodh Chandrodya
(d) Swapanvasav dattam.

37. The Pala king who founded the Vikramasila University was
(a) Dharmapala (b) Devapala
(c) Narayanapala (d) Ramapala.

38. The Pala king who was defeated by Rajendra Chola was
(a) Gopala (b) Devapala
(c) Vigrahapala (d) Mahipala I.

39. The capital of the Palas was probably
(a) Kanauj (b) Pataliputa
(c) Tamralipti (d) Monghyr.

40. The greatest of the Pala kings and one of the most powerful of the kings that ever ruled in Bengal was?
(a) Gopala (b) Dharmapala
(c) Devapala (d) Mahipala.

41. Gopala established the Pala dynasty in the Bengal region. What his chief claim to renown?
(a) He founded the Pala dynasty
(b) He was first to capture Kanauj

(c) He was not a hereditary king but was elected by the people
(d) He defeated both Partiharas and Rastrakutas.

42. The tripartite struggle lasted for about......years.
(a) 100 (b) 200
(c) 300 (d) 400.

43. The Rashtrakuta king who defeated the Pratihara ruler Nagabhatta was
(a) Amoghavarsha I (b) Govinda III
(c) Indra III (d) Krishna III.

44. The Sanskrit poet Sri Harsa, the author of Naishadhiya Charitan lived at the court of
(a) Jaichandra (b) Vijaychandra
(c) Govindachandra (d) Harish Chandra.

45. Which of the following was the first to wrest the control of Kanauj from Dharmapala?
(a) Pratihara ruler Vatsaraja
(b) Rashtrakuta king Dhruva
(c) Pratihara king Nagabhatta II
(d) Rashtrakuta ruler Govinda III.

46. The first Pala ruler to plunge into the tripartite struggle was
(a) Gopala (b) Dharmapala
(c) Devapala (d) Mahipala I.

47. The memorable tripartite struggle was fought by the Palas and the Gurjara Pratiharas because both powers were keen to
(a) Establish supremacy over Kanauj
(b) Reduce Kanauj as their feudatory state
(c) Capture river bound trade route through the Ganga
(d) Break the Rashtrakuta Ayudha alliance.

48. In which of the following early medialval states did women play a leading role in its history?
(a) Gujarat (b) Malwa
(c) Kashmir (d) Mewar.

49. Kalhana was a contemporary of the Lohara King of Kashmir named?
   (a) Harsha (b) Utakarsha
   (c) Kalasa (d) Ananta.

50. The main targets of Mahmud Ghazni's attacks were large towns and temples because
   (a) Victory over them would have given him greater renown
   (b) Destruction of large towns and temples shattered morale of Indian people
   (c) They were repositories of immense wealth
   (d) All of the above.

ANSWERS

1.	(c)	2.	(d)	3.	(d)	4.	(c)
5.	(b)	6.	(c)	7.	(d)	8.	(d)
9.	(a)	10.	(d)	11.	(d)	12.	(a)
13.	(d)	14.	(b)	15.	(c)	16.	(b)
17.	(c)	18.	(c)	19.	(a)	20.	(d)
21.	(c)	22.	(a)	23.	(c)	24.	(a)
25.	(b)	26.	(b)	27.	(d)	28.	(b)
29.	(d)	30.	(c)	31.	(c)	32.	(b)
33.	(c)	34.	(b)	35.	(d)	36.	(b)
37.	(a)	38.	(d)	39.	(d)	40.	(b)
41.	(c)	42.	(a)	43.	(b)	44.	(a)
45.	(a)	46.	(b)	47.	(a)	48.	(c)
49.	(a)	50.	(c)				

13
DELHI SULTANATE

1. Which of the following sultans tried to organise the army on the decimal system on the Mangal pattern?
   (a) Ghiyasuddin Balban
   (b) Alauddin Khalji
   (c) Muhammad bin Tughluq
   (d) Firuz Tughluq.

2. The fiscal policy of the sultanate was modelled can the theory of finance of the Hanafi school of Muslim jurists. From whom did the sultans borrow this system?
   (a) The Mongols (b) The Caliphato
   (c) The Ghaznavids (d) The Ghurids.

3. The largest standing army of the sultanate directly paid by state was created by
   (a) Iltutmish
   (b) Alauddin Khalji
   (c) Muhammad bin Tughluq
   (d) Sikander Lodi.

4. Which of the following was not one of the major taxes during the sultanate period?
   (a) Kharaz or land tax from non Muslims varying from one tenth to one half
   (b) Jeziah or poll tax charged only from the non-muslims
   (c) Khums or one-fifth of the spoils of war
   (d) A tax on purchase and sale of commodities.

5. Abwabs were
   (a) Religious taxes such as Zakat
   (b) Toll taxes
   (c) Miscellaneous kinds of taxes like the house taxes grazing tax, irrigation tax etc.
   (d) Taxes on merchandise and custom duties.

6. The exemption of Brahmins from payment of Jaziah was not provided for in the muslim law. Which of the following sultans withdrew this exemption and levied Jaziah on Brahmins also?
   (a) Ghiyasuddin Balban
   (b) Alauddin Khalji
   (c) Muhammad bin-Tughluq
   (d) Firuz Tughluq.

7. Which of the following was not one of the imposts levied during the sultanate period?
   (a) Tax on butchers, brokers or entertainers and on writers
   (b) Sales tax on indigo, fish, rapes etc.
   (c) Tax on soap and oil making, gambling dens, patterns and brick kilns
   (d) Tax on eating houses and professional singers.

8. Which of the following explains 'Khums Ghanin' one of the biggest sources of state income?
   (a) Four parts of the body appropriated by the sultan
   (b) Tribute from the tributary states
   (c) Pilgrim tax realised from the non-muslims
   (d) House tax.

9. Which of the following explains the term khidmati?
   (a) It was a tribute realised from the subjugated Indian Chiefs
   (b) Gifts from the nobles and high officials of the state to the sultan
   (c) It was the state's share of land revenue given by maqitais
   (d) It was a tax on service tenures.

10. The provincial governors during the sultanate period were designated as
    (a) Wali
    (b) Muqti or Muqtai
    (c) Naib
    (d) All of the above.

11. The administrative officer whose functions and duties are not matched properly is
    (a) Wakil-i-dar-Controller of the royal household
    (b) Hamir-i-hajib Master of cremonies at the court
    (c) Akhurbck Superintendent of royal houses
    (d) Naib-i-mulk Deputy Prime Minister.

12. The greatest check on the tyranny of the governors during the sultanate period was
    (a) Right of recall by the Sultan
    (b) People's right of appeal to the Sultan against oppression of the governors
    (c) Transfer of governors from one province to another
    (d) In matters of justice, appeals from the provincial courts could always be filed with the centre.

13. Which of the following gives the administrative divisions of the empire in the correct descending order?
    (a) Provinces, Shiqs parganas and villages
    (b) Parganas, Shiqs, villagers
    (c) Shiqs, parganas, qasbahs
    (d) Iqtas, parganas shiqs and villages.

14. The motive of Alauddin Khalji in invading South India was/were to
    (a) Secure fabulous wealth
    (b) Force the Deccan states to accept the suzerainty of the Sultanate
    (c) Both (a) and (b)
    (d) Annex the south to the Sultanate of Delhi.

15. The maximum number of Mongol invasions took place during the reign of

(a) Balban
(b) Alauddin Khalji
(c) Muhammad bin Tughluq
(d) Firug Tughluq.

16. One of the following officers who was the chief revenue collector and was also empowered to settle revenue disputes at pargana level, was

(a) Amil (b) Munsif
(c) Wali (d) Sahib-i-diwan.

17. The first Sultan to adopt the principle of measurement of cultivable land for determining land revenue was

(a) Iltutmish (b) Balban
(c) Alauddin Khalji (d) Ghiyasuddin Tughluq.

18. The administrative set up to look after and regulate the market central system introduced by Alauddin Khalji was under the purview of

(a) Diwan-i-riyasat (b) Diwan-i-risalet
(c) Diwan- i-insha (d) Diwan-i-arz.

19. Alauddin Khalji's market central system died instantaneously with his death because

(a) It was not based on the principle of demand and supply.
(b) The whole system was kept alive by the use of brute force
(c) Both (a) and (b) above.
(d) Alauddin Khalji's successors had no will to continue the system.

20. Several types of iqtas were granted during the Cultanate period which of the following was the most important iqta?

(a) The administrative iqta in the form of military grant
(b) Iqta-i-tamlik or iqta of appropriation
(c) Iqta-i-istightal or iqta of stipends
(d) Iqta for charitable purposes.

21. Which of the following was the most important contribution of Balban in the evolution of Iqta system?
    (a) He instituted an inquiry in the terms and tenure of the iqta given to the Turkish soldiers in the Doab.
    (b) The principle of hereditary iqta was completely rejected by him
    (c) He appointed a minister to watch and central the activities of the iqtadars
    (d) He defined the state's central over the iqtas.

22. To curb hoarding and black marketing Alauddin Khalji ordered that
    (a) Land revenue should be collected in kind
    (b) Cultivators should sell the harvested crops on the field only
    (c) Merchants should sell all commodities in the open
    (d) All of the above.

23. Which of the following changes in the iqtadari system was not introduced by Firuz Shah Tughluq?
    (a) He restored the system of payment of salaries to soldiers by land assignments now called wajaf
    (b) The wajafdars, holders of such assignments were another group of iqtadars
    (c) The system of sub-assignment of land by muqtais to their soldiers was also started
    (d) He rigidly enforced the non- transfer of assignments.

24. The most important change in the iqtadari system introduced during the reign of Sikandar Lodi was
    (a) Muqtas seem to have been called wajafdars
    (b) The wajafdars, Muqtas or hakims had no right over the land grants
    (c) If any noble was reported to oppressed anyone he was punished severely
    (d) No noble could occupy any land which was not specifically mentioned in the farman of assignment.

25. Which of the following regarding the ownership of land during the sultanate period is not true?
    (a) The peasant was the proprietor of the sail
    (b) The king or his jagirdars had a claim only on a share of its produce
    (c) The state enjoyed only usufructuary rights and not proprietary rights
    (d) With the coming of the Turks the basic concepts regarding the ownership of land materially changed.

26. From which of the following categories of land was income not derived by the state?
    (a) Khalisa or crown lands
    (b) Iqtas or land granted to officers and others
    (c) Principalities of the Hindu chiefs who had come to terms with the sultans
    (d) Land given away to Muslim scholars and saints in gift or waqf lands.

27. The term iqta means
    (a) An administrative grant or fief
    (b) Revenue assignment of a particular area in lieu of cash salary
    (c) Assignment of land as reward or pension
    (d) Both (b) and (c).

28. The Sultan who is said to have raised the land revenue to one-half of the produce was
    (a) Ghyasuddin Balban
    (b) Ghiyasuddin Khalji
    (c) Alauddin Khalji
    (d) Mummad bin-Tughluq.

29. For the collection of land revenue the farming system was prevalent. Which of the following did not usually act as a tax farmer?
    (a) Village headman (b) Patwari
    (c) Governor (d) Tributary Chief.

30. Which of the following was not one of the popular methods of land revenue assessment?
(a) Sharing (b) Measurement
(c) Qabuliat (d) Kankut.

31. The term used for measurement of land in the Sultanate period was
(a) Kismat-i-ghalla (b) Ghalla Bakshi
(c) Masahat (d) Ghazi.

32. The iqta system has been called the "control pillar" of the administrative system of the sultanate of Delhi: because
(a) The collection of land revenue in the noncrown lands was assigned to iqtadar
(b) The troops maintained by iqtadars constituted the largest chunk of the army of the sultanates
(c) Almost all civil and military officers of the sultanate were iqtadars
(d) All of the above.

33. The land revenue yielding territories of the sultante were divided into Khalisa or crown lands and lands
(a) Iqta (b) Inam
(c) Waqf (d) Barren.

34. Which of the following was not one of the changes made in the agrarian system by Alauddin Khalji?
(a) He revoked most of the small iqtas granted by previous sultans
(b) Land was reassessed and fresh grants were made
(c) The state's share of the revenue was increased to one half of the produce
(d) Increased tax was to be realised irrespective of damage to the crops due to natural calamities.

35. Why did Alauddin enjoin collection of land revenue in kind in lieu of cash?
(a) It reduced the possibilities of misappropriation
(b) It ensured collection against fluctuations in prices

(c) It ensured the availability of food grains in the town and helped him in his economic regulations or market control

(d) It was conducive to prompt realisation of demand.

36. What was the over all objective of the changes and reforms introduced by Alauddin in the agrarian system?

(a) To reduce the atrocities of the iqtadars and revenue collectors on the peasants

(b) To enrich his treasury with additional land revenue

(c) To eliminate and military considerations

(d) On political and military considerations.

37. Which of the following was the greatest contribution of Alauddin Khalji in the field of agrarian administration?

(a) He brought the peasant in direct relation with the state

(b) He tried to curb and check the intermediaries

(c) He was the first to introduce the system of measurement of land for the assessment of revenue

(d) The records of the village accountant were audited.

38. Which of the following agrarian measures was not taken by Ghiyasuddin Tughluq?

(a) He discarded measurement in favour of sharing

(b) The chiefs and headmen of villages were given back their perquisites

(c) The basis of the demand by the government was to be hasil enough provision for crop failures

(d) He made a large reduction in the scale of revenue of fixed by Alauddin and brought it down to one- sixth of the grass produce.

39. Muhammad bin-Tughluq created the Diwan-i-Kohi or department of agriculture primarily to

(a) Bring uncultivated land under cultivation by direct state management and financial support

(b) Introduce state-promoted irrigation

(c) (a) and (b)

(d) Improve irrigation and introduce superior crops.

40. Ghiyasuddin Tughluq attempted to improve agricultural production by
    (a) Discarding the system of measurement of land for the assessment of land revenue
    (b) Encouraging the cultivators to bring the unreclaimed lands under the plough
    (c) Giving up the oppressive methods for the collection of land revenue
    (d) All of the above.

41. The state-promoted canal irrigation system was initia ed by
    (a) Muhammad bin Tughluq
    (b) Ghiyasuddin Tughluq
    (c) Firuz Tughluq
    (d) Alauddin Khalji.

42. The conquest of South India was completed during the reign of
    (a) Ghiyasudin Tughluq
    (b) Alauddin Khalji
    (c) Muhammad bin Tughluq
    (d) Mubarak Shah Khalji.

43. The credit for completing the conquest of South India goes to
    (a) Muhammad bin Tughluq
    (b) Jalaluddin Khan
    (c) Malik Kafur
    (d) Nusrat Khan.

44. Which of the following was not one of the steps taken by Firuz Tughluq to encourage agriculture?
    (a) He repaired and dug a number of irrigation canals
    (b) He undertook reclamation of waste lands
    (c) Cultivation of superior crops such as wheat, sugarcane, lentils etc. was encouraged
    (d) New agricultural colonies were settled along the canals.

45. Which of the following was not a defect in the agrarian policy of Firuz Tughluq?
   (a) He farmed out the revenue of even the provinces to the Government officials
   (b) He was lavish in paying his officials in the shape of jagirs
   (c) He extended the operation of jeziah
   (d) He permitted the sale, purchase and mortgage of the iqtas.

46. The south Indian ruler whose kingdom could not be annexed to the sultanate of Delhi by the Tughluqs was
   (a) Yadavas of Devagiri
   (b) Kakatiyas of Warangal
   (c) Hysalas of Dwarasamudra
   (d) Pandyas of Madurai.

47. The Sultan who first formulated the "Famine code" to provide relief to famine-affected people, was
   (a) Balban
   (b) Alauddin Khalji
   (c) Muhammad bin Tughluq
   (d) Firuz Tughluq.

48. The most learned medialval muslim ruler who was well-versed in branches of learning including astronomy, mathematics and medicine was
   (a) Iltutmish
   (b) Alauddin Khalji
   (c) Muhammad bin Tughluq
   (d) Sikandar Lodi.

49. Which of the following progressive concepts is not associated with Muhammad bin Tughluq?
   (a) He tried to strengthen the geo-political and cultural unity of India
   (b) He wanted to break all barriers between North and South India

(c) He discarded all communal discrimination in matters of state policy

(d) He was the first to introduce sufism and Islamic culture in South India.

50. Muhammad bin Tughluq's experiment of introducing token currency failed on account of

(a) Rejection of token coins by foreign merchants.

(b) Large-scale minting of spurious coins.

(c) Poor quality of token currency.

(d) Melting of token coins.

51. The story that Alauddin Khalji invaded Chittor to secure Padmini, the queen of Rana Ratna Singh of Mewar was vividly described by?

(a) Amir Khusrau in Khazain ul Futuh

(b) Col. J. Todd in Annals and Antiquities of Rajasthan

(c) Malilk Muhammad Jayasi inn his epic Padmavat

(d) Ibn Batula in his Rehla.

52. The military officer of the sultanate who was the highest in the military gradation was?

(a) Khan (b) Malik

(c) Amir (d) Wali.

53. The most important branch of the army of the Sultanate was?

(a) Infantry (b) Artillery

(c) Cavalry (d) Elephants.

54. A Persian historian of the sultanate period who accompanied Alauddin Khalji on his expedition to Chittor was?

(a) Amir Khusrau (b) Minhaj-us-Siraj

(c) Ziauddin Barani (d) Shamar-i-Siraj Afif.

55. The most hard earned conquest of Alauddin Khalji in which he gained success after nearly a year-long campaigning was of

(a) Ranthambhor (b) Chittor

(c) Gujarat (d) Devagiri.

56. Which of the following held the highest and extraordinary position in the Central Government?
    (a) Qazi-ul-quzat
    (b) Head of the majlis-i-khalawat
    (c) Wazir
    (d) Naib-i-mulk or regent of the state.

57. Who were the barids?
    (a) The craftsmen who worked in royal Karkhanas
    (b) The king's bodyguards
    (c) The officers in-charge of accounts and receipts
    (d) The news reporters and secret spies.

58. Which of the following was the most well known, powerful and the earliest nobility created during the sultanate period?
    (a) Amiran-i-Sadah
    (b) Turkan-i-Chahalgani
    (c) Umarah
    (d) Alaiamir.

59. A group of officers to be collectively known as umarahs were?
    (a) Nobles
    (b) Provincial governors
    (c) Iqtadars
    (d) Revenue officials.

60. The nobility of the Sultanate was largely composed of
    (a) Arabs (b) Afghans
    (c) Turks (d) Composite elements.

61. Which of the following did not exercise some check or limits on the authority of the sultans?
    (a) Wazir
    (b) The nobles
    (c) The Ulema
    (d) The soldiers of the standing army.

62. The decisive factor in the succession in the throne was?
    (a) Priority of Birth
    (b) Law of Primogeniture
    (c) Nomination by the previous sultan
    (d) Wishes of the nobles and the personal power and force of the incumbent.

63. The main motive of Alauddin Khalji introducing market central measures or economic regulations was?
    (a) General welfare of the people
    (b) To keep his soldiers contented of a meagre salary
    (c) To control the Hindu merchants and traders
    (d) To stop illegal trade practices.

64. What was the real source of the Sultan's authority?
    (a) The will of the people
    (b) Military strength
    (c) The support of the caliph
    (d) Recognition of his authority by the Ulema.

65. To prevent the frequent occurrence of rebellions Alauddin Khalji ordered
    (a) Appropriation of all pensions and endowments to the state
    (b) Establishment of an efficient intelligence system
    (c) Total prohibition on the sale of intoxicants
    (d) All of the above.

66. The Sultan who refused to recognise the authority of the caliph was?
    (a) Alauddin Khalji
    (b) Ghiyasuddin Tughluq
    (c) Muhammad bin Tughluq
    (d) Qutbuddin Mubarak

67. The first Sultan who requested and obtained letters of investiture from the caliph was?
    (a) Iltutmish (b) Jalaluddin Khalji
    (c) Firuz Tughluq (d) Balban.

68. Which of the following was the first ruler of the Delhi Sultanate to put forward the view that kingship should be based on the willing support of the governed?
    (a) Ghiyasuddin Tughluq
    (b) Jalaluddin Khalji
    (c) Alauddin Khalji
    (d) Firuz Tughluq.

69. The Sultan who styled himself "the second Alexander" was?
    (a) Balban
    (b) Alauddin Khalji
    (c) Muhammad bin Tughluq
    (d) Sikander Lodi.

70. In a formal sense, which of the following correctly describes the nature of the state during Sultanate period in India ?
    (a) Theocracy (b) Democracy
    (c) Autocracy (d) Oligarchy.

71. Who selected the site for the city of Agra as his Capital?
    (a) Alauddin Khalji
    (b) Muhammad bin Tughluq
    (c) Bahlul Lodi
    (d) Sikander Lodi.

72. Alauddin's theory of kingship was based on the concept that?
    (a) Kingship knows no kinship
    (b) As a ruler he was a law unto himself
    (c) The good of the state and the benefit of the people is the highest ideal
    (d) All of the above.

73. Which of the following cities was not founded by Firuz Tughluq
    (a) Fatehabad (b) Jaunpur
    (c) Fatehpur (d) Hissar.

74. The original name of Alauddin Khalji was ?
(a) Almas Beg (b) Ali Gurshap
(c) Alaul Mulk (d) Alp Khan.

75. The token currency introduced by Muhammad bin Tughluq was the tanka of the inferior metal in place of the prevalent silver tanka. Which of the following metals was used by him for issuing the token currency?
(a) Copper (b) Bronze
(c) Nickel (d) Brass.

76. Alauddin Khalji captured the throne after securing fabulous wealth from?
(a) Chanderi (b) Gujarat
(c) Devagiri (d) Chittor.

77. To streamline the working of the Military Department Alauddin Khalji introduced
(a) Preparation of a regular master of the armed forces
(b) Introduction of the system of branding of horses
(c) Payment of cash salaries to soldiers
(d) All of the above.

78. The coming of Khaljis to power is known as the
(a) Khalji imperialism (b) Khalji revolution
(c) Khalji usurpation (d) Khalji coup.

79. The Chalisa or the Group of Forty was liquidated by
(a) Balban
(b) Alauddin Khalji
(c) Mubarak Shah Khalji
(d) Ghiyasuddin Tughluq.

80. Who founded the fortress city of Tughluqabad near Delhi?
(a) Ghiyasuddin Tughluq
(b) Muhammad bin-Tughluq
(c) Firuz Tughluq
(d) Tughluq Shah.

81. Spot the most controversial of the following:
    (a) Ghiyasuddin Balban
    (b) Alauddin Khalji
    (c) Muhammad bin Tughluq
    (d) Firuz Tughluq.

82. About whose kingdom is it said, "The dominion of the Lord of the Universe extended from Delhi to Palam"?
    (a) Qutbuddin Mubarak
    (b) Nasiruddin Mahmud Tughluq
    (c) Ibrahim Lodi
    (d) Alauddin Alam Shah.

83. The reign of which of the following Sultans is said to mark the highest point of territorial expansion of the Sultanate?
    (a) Alauddin Khalji
    (b) Muhammad bin Tughluq
    (c) Firuz Tughluq
    (d) Sikander Lodi.

84. The rulers of the Lodi dynasty were
    (a) Pure Turks
    (b) Timurid Turks
    (c) Pure Afghans
    (d) Turks settled in Afghanistan.

85. During whose reigon did Timur a centrol Asian Turk, invade India and sack Delhi?
    (a) Tughluq Shah
    (b) Nasiruddin Muhammad
    (c) Nasiruddin Mahmud Tughluq
    (d) Daulat Khan Lodi.

86. Which of the following come to the throne immediately after the death of Nasiruddin Mahmud the last ruler of the Tughluq dynasty?
    (a) Dault Khan Lodi (b) Khizr Khan
    (c) Muhammad Shah (d) Abu Baqr.

87. Which of the following was the low caste Hindu convert who usurped the throne from the Khalji's before the establishment of the succeeding Tughluq dynasty?
   (a) Malik Kafur
   (b) Khusru Khan
   (c) Amir Khusrau
   (d) Qutbuddin Mubarak.

88. The greatest contribution of Balban was/were?
   (a) He propounded the theory of kingship
   (b) He restarted peace in the Doab
   (c) He took vigorous measures to check the Mongol inroads
   (d) Both (a) and (b) above.

89. The Diwan-i-arz or the Department of Military Affairs was created by?
   (a) Allauddin Khalji
   (b) Balban
   (c) Ghiyasuddin Tughluq
   (d) Firuz Tughluq.

90. The Sultan who called himself Naib-i-Khudai or Deputy of the God, was?
   (a) Iltutmish (b) Balban
   (c) Alauddin Khalji (d) Ghiyasuddin Tughluq.

91. Razia's claim to fame lies in the fact that she was?
   (a) The muslim woman ruler in medialval India
   (b) The only ruler to ascend the throne with the support of the people
   (c) All of the above
   (d) Accepted as a ruler against Islamic injunctions.

92. From the death of Iltutmish till the accession of Balban the actual power was wielded by?
   (a) The army (b) The nobility
   (c) The theologians (d) (b) and (c) above.

93. The Chalisa or the Group of forty was the nickname of the
   (a) Forty great scholars at the court of Iltutmish
   (b) Turkish nobility created by Iltutmish
   (c) Turkish commanders of Iltutmish
   (d) Forty leading slave officers of Iltustmish.

94. The first Sultan of Delhi to issue regular currency and declare Delhi as the Capital of his empire was?
   (a) Aram Shah (b) Iltutmish
   (c) Nasiruddin Mahmud (d) Balban.

95. The first sovereign ruler of the Sultante of Delhi was
   (a) Qutbuddin Aibak
   (b) Aram Shah
   (c) Iltutmish
   (d) Nasiruddin Mahmud.

96. The Sultans of the so-called slave Dynasty are also sometimes known as "Ilbari Turks" because they belonged to the tribe of Ilbari in Turkestan. Which of the following rulers did not belong to Ilbari tribe?
   (a) Qutbuddin Aibak (b) Iltutmish
   (c) Nasiruddin Mahmud (d) Ghiyasuddin Balban.

97. The foreign traveller whose account does not throw light on the history of the sultanate is?
   (a) Ibn Batutah
   (b) Marco Polo
   (c) Abdur Razzaq
   (d) Athanasius Mikitin.

98. Which of the following was not a Chronicler of the history of the Sultanate?
   (a) Abbas Khan Shawani
   (b) Amir Khusrau
   (c) Ziauddin Barani
   (d) Minhaj-us-Siraj.

99. The part of Delhi where Qutbuddin Aibak laid the foundation of the first so-called "seven cities" of medialval Delhi, was

(a) Siri (b) Tughluqabad

(c) Mehrauli (d) Hauz Khas.

100. Qutbuddin Aibak cannot be called the sovereign ruler of the Sultanate because he

(a) Did not assume the title of Sultan

(b) Issued no coins nor the Khutba was read in his name

(c) Both (a) and (b) above

(d) Instead of Delhi he mostly stayed in Lahore.

ANSWERS

1.	(c)	2.	(c)	3.	(b)	4.	(d)
5.	(c)	6.	(d)	7.	(d)	8.	(a)
9.	(a)	10.	(a)	11.	(d)	12.	(d)
13.	(b)	14.	(a)	15.	(c)	16.	(b)
17.	(b)	18.	(c)	19.	(a)	20.	(c)
21.	(a)	22.	(b)	23.	(d)	24.	(d)
25.	(a)	26.	(d)	27.	(d)	28.	(b)
29.	(c)	30.	(b)	31.	(c)	32.	(c)
33.	(d)	34.	(a)	35.	(d)	36.	(c)
37.	(d)	38.	(c)	39.	(d)	40.	(b)
41.	(d)	42.	(b)	43.	(a)	44.	(a)
45.	(b)	46.	(d)	47.	(c)	48.	(c)
49.	(c)	50.	(b)	51.	(c)	52.	(a)
53.	(b)	54.	(a)	55.	(c)	56.	(a)
57.	(d)	58.	(b)	59.	(a)	60.	(c)
61.	(a)	62.	(d)	63.	(a)	64.	(b)
65.	(d)	66.	(d)	67.	(a)	68.	(b)
69.	(b)	70.	(c)	71.	(d)	72.	(d)
73.	(c)	74.	(b)	75.	(b)	76.	(c)
77.	(d)	78.	(b)	79.	(a)	80.	(a)
81.	(c)	82.	(b)	83.	(b)	84.	(c)
85.	(c)	86.	(a)	87.	(b)	88.	(d)
89.	(b)	90.	(b)	91.	(c)	92.	(b)
93.	(b)	94.	(b)	95.	(c)	96.	(a)
97.	(c)	98.	(a)	99.	(c)	100.	(c)

14
MOGHAL PERIOD

1. The first Rajput Chief who entered into matrimonial alliance with Akbar was
   (a) The Ruler of Ranthambor
   (b) The Ruler of Mewar
   (c) The Ruler of Jaipur
   (d) The Ruler of Kalinga.
2. The only state in Northern India which Akbar failed to annex was
   (a) Kashmir (b) Malwa
   (c) Mewar (d) Gondwana.
3. The famous Battle of Haldighati was fought between Rana and Akbar in
   (a) 1576 AD (b) 1578 AD
   (c) 1568 AD (d) 1580 AD.
4. Which of the following states of southern India was completely annexed by Akbar
   (a) Ahmednagar (b) Bijapur
   (c) Khandesh (d) Golkunda.
5. The first step that Akbar to make him free from the influence of the ulemas was to read the Khutba in his own name from the mosque at Fathepur Sikri on the
   (a) 22nd Oct. 1573
   (b) 22nd June 1579
   (c) 3rd March 1574
   (d) 3rd March 1580.

6. Akbar followed the policy of conciliation towards the Rajputs with a view to
   (a) Marrying Rajputs ladies
   (b) Annexing Rajput states
   (c) Isolating Muslim rivals
   (d) Strengthening the mughals empire.

7. Jahangir ascended the throne in the year:
   (a) 1600 AD (b) 1605 AD
   (c) 1590 AD (d) 1627 AD.

8. Who was the first Mughal ruler to introduce prohibition?
   (a) Babar (b) Akbar
   (c) Humayun (d) Jahangir.

9. What was the immediate cause of the Satnami revolt against Aurangzeb?
   (a) Aurangzeb enslaved them
   (b) Aurangzeb took away all the land belonging to them
   (c) A Satnami peasent was murdered by a mughal foot soldier
   (d) Satnami were prone to rebel.

10. The Yusufzais rose in revolt against Aurangzeb in the year
    (a) 1658 AD (b) 1667 AD
    (c) 1678 AD (d) 1687 AD.

11. Who was the leader of the Jet rebellion in the Mathura region during the reign of Aurangzeb?
    (a) Jujhar Singh (b) Jai Singh
    (c) Durga Das (d) Gokul.

12. Who was the Maratha King who gave shelter to prince Akbar, son of Aurangzeb?
    (a) Shivaji (b) Rajaram
    (c) Sambhuji (d) Sahu.

13. What was the name of the sikh Guru who was executed by Aurangzeb?
    (a) Guru Hargovind (b) Guru Har Rai
    (c) Guru Arjan Dev (d) Guru Teg. Bahadur

14. Who among the following Mughal emperors, was the most pious in his personal idealism.
    (a) Babar (b) Akbar
    (c) Aurangzeb (d) Shah Jahan.

15. The 'chain of Justice' is associated with
    (a) Akbar (b) Jahangir
    (c) Nur Jahan (d) Shah Jahan.

16. Which Mughal Emperor was known as Shaiku Babu
    (a) Jahangir (b) Shah Jahan
    (c) Akbar (d) Aurangzeb.

17. The Mughal Empire reached the territorial climax under
    (a) Akbar (b) Jahangir
    (c) Shah Jahan (d) Aurangzeb.

18. In the hierarchy of nobles , who of the following was considered their head?
    (a) Diwan-i-ala (b) Mir Bakhshi
    (c) Sadar-us-Sudur (d) Qazi-ul-Qazat.

19. Who of the following was the head of the civil as well as military administration of the province?
    (a) Diwan (b) Nazim
    (c) Bakhshi (d) Faujdar.

20. Who was responsible for the administration of a village under the Mughals?
    (a) The Shiqdar
    (b) The Faujdar
    (c) The Amil
    (d) The Village Panchayat.

21. Which of the following was not the part of the Armed forces of Akbar?
    (a) Infantry (b) Navy
    (c) Cavalry (d) Artillery.

22. The origin of the Mansabdari system introduced by Akbar in the Mughal army can be traced back to :
(a) Khalifa Abba Said
(b) Chingiz Khan
(c) Amir Timur
(d) Alauddin Khalji.

23. What were the person holding ranks from 500 to 2500 known as
(a) Mansabdars (b) Amirs
(c) Amir-i-Umda (d) Umda-i-Azam.

24. Which was the most important source of income of the state during the Mughal rule?
(a) Custom duty (b) Minerals
(c) Chachar (d) Banjar.

25. Almost all the great Mughal emperors realised the land revenue at the rate of
(a) 1/5 of the produce
(b) 1/2 of the produce
(c) 1/3 of the produce
(d) 1/6 of the produce.

26. The revenue collector incharge of the district was called
(a) Muqaddam (b) Faujdar
(c) Qanungo (d) Amal Guzar.

27. During the Mughal period, sugarcane was mostly produced in
(a) Bengal and Sindh
(b) Bengal and Bihar
(c) Punjab and North West provinces
(d) Sindh.

28. During whose reign tobacco was introduced in India for cultivation?
(a) Humayun (b) Akbar
(c) Jahangir (d) Shah Jahan.

29. The most important industry during the Mughal period was
    (a) Silk (b) Sculpture
    (c) Cotton (d) Handicrafts.

30. The position of woman during the Mughal period
    (a) The same as it was in the Sultanate period
    (b) Deteriorated
    (c) Improved
    (d) Highly respectable.

31. Who was the designer of Taj Mahal?
    (a) Ustad Ahmed Lahori
    (b) Ali Mardan
    (c) Abdus Samad
    (d) Sanwal Das.

32. Who was the founder of Mughal Dictorial art during the reign of Akbar?
    (a) Mir Sayed Ali (b) Khwaja Abdus Samad
    (c) Mukund (d) Madhu.

33. The Mughal painting reached to its zenith at the time of
    (a) Jahangir (b) Akbar
    (c) Shahjahan (d) Aurangzeb.

34. During whose reign portrait painting made special progress
    (a) Humayun (b) Akbar
    (c) Jahangir (d) Shah Jahan.

35. Who wrote 'Ain-i-Akbari' and Akbarnama?
    (a) Rahim Khan Khana (b) Faizi
    (c) Naqib Khan (d) Abul Fazal.

36. Which book is regarded as the greatest digest of Muslim law made in India?
    (a) Masir-i-Alamgiri
    (b) Muntakhab-ul-Lubab
    (c) Khulasal-ul-Tawarikh
    (d) Fatwa-i-Alamgir.

37. Who, among the following scholar's translated Ramayana into persian

(a) Badauni (b) Abu Fazal
(c) Faizi (d) Khafi Khan.

38. Which one of the following is not a cultural contribution of the Great Mughals?

(a) Calligraphy
(b) Rage drupad and Raga darbari
(c) Kathak
(d) Decorative work.

39. Akbar was the great lover of music and is said to be adept at playing

(a) Shehnai (b) Veena
(c) Dholak (d) Nakkarah.

40. Which one of the following Mughal Emperor was an accomplished Veena player

(a) Akbar (b) Jahangir
(c) Shah Jahan (d) Aurangzeb.

41. Babar captured Samarquad thrice but failed to keep it under his control because of the resistance of the

(a) Uzbegs (b) Persians
(c) Turks (d) Afghans.

42. Which Battle did Babar fight against the Afghans?

(a) Panipat (b) Ghaghara
(c) Khanua (d) Chanderi.

43. Humayun fought his decisive battle against Sher Shah at

(a) Chausa (b) Chunargarh
(c) Bilgram (d) Panipat.

44. Akbar was born at

(a) Lahore (b) Ghazni
(c) Kabur (d) Amarkot.

45. Bairam Khan worked as regent of Akbar between the period
   (a) 1556-1558 A.D. (b) 1556-1564 A.D.
   (c) 1556-1560 A.D. (d) 1556-1605 A.D..

46. The Second battle of Panipat was fought in 1556 A.D between
   (a) Akbar and Udaya Singh
   (b) Akbar and Rana Pratap
   (c) Akbar and Hemu
   (d) Akbar and Raja Surjan Rai.

47. Which was of the following statements about Aurangzeb comes closer to the truth
   (a) He was the greatest Mughal emperor
   (b) He worked for the glory of the Mughal dynasty
   (c) He tried to transform India into an Islamic state
   (d) He was a statesman.

48. The greatness of Shivaji was that he
   (a) was the father of the Maratha nation
   (b) defeated the Mughal forces
   (c) was a benevolent ruler
   (d) checked Mughal expansion in the south.

49. The finest of Mughal architecture in Marble is the
   (a) Diwan-i-Am (b) Taj Mahal
   (c) Peacock throne (d) Pearl Mosque.

50. Guru Nanak preached
   (a) the brotherhood of man
   (b) about making Sikhs a militant organisation
   (c) Sikhism as a religion
   (d) the unity of Sikhs.

51. Painting in the Mughal period was at its prime during the reign of
   (a) Jahangir (b) Shahajahan
   (c) Aurangzeb (d) Akbar.

52. Which of the following is not characteristic of the paintings of the Mughal period? The depiction of
    (a) Religious scenes
    (b) Court and Cultural scenes
    (c) Scenes of battle
    (d) Mythological themes.

53. Who was the first Muslim ruler to formulate the theory of kingship similar to the theory of divine right of the kings?
    (a) Aibak (b) Iltutmish
    (c) Balban (d) Alauddin.

54. In the third battle of Panipat, the Marathas were defeated by the
    (a) Mughals (b) Afghans
    (c) English (d) Ruhella.

55. The most important limitation that generally served a check on the obsolutism of the Sultans of Delhi was the power of the
    (a) Wazir (b) Ulemas
    (c) Quran (d) Caliph.

56. European painting was introduced in the court of
    (a) Humayun (b) Akbar
    (c) Jahangir (d) Shahjahan.

57. When the East India Company started its business legally in India?
    (a) 1500 A.D.
    (b) 1600 A.D.
    (c) 1650 A.D.
    (d) 1700 A.D..

58. The greatness of Sher Shah lies in his
    (a) Victories against Humayun
    (b) Superior generalship
    (c) Administrative reforms
    (d) Secular attitude.

59. The Mughals were
    (a) Turks (b) Mongols
    (c) Arabs (d) Chaghtais.

60. The second battle of Panipat was fought in 1556 A.D. between
    (a) Akbar and Udaya Singh
    (b) Akbar and Rana Pratap
    (c) Akbar and Hemu
    (d) Akbar and Raja Surjan Rai.

61. Many English merchants are said to have visited India during the reign of Akbar, but one of them was taken into royal service at Fatehpur Sikri who was he?
    (a) John Newbery (b) William Leeds
    (c) Ralph Fitch (d) John Milldeihall.

62. Abul Fazl list 18 members of Din-i-Ilahi, in the Ain-i-Akbari amongst whom one was a Hindu who was he?
    (a) Todar Mal (b) Man Singh
    (c) Birbal (d) Bhagwandas.

63. Akbar promulgated Din-i-Ilahi in 1582. It was
    (a) Islamic doctrine
    (b) Code of conduct
    (c) Hindu Law influenced by Islam
    (d) None of the above.

64. The reconciliation between Akbar and prince Salim was achieved with the efforts of
    (a) Salina Sultan Begum
    (b) Khan Azam
    (c) Man Singh
    (d) Hamida Banu Begum.

65. Akbar erected the 'Ibadat Khana' for
    (a) Holding royal durbars
    (b) Receiving royal guests
    (c) To entertain his Rajput Wives
    (d) Holding religious discussions.

66. What was Nur Jahan real name?
    (a) Arjumand Banu Begum
    (b) Meher-un-nisa
    (c) Hamida Begum Banu
    (d) Ruqaiya Begum.

67. A war of succession was fought among the son of Shah Jahan in 1657-58, who was they?
    (a) Kam Baksh, Murad, Dara, Aurangzeb
    (b) Shuja, Aurangzeb, Dara, Kam Baksh
    (c) Dara, Aurangzeb, Murad, Shuja
    (d) Dara, Kamran, Aurangzeb, Murad.

68. Which of the following Rajput Chiefs fighting against Aurangzeb, was called the flower of the Rajput Chivalry?
    (a) Jai Singh of Mewar
    (b) Raja Singh of Mewar
    (c) Durga Das of Mewar
    (d) Ajit Singh of Mewar.

69. Aurangzeb reimposed Jaziya in
    (a) 1675 A.D. (b) 1619 A.D.
    (c) 1681 A.D. (d) 1682 A.D..

70. Who among the following, was the revenue officer of a Sarkar?
    (a) Amal Guzar (b) Amil
    (c) Bitikchi (d) Khazandar.

71. The range of the Mansabs as organised by Akbar was
    (a) 100 to 5000 (b) 10 to 5000
    (c) 10 to 7000 (d) 10 to 10000.

72. During the Mughal rule, wealth was mostly concentrated in
    (a) Emperors and Nobility
    (b) Mosques
    (c) Traders
    (d) Peasants.

73. The text of the Khutba declaring Akbar as the Supreme head of Muslim Church was prepared by

(a) Abul Fazl (b) Faiza
(c) Sheikh Mubarak (d) Mullah Abdullah.

74. Which Deccan state was conquered by Aurangzeb who belonged to the concerned power

(a) Travancore (b) Golkunda
(c) Bijapur (d) Mewar.

75. Name the emperor during whose tenure, the office of the Vakil came into prominence?

(a) Jahangir (b) Aurangzeb
(c) Akbar (d) Shahjahan.

76. The Nasaq system of land revenue collection during the time of Akbar prevailed in

(a) Bengal, Barar, Khandesh, Sind
(b) Bengal, Barar, Rajputana
(c) Barar, Khandesh, Gujarat
(d) Malwa, Gujarat and Rajputana.

77. "Humayun tumbled through the life and tumbled out of it", whose words are these?

(a) V.A. Smith (b) Lane Poali
(c) Percival Spear (d) S.A.A. Rizvi.

78. Once Sher Shah exclaimed that he had lost the empire of Hindustan for a handful of Bajra. What does this mean?

(a) Once he got standed in the desert of Rajasthan without getting food for 17 days and he would have been killed but for timely supply of bajra rotis by the Rajput king, Maldev
(b) Sher Shah never gave such an exclamation
(c) The troops of Jaita and Kampa, two famous generals of Maldev, the Rajput king of Jodhpur (Marwar) cut their way to the very heart of Sher Shah camp and he would have been killed but for timely help
(d) One of the Rajput kings served him with bajra rotis containing poison and he would have been killed but for timely medical help.

79. What is the significance of the second Battle of Panipat?
   (a) It marked the final triumph of the Mughals in their contest with the Afghan for supremacy in India
   (b) It marked the final triumph of the Mughal in their contest with the Rajput for supremacy in India
   (c) It marked the supremacy of artellery over the cavalry in India conditions of warfare
   (d) It marked the supremacy of infantry supported by artellery over the cavalry in Indian conditions of warfare.

80. What made Bairam Khan rebel against Akbar?
   (a) He was a man of masterful personality
   (b) He was incensed by the outrageous conduct of Pir Muhammad, his old servant now in Akbar's favour, who wanted to hustle him out of the country
   (c) He was stung by the outrageous conduct of Akbar, who dismissed him and asked him to go Mecca
   (d) He was tempted by the youth of Akbar and wanted the throne for himself.

81. Which of the following cause was responsible for Akbar's invansion of Mewar?
   (a) Rana Udai Singh had given shelter to Baz Bhadur of Malwa who was the enemy of the Mughals
   (b) Without capturing Mewar Akbar could not claim to be an emperor of whole north India
   (c) Rana Udai Singh was interested to conquer Delhi
   (d) Rana Udai Singh of Mewar opposed Islam.

82. According to V.A Smith, "The Conquest of Gujarat marks an important epoch in Akbar's history", why?
   (a) The conquest of Gujarat was made in unfavourable conditions and there by boosted the morals of Akbar's army
   (b) This annexation enabled Akbar and his successor's to prevent the intrusion of European trader's in the coming years

(c) The annexation of Gujarat secured for the Mughals free access to the sea and brought them in contact with the Portuguese

(d) For the first time in Mughal history, the conquest was led by Hindu generals alone.

83. Akbar would not claim one of the following as his achievement in the Deccan?

(a) In 1595-96 he invaded Ahmadnagar and forced it to code the province of Berar to the Mughal empire

(b) Subsequently Chand Bibi of Ahmadnagar formed a front with Bijapur and Golkunda against the Mughals, but with the death of Chand Bibi all opposition collapsed

(c) In 1601 Asirgarh was seized and Khandesh was annexed to the Mughal empire

(d) Todarmal's revenue system was introduced in the Deccan.

84. Why was Akbar interested in extending his way to the south of Narmada and which one of the following factors did not shape his Deccan policy in this regard?

(a) His desire to bring the whole of India under his way and to repeat the experiment of the Sultans of Delhi in Deccan

(b) For the expulsion of the Europeans, particularly the Portuguese, the annexation of the Deccan was essential

(c) The Deccan had became the centre of bitter religious controversies, which would have disturbed the religious peace he was trying to restore in the North

(d) As in the case of Ala-ud-din Khalji, the wealth of the south was one of the biggest inducements to him.

85. It is generally held that Jahangir as a prince was in love with mehr-un-nisa when she was a maiden and the emperor arranged the murder of her husband Sher Afghan to marry her. Dr. Beni Prasad attempts to exonerate Jahangir of this charge which of the following reasons have not been advanced by Dr. Beni Prasad in support of this thesis?

(a) No contemporary chronicle has made the charge against the emperor

(b) Contemporary European writers who are otherwise critical of Jahangir do not impute the crime of Jahangir

(c) If Jahangir as a prince took she Afghan as his rival in love , he would have got him killed when she Afghan was placed under prince Salim

(d) The chronicler's of Shah Jahan reign also make no mention of the affair.

86. Which of the following causes was not responsible for the execution of Guru Arjan by Jahangir?

(a) Jahangir was doubtful about Guru Arjan that he had supported a rebel

(b) Jahangir was a religious bigot

(c) Guru Arjan gave shelter to Khusra

(d) Guru Arjan refused to pay a fine of one lakh rupee which was imposed on the Guru by Jahangir.

87. What was the basic reason of the conflict between Jahangir and Prince Khurram?

(a) Khurram became very powerful, and this was a great threat of Jahangir

(b) Jahangir wanted Khusraw to succeed him

(c) Nur Jahan wanted Shahryar to succeed Jahangir

(d) Jahangir wanted to marry Mumtaz Mahal.

88. The main cause for the war of succession among Shah Jahan's son was

(a) The non-acceptance of the law of primogeniture

(b) Precedents of fratricidal wars

(c) Aurangzeb was over ambitious

(d) The Shah Jahan wanted the victor of the wars to succed him.

89. Why did Aurangzeb reimpose Jaziya and pilgrim tax on the Hindus?

(a) He needed money to meet the revolts of the Rajputs

(b) It was a matter of punishment to the Hindus for their disloyality to the emperor

(c) He wanted to spread Islam and discourage the infidel practices
(d) He wanted money for the conquest of the South India.

90. The best means by which Aurangzeb tried to serve the best interests of his subject was
(a) To develop the growth of agriculture
(b) To spread Islam in every corner of India
(c) To establish political unity in the state
(d) To increase the export and Import of India.

91. As compared to the ruler of the Delhi Sultanate the Mughal emperors brought a fundamental change in the policy of the state. The change was
(a) There was no interference in the working of village panchayats
(b) The Mughal rulers believed in the theory of Divine Rights
(c) The administration was centralized
(d) There was no theoratic rule.

92. Which of the following was not a duty of the Mir-Bakshi under the Mughals?
(a) He supervised the branding of horses
(b) He was responsible for enforcing the royal regulation regarding the army
(c) He represented the emperor in latter's absence
(d) All order were passed to mansabs through him.

93. The Diwan was most powerful functionary under the Mughal's but his power did not include
(a) Head of Revenue department
(b) Superior over all other departments
(c) Power to recommend appointments and dismissal of other heads of departments
(d) Issue all imperial farmans.

94. Which of the following was not a duty of the Subahdar under the Mughal's?
 (a) He enforced emperial order's in the province
 (b) He was responsible for the maintenance of law and order in the provinces
 (c) He helped in the collection of revenue in the province
 (d) He appointed the provincial sadars.

95. Akbar brought out several reforms in the arms. However, which among the following was not one of them?
 (a) Forcing the Mansabdar's to keep the number of their soldier's according to the number of their mansabs
 (b) Keeping of the descriptive roll (Hurriya) of the soliders
 (c) Branding (Dagh) of the horses
 (d) Occasional inspection by the emperor of the armies of the nobles and Subahdar.

96. Shah Jahan modification in the Mansabdari system were aimed at
 (a) Increasing the number of Sawars a noble was required to maintain
 (b) Decreasing the number of Sawars a noble was required to maintain
 (c) Doing away with the Sawar rank and increasing the zat rank
 (d) None of these.

97. During Akbar's reigin the Qanungos were hereditary holder's of land as well as local offcicals conversant with local condition. What was their main function?
 (a) They calculated land revenue
 (b) The reported on the actual produce and state of cultivation along with local prices
 (c) Both (a) and (b)
 (d) None of these.

98. What was the revenue policy behind different rates of assessment for different classes of land?
 (a) To retain discretion for granting concessions
 (b) To avoid hardship to peasants

(c) To help in bringing virgin and uncultvated waste land under cultivation
(d) To leave scope for the Jagirdars and Zamindars to raise their share of revenue.

99. The Nasaq system of land revenue collection during the time of Akbar prevailed in
(a) Bengal, Berar, Khandesh and Sind
(b) Bengal, Berar and Rajputana
(c) Brar, Khandesh and Gujarat
(d) Malwa, Gujarat and Rajputana.

100. A Deshmukh during the Mughal period was
(a) A chief in the southern parts of India
(b) Equivalent to the North Indian Chaudhari
(c) Equivalent to a Zamindar in south India
(d) Equivalent to the Talukdar in North India.

101. Which one of the following was not the feature of educational system in the Mughal times?
(a) Education was compulsory
(b) The Christians opened their missionary school
(c) The elemaetary school were attached to the mosques
(d) Female education was confined a very few numbers.

102. Which one of the following was the improved feature of Indian society during the Mughal period?
(a) Close cultural relations between the Hindus and Muslims
(b) Interdining and inter marriages between the Hindu and Muslims
(c) Improvement in education
(d) Improvement in the position of women.

103. 'Pietra Dura', means.
(a) Decorating walls with miniature paintings
(b) Decorating walls with floral designs made of semi-precious stones
(c) Construction of buildings with glazed tiles
(d) Indo-muslim architecture.

104. Why did Aurangzeb reimpose Jaziya and Pilgrim tax on the Hindus?
   (a) He needed money to meet the revolt of the Rajputs
   (b) It was a matter of punishment to the Hindu for their disloyality to the emperor
   (c) He wanted to spread Islam and discourage the infidels practices
   (d) He wanted money for the conquest of the south India.

105. Which chronological order of Babur's battles in Hindustan is correct?
   (a) Panipat, Ghaghara, Chanderi, Khanua
   (b) Panipat, Chanderi, Khanua, Ghaghara
   (c) Panipat, Khanua, Chanderi, Ghaghara
   (d) Panipat, Khanua, Ghaghara, Chanderi.

106. Which of the following was not a result of the Rajput policy of Akbar?
   (a) The Rajputs gave co-operation to the administrative machinery of Akbar
   (b) The Rajputs gave help to the melitary achievements of Akbar
   (c) It developed the Indo-Islamic culture
   (d) The co-operation of the Rajputs changed the minds of orthodox muslim ulemas and they became liberal.

107. Which of the following is correct?
   (a) Shah Jahan conquered Qandahar but lost to the Uzbegs at Balkh
   (b) Shah Jahan did not conquer Qandahar but defeated the Uzbegs at Balkh
   (c) Shah Jahan both conquered Qandahar and defeated the Uzbegs at Balkh
   (d) Shah Jahan failed both in conquered Qandahar and in fighting the Uzbegs at Balkh.

108. Check one of the follwoing statement about the Mughal administration that is incorrect.
   (a) It was essentially military in nature and the civil servants were either mansabdars or members of the army
   (b) It was necessary a centralised autocracy and the emperor had unlimited powers
   (c) The emperor had obey the scriptures and Islamic tradition
   (d) The minister's had no claim to be consulted as a matter of right, and to accept or not to accept their advice was a matter of the emperor's discretion.

109. Which points on the Jagirdari system is not correct?
   (a) The increase in the number of mansabdars and a new posting after the time of Akbar, led to a chain of Jagir transfers
   (b) The confiscation of Wasan Jagirs in Rajasthan was an important factor in the Rajput rebellion
   (c) All the Jagirs were transferred to the emperor after the death of the Jagirdars
   (d) This system made the Jagirdar's rebellious while they exploited the peasantry.

110. Which statement on the jagirdari system of Mughals is incorrect?
   (a) The Jagir were assigned to offcials of Mansabdar's in liew of their pay
   (b) A Mansabdar continued to enjoy the same jagir throughout his life
   (c) The Jagirs existed in every pargana
   (d) By the mid 17th centurary over 61% of the revenue income was taken over by nearly 450 mansabdars.

111. Which statement on the landless in the Mughal period is not correct?
   (a) The landless people were generally of the lower castes
   (b) They worked in the fields of Zamindars, the peasants
   (c) The menial castes, too, owned land

(d) Caste system was a determining factor in the working conditions.

112. Which statement on the peasants in Mughal India is not correct?

(a) The rights to cultivate was hereditary but the peasant was rarely exempted from this obligation

(b) The landless were not many in numbers

(c) The zamindari right had a caste basis since the zamindari and the retainers normally belonged to the same caste

(d) The sale of lands by peasants was extremely rare.

113. Which statement on the peasants and the rulers in the Mughal period is not correct?

(a) Prices were kept low resulting in the peasant not getting any reasonable return for his surpluses

(b) The soldiers on march were encouraged to lost the peasants to obtain grain

(c) The granting of jagirs went against the interest of the peasants

(d) The peasantry was through oppressed there were no conflicts between them and the ruler rich.

114. Which of the following statement regarding the life of the peasant in the Mughal period is incorrect?

(a) As the Mughals made an attempt to integrate the village into the administrative machinery the muqaddams, chaudharies and khuts took away what ever the surplus that was left with the peasant after the payments were made to the royal treasury

(b) They consumed only inferior foodgrains

(c) The food consumed by the peasant was poor in nutrition

(d) Salt was more expensive than wheat.

115. Which points on trade and commerce is the Mughal period is not correct?

(a) Jahangir, his mother, Nur Jahan and Prince Khurram owned their own ships

(b) Princess Jahan Aara had her own ships and even hired the Dutch and the English vassels

(c) Jahangir and Shah Jahan had their own flets

(d) Nobles and clergymen had no share in trade.

116. Which statement on the Zamindar in the later part of Mughal Empire is not correct?

(a) There grew a tension between the emperial authority and the zamindars with regard to the share in the surplus produced by the peasants

(b) The zamindars had their own retainer and they were stranger to the peasant

(c) As the imperial share in the land revenue increased the zamindar found that they were unable to collect their share

(d) The revolts of the jats, Satnamis and sikhs were led by the zamindars.

117. Towards the end of the Mughal period the institution of zamindari under went change but one of them is incorrect.

(a) The zamindars made common cause with the peasant and started peasant revolt like these of jats, sikhs and satnamis

(b) Whenever the Marathas or jat zamindar suceeded in their rebellions, they assumed the role of both rulers and zamindars

(c) By the time the British rule was established the zamindars were exercising greater authority than during the Mughal period

(d) The other revenue farmers did not claim to zamindari rights.

118. Which one of the following statement about the institution of slavery during the Mughal rule is not correct?

(a) It was a recognized institution in the society

(b) Slaves were treated badly and cruely

(c) They should never rise to distinguished position in the state

(d) The state en couraged low treatment with slaves.

119. Which statement of Shah Jahan architecutre is not correct?
   (a) White marbel used on a great scale
   (b) There was change of building materials, but surface decoration did not change
   (c) The dome assumed a bulbous shape placed on a high drum
   (d) The pillars have faliated bases.

120. Which of the following statement is incorrect regarding the social life of the people in the time of the Mughals?
   (a) Both Hindus and Muslims believed in astrology
   (b) Sati system, child marriage and dowry system was in practice
   (c) Widow remarriage were prevalent
   (d) The Mughal government banned child marriage and sati system.

121. Regarding Fatehpur Sikri which statement is incorrect?
   (a) It took nearly one generation to build it
   (b) Without exception sand stone of a rich red colour was used
   (c) The house of Mariam is decorated with Persian murals
   (d) The structures are both secular and religious.

122. Which statement of Jahangir and Mughal paintings is not correct?
   (a) Miniature painting was given great impetus
   (b) Ustad Mansur painted birds
   (c) Stress was laid on depicting natural beauty
   (d) Jahangir had no taste for painting.

123. Which of the following points relating to Akbar and Mughal painting is not correct?
   (a) There were more than 1000 painters
   (b) Portraits and big illustrations were the principal features of Akbar era
   (c) The two chief painter of Humayun continued to adom the court of Akbar

(d) There were no foreign influence on paintings during the time of Akbar.

124. Which feature is not true of the Rajasthani paintings?
(a) Presentation of nature reached the level of landscape paintings
(b) Importance attached to animal
(c) Human figures play an insignificant part
(d) Human figures stand out clearly.

125. Which of the following statement regarding the later day influence of Mughal painting is not correct.
(a) Aurangzeb had no interest but he only wanted his father's portrait to be painted from time to time in order to see how he was fairings in the dungeons
(b) Since Aurangzeb did not patronize painter painting moved to provincial capital such as Rajput school and later to the hill states of Basholi, Nandi, Chamba, Kangra and Rampur
(c) The Mughal painting faded away with time and it had no influence after the nineteen century
(d) Painting were continued during the time of Aurangzeb but they show an artificial rendering.

126. Match the arcthitectural characteristic with the dynasty that used them

A. Uses of large stone blocks and minimum ornamentation	1. Lodi dynasty
B. True arch	2. Slave dynasty
C. Half-dome portal	3. Mughal dynasty
D. Double domes and thick wall	4. Tughluq dynasty

(a) A-4, B-1, C-2, D-3 (b) A-4, B-2, C-3, D-1
(c) A-1, B-2, C-4, D-3 (d) A-4, B-2, C-1, D-3.

127. Match the following kingdoms which were annexed by the Mughal Gradually.

A. Berar	1. Aurangzeb
B. Bijapur and Golkunda	2. Shahjahan

C. Ahmadnagar — 3. Akbar
D. Kangra — 4. Jahangir

(a) A-4, B-1, C-3, D-2 (b) A-3, B-4, C-1, D-2
(c) A-3, B-1, C-2, D-4 (d) A-4, B-1, C-2, D-3.

128. Match the following:

A. Battle against Amar Singh of Mewar — 1. Babar
B. Battle of Chausa — 2. Humayun
C. Battle of Khanwa — 3. Akbar
D. Second battle of Panipat — 4. Jahangir

(a) A-3, B-2, C-1, D-4
(b) A-3, B-1, C-2, D-4
(c) A-4, B-2, C-3, D-1
(d) A-4, B-2, C-1, D-3.

129. Match the IndoIslamic architectural feature with the phase which it is most characteristic of and select the correct answer code.

A. Emergence of true dome with recessed arches under the squich — 1. Shah Jahan and Jahangir
B. The four centered arch which was reinforced with a supporting beam i.e. arch beam combination was adopted — 2. Jahangir
C. The dome developed a bulbous form with stifled neck Double domes become very common — 3. The Khaljis
D. A new device of inlay decoration was adopted — 4. The Tughlaks

in which semi precious stones were embedded in the marble in graceful fatigue

(a) A-3, B-1, C-4, D-2 (b) A-3, B-4, C-1, D-2
(c) A-4, B-3, C-1, D-2 (d) A-4, B-2, C-1, D-3.

130. Match the following:

A.	Abolition of Jaziya	1.	A.D. 1563
B.	Abolition of Pilgrims Tax	2.	A.D 1564
C.	Abolition of enclaving war prisoner	3.	A.D 1562
D.	Fall of Bairan Khan	4.	A.D 1560

(a) A-2, B-1, C-3, D-4 (b) A-4, B-1, C-3, D-2
(c) A-1, B-2, C-3, D-4 (d) A-3, B-4, C-2, D-1.

131. Match the following:

A.	Battle of Bahadurpur	1.	fought between Dara and Shuja
B.	Battle of Dharmat	2.	fought between Dara and Aurangzeb
C.	Battle of Samugarh	3.	fought between Dara and combined armies of Aurangzeb and Murad

(a) A-1, B-3, C-2 (b) A-2, B-3, C-1
(c) A-1, B-2, C-3 (d) A-3, B-1, C-2.

132. Match the follwoing government officials with this respective functions

A.	Khan-i-Saman	1.	House hold department and Karkhanas
B.	Sadar-us-Sudur	2.	Chief adviser to the emperor on eccsiastial affairs and thief justice of the empire

C. Wazir — 3. Prime Minister and the intermediary between the ruler and the rest of the officials

D. Vakil — 4. Finance Minister

(a) A-1, B-2, C-3, D-4 (b) A-2, B-3, C-1, D-4
(c) A-4, B-3, C-2, D-1 (d) A-1, B-2, C-4, D-3.

133. Match the following categories of land with the respective names assigned to them.

A. Polaj — 1. Land which was cultivated almost every year

B. Paravti — 2. Land which had been follow for one or two years

C. Chachar — 3. Fallow land

D. Banjar — 4. Land which had been fallow for three or four years

(a) A-1, B-2, C-4, D-3 (b) A-3, B-1, C-4, D-2
(c) A-1, B-3, C-4, D-2 (d) A-2, B-1, C-4, D-3

134. Match the following:

A. An architectural form in which the main opening are made by beams supported on pillars, was extensively used by Akbar — 1. Piettradura

B. An ornamental lazuli, marble etc. — 2. Trabcate

masic of lapis

C. of the faliation, was the dominat form employed. It is characterised by a continuous stem which — 3. Arabesque

spilts regularly, producing a series of leafy secondary stems which in turn can split again or reintegrate into the main stem. The repetition of this pattern produce a beautiful balanced design with a three dimensional effect.

D. Ornamentation done by carving ime plaster — 4. Stucco

(a) A-3, B-1, C-3, D-4 (b) A-1, B-2, C-4, D-3
(c) A-2, B-3, C-4, D-1 (d) A-2, D-1, C-4, D-3.

135. Put in ascending chronological order

A. First battle of Panipat
B. Second battle of Tarrain
C. Shifting of the Capital from Delhi to Deogiri
D. Ahmad Shah Abdali invasion

(a) ABCD (b) BACD
(c) CBAD (d) BCAD.

136. Put the following social legislation in a chronological order.

A. The practice of human sacrifice was outlawed
B. The Act declared slavery illegal in India
C. The Caste Disabilities Removal Act
D. The Act that legalised the marriages of widow

(a) BACD (b) ABCD
(c) ABDC (d) BCAD.

137. Which chronological order of Babar battle in Hindustan is correct?

(a) Panipat, Ghaghara, Chanderi, Khanua
(b) Panipat, Chanderi, Khauna, Ghaghara
(c) Panipat, Khanua, Chanderi, Ghaghara
(d) Panipat, Khanua, Ghaghara, Chanderi.

138. Arrage chronologically
   1. Construction of Ibadat Khana
   2. Promulgation of Din-i-Ilahi
   3. Issuing of Mazharnama

   (a) 1,2,3 (b) 3,1,2
   (c) 1,3,2 (d) 2,3,1.

139. Mention one of the following that sets out the hierarchy of the Mughal empire in the descending order?
   (a) Subah, Mugta, Pargana
   (b) Shiq, Muqta, Pargana
   (c) Subah, Sarkar, Pargana
   (d) Subah, Amir, Sarkar.

140. TodarMal classified the land, into four, they are
   1. Polaj 2. Paravti
   3. Krori 4. Chachar
   5. Potdar 6. Banjar

   (a) 1,2,4,6 (b) 1,2,3,4
   (c) 1,3,5,6 (d) 2,3,4,5.

141. "I had ordered", write Babar, "that the two Swords he had girt to his waist to fight me with, should be hung from his neck--------", who was the man Babur referred to?
   (a) Alam Khan Lodhi (b) Daulat Khan Lodi
   (c) Rana Sanga (d) Ibrahim Lodi.

142. "The infallibility decree assured to Akbar so far as many written instrument could have such effect, the utmost power that any man could claim to exercise with in the limits of Islam," which of the following historians express the above view about the infallibility decree?
   (a) Stanley Lane Poole (b) V.A. Smith
   (c) Edwards and Garret (d) S.R. Sharma.

143. "In his age he stood alone, not in Islam, but in the whole world; catholic and protestants christiandom might both have gone and sat at his feet". Whose words are these?
   (a) V.A. Smith (b) Freeman
   (c) Stanely Lane Poole (d) Edwards and. Garret.

144. The reign of Shah Jahan saw the worse famine in the Deccan in which according to Abdal Hamid Lahori, "destitution at length reached such a pitch that man began to devour each other and the flesh of a son was preferred to his love". In which year of the reign did this terrible famine take place?

(a) 1628 A.D. (b) 1631 A.D.
(c) 1638 A.D. (d) 1648 A.D..

145. Shah Jahan wrote, "And thou, my son, art a Marvellous Mussalman, as thou causes me in life to lament". What made him write this?

(a) Aurangzeb imprisoned Shah Jahan in the Agra Fort
(b) Shah Jahan was made to suffer in solitude
(c) Shah Jahan was dethroned
(d) Aurangzeb cut off the water fupply to Agra fort.

146. Who among the following historians, has described Aurangzeb as "greatest among the great Mughal except one"?

(a) J.N. Sarkar
(b) Ishwari Prasad
(c) Lane Poole
(d) V. A Smith.

147. Which building bore the persian inscription "if on earth be an Eden of bliss it is this, none but this".

(a) Diwan-i-Khas in Delhi fort
(b) Diwan-i-khas in Fatepur Sikri
(c) Buland Darwaza
(d) Taj Mahal.

148. Who said, "If there were similar portraits finished by several artists, I could point out the painter of each------"?

(a) Akbar (b) Jahangir
(c) Shah Jahan (d) Humayun.

149. Who wrote 'Ain-i-Akbari' and 'Akbarnama'?

(a) Rahim Khan Khana (b) Faizi
(c) Naquib Khan (d) Abul Fazal.

150. Which book is regarded as the greatest digest of Muslim law made in India?

(a) Masir-i-Alamgiri (b) Muntakhab-ul-bab
(c) Khulasat-ul-Tawarikh (d) Fatwa-i-Alamgir.

151. A famous historical work 'Padshahnama' written by Abdul Hamid Lahori gives us important information about the reign of which Mughal ruler?

(a) Akbar (b) Aurangzeb
(c) Shah Jahan (d) Jahangir.

152. Khafi Khan wrote contemporary history in secrecy because Aurangzeb was opposed to it. That book is

(a) Alamgirnamah
(b) Fatwa-i-Alamhgiri
(c) Muntakhab-ul-Lubab
(d) Khulasat-ul-Tawarikh.

153. Abul Fazal and Faizi Sarhindi gave same title to one of their works: It was

(a) Akbarnama (b) Ain-i-Akbari
(c) Tabaqat-i-Akbari (d) Tofan-i-Akbarshahi.

154. Who was the author of Tuzuk-i-khan?

(a) Abdur Rahim Khan-i-Jahangiri
(b) Badauni
(c) Kamgar Khan
(d) Emperor Jahangir.

155. Who was the author of Iqbal nama Jahangiri?

(a) Baqir Khan
(b) Mutamad Khan
(c) Emperor Jahangir
(d) Ahmand Yadgari Mirza.

156. Which well known scholar has translated 'Memories of Babar from its original text Turki into English?

(a) Mrs. A.S. Beveridge (b) Leyden and Erskine
(c) V.A. Smith (d) Marti Wheeler.

157. Who, among the following daughters of Shah Jahan has been regarded as a good poetess?
(a) Jahan Ara (b) Roshan Ara
(c) Gauham Ara (d) None of the above.

158. Aurangzeb was a scholar of
(a) Poetry
(b) Muslim theology and Jurisprudence
(c) Persian literature
(d) Persian warfare.

159. Who, among the following sons of Shah Jahan, was the author of Majmaul Bahrain?
(a) Shah Shuja (b) Dara Shaukoh
(c) Aurangzeb (d) Murad.

160. The important religious work named 'Dabistan Mazahab' was written by
(a) Khafi Khan (b) Mutamad Khan
(c) Mohsin Fani (d) Naquib Khan.

161. Who was the author of Humayun Nama?
(a) Abul Fazal (b) Amir Khusrau
(c) Gulbadan Begum (d) Khan Khana.

162. Who, among the following Muslim scholars made a valuable contribution towards Hindi literature?
(a) Khafi Khan
(b) Abul Fazal
(c) Faizi
(d) Abdur Rahim Khan-i-Khana.

163. Who was given the tittle Zarrinqalam (Gold Pen) by Akbar?
(a) Birbal (b) Tulsidas
(c) Muhammad Hussain (d) Kasiramadas.

164. "Vinapatrika" was written by
(a) Surdas (b) Tulsidas
(c) Valmiki (d) Badauni.

165. Which of the following was patronized by Aurangzeb?
   (a) Music (b) Calligraphy
   (c) Painting (d) Sculpture.

166. Mughal culture greatly influenced India.
   (a) Sculpture (b) Painting
   (c) Architecture (d) Dance.

167. The Shalimar garden at Srinagar was raised by
   (a) Akbar (b) Shah Jahan
   (c) Jahangir (d) Aurangzeb.

169. What was described as a "Romance in stone"?
   (a) Taj Marble (b) Jani-i-Masjid
   (c) Diwan-i-Am (d) Buland Darwaza.

170. The term 'Krori' become synonymous under the Mughal with
   (a) Khalsa land (b) A revenue collector
   (c) Ijaradar (d) Revenue free lands.

ANSWERS

1.	(c)	2.	(c)	3.	(a)	4.	(c)
5.	(c)	6.	(d)	7.	(d)	8.	(d)
9.	(c)	10.	(b)	11.	(d)	12.	(b)
13.	(d)	14.	(d)	15.	(b)	16.	(a)
17.	(d)	18.	(b)	19.	(b)	20.	(d)
21.	(b)	22.	(b)	23.	(b)	24.	(a)
25.	(b)	26.	(b)	27.	(b)	28.	(c)
29.	(c)	30.	(b)	31.	(a)	32.	(b)
33.	(a)	34.	(c)	35.	(d)	36.	(d)
37.	(a)	38.	(d)	39.	(c)	40.	(d)
41.	(a)	42.	(b)	43.	(c)	44.	(d)
45.	(c)	46.	(c)	47.	(c)	48.	(d)
49.	(b)	50.	(a)	51.	(a)	52.	(a)
53.	(c)	54.	(b)	55.	(b)	56.	(c)
57.	(b)	58.	(c)	59.	(d)	60.	(c)
61.	(b)	62.	(c)	63.	(b)	64.	(a)
65.	(d)	66.	(b)	67.	(c)	68	(c)

69.	(b)	70.	(a)	71.	(d)	72.	(a)
73.	(b)	74.	(b)	75.	(c)	76.	(a)
77.	(b)	78.	(c)	79.	(a)	80	(b)
81.	(b)	82.	(b)	83.	(d)	84.	(d)
85.	(c)	86.	(b)	87.	(a)	88.	(a)
89.	(c)	90.	(a)	91.	(d)	92.	(c)
93.	(c)	94.	(d)	95.	(a)	96.	(b)
97.	(b)	98.	(c)	99.	(a)	100.	(a)
101.	(b)	102.	(a)	103.	(b)	104.	(c)
105.	(c)	106.	(d)	107.	(c)	108.	(c)
109.	(d)	110.	(b)	111.	(c)	112.	(b)
113.	(d)	114.	(c)	115.	(d)	116.	(b)
117.	(d)	118.	(d)	119.	(b)	120.	(d)
121.	(a)	122.	(d)	123.	(d)	124.	(c)
125.	(b)	126.	(b)	127.	(c)	128.	(d)
129.	(b)	130.	(a)	131.	(a)	132.	(d)
133.	(a)	134.	(a)	135.	(a)	136.	(b)
137.	(c)	138.	(c)	139.	(c)	140	(a)
141.	(b)	142,	(b)	143.	(c)	144.	(b)
145.	(d)	146.	(a)	147.	(a)	148.	(b)
149.	(d)	150.	(d)	151.	(c)	152.	(c)
153.	(a)	154.	(d)	155.	(b)	156.	(a)
157.	(a)	158.	(b)	159.	(b)	160.	(a)
161.	(c)	162.	(d)	163.	(c)	164.	(b)
165.	(b)	166.	(c)	167.	(d)	168.	(b)
169.	(b)	170.	(b)				

15
HISTORY OF INDIAN NATIONAL MOVEMENT

1. Who among the following was the first President of the All India Congress.
   (a) A.O. Hume (b) Feroze Gandhi
   (c) W.C. Banerjee (d) Dada Bhai Naoroji.

2. The first Indian National Congress consisted of
   (a) 65 delegates (b) 72 delegates
   (c) 76 delegates (d) 80 delegates.

3. The first split in Congress occurred in 1907 at the
   (a) Bombay Session (b) Surat Session
   (c) Lucknow Session (d) Nagpur Session.

4. Identify the first public association to be formed in modern India in 1837?
   (a) Bengal British Indian Society
   (b) British India Association
   (c) Landholder's Society
   (d) Madras Native Association.

5. Name one of the following which earned the recognition of Dadabhai Naoraji?
   (a) East Indian Association, 1866
   (b) Poona Sarvajanik Sabha, 1870
   (c) Madras Mahajan Sabah, 1881
   (d) Bombay Presidency Association, 1885.

6. Which one of the following was founded by Ferozeshah Mehta?
   (a) Bombay Presidency Association
   (b) Indian Association
   (c) Madras Mahajan Sabha
   (d) Hindustan Socialist party.

7. Who was the political Guru of Gokhale?
   (a) Ranade
   (b) Rabindranath Tagore
   (c) Raja Ram Mohan Roy
   (d) Iswar Chand Vidyasagar.

8. Which one of the following was not an Extremist Leader?
   (a) Bipin Chandra Pal
   (b) Lala Lajpat Rai
   (c) Pherozeshah Mehta
   (d) Aurobindo Ghosh.

9. King Emperor George V visited India in
   (a) 1911 (b) 1909
   (c) 1912 (d) 1913.

10. At which Viceroy was a bomb thrown on the occassion of his state entry into Delhi?
    (a) Lord Curzon (b) Lord Wavell
    (c) Lord Minto (d) Lord Hardinge.

11. Who made the famous announcement of August 20, 1916?
    (a) Austin Chamblreain
    (b) Lord Moutague
    (c) Chelmsford
    (d) Lord Morley.

12. The Congress which split into two groups of moderates and Extremists again united at the Lucknow session held in
    (a) 1915 (b) 1916
    (c) 1920 (d) 1921.

13. Which of the following leaders played a leading role in bringing about an understanding between the Congress and the All India Muslim league which culminated in the Lucknow pact?
    (a) Ali Brothers
    (b) Maulana Abul Kalam
    (c) Bal Gangadhar Tilak
    (d) Mahatama Gandhi.

14. The reversal of partition of Bengal was carried out during the time of
    (a) Lord Curzon (b) Lord Minto
    (c) Lord Hardinge (d) Lord Mountbatten.

15. Which one of the international happenings had the greatest impact on the freedom struggle?
    (a) French Revolution
    (b) Russian Revolution
    (c) First World War
    (d) Second World War.

16. Who formed the Ghadar party in the United States of America in 1913?
    (a) V.D. Sarvarkar (b) Lala Hardayal
    (c) Madame Cama (d) Madan Lal Dhingra.

17. Which event pushed Gandhiji into the arena of freedom struggle?
    (a) Rowlatt Act
    (b) Jallianwala Bagh Massacre
    (c) The death of Tilak
    (d) Outbreak of the First World War.

18. In which of the following movement spearheadedby Mahatma Gandhi did Sardar Patel play a leading role?
    (a) Champaran movement
    (b) Khaira movement
    (c) Bardoli Satyagrah
    (d) Ahmedabad Mill workkers strike.

19. The Satyagraha sabha, to carry on passive ressistance against the Rowlatt Acts was formed by
    (a) Mahatama Gandhi (b) Lala Lajpat Rai
    (c) J.L.Nehru (d) Bal Gangadhar Tilak.

20. Which of the following did not belong to the responsivists group which believed in co-operation with the British Government to protect Hindu interest?
    (a) Lokamanya Tilak
    (b) Madan Mohan Malviya
    (c) Lala Lajpat Rai
    (d) N.C Kelkar.

21. When the Turkish empire after the world war first was dismembered, which of the following territories were taken away by Britain and her allies?
    (a) Montenegro (b) Serbia
    (c) Bosnia (d) Thrace.

22. The non-co-operation movement was suspended in
    (a) 1921 (b) 1922
    (c) 1925 (d) None of the above.

23. Those who opposed participation in the legislative councils and their non-cooperation with the government were known as 'No changers' in 1923. Whose name does not belong to the 'No changer's'?
    (a) Sardar Vallabh Bhai patel
    (b) Rajendra Prasad
    (c) C. Rajagopalachari
    (d) Motilal Nehru.

24. Madan Mohan Malviya, Lala Lajpat Rai and Kelkar wanted to co-operate with the government to protect the interests of Hindus, but accused one of the following of letting down Hindus by eating beef and being anti Hindu, who was it?
    (a) Moti Lal Nehru
    (b) J.L. Nehru
    (c) Subhash Chandra Bose
    (d) Durabhai Deshmukh.

25. Which event was known as the Muslim War of National Independence?
(a) Aligarh movement (b) Wahabi movement
(c) Moplah Revolt (d) Khilafat movement.

26. Who can be called the father of the idea of Pakistan?
(a) Iqbal (b) Mohd. Ali Jinnah
(c) Fazlul Huq (d) Abdul Ghaffar Khan.

27. Who said, "I cannot close my eyes to the belief that race is to reconcilate the Hindu"?
(a) Lord Ellenborough (b) Lytton
(c) Curzon (d) Minto.

28. Who published in 1929 the famous Fourteen points to run counter to the most important suggestions in the Nehru Committee Report?
(a) Jinnah (b) Abul Kalam Azad
(c) Agha Khan (d) Allah Bux.

29. The idea of Pakistan had its birth in the year
(a) 1930 (b) 1940
(c) 1936 (d) 1937.

30. Who was the principal of Aligarh college who encouraged Muslim communalism in the first decade of the 20th century?
(a) Archibold (b) Dunlop Smith
(c) Minto (d) Mr. Beck.

31. Who was the partriot to the flogged for ridiculing the court by giving his name as 'AZAD' father's name 'Swatantra' and his address as prison?
(a) Jitendra Nath Das (b) Bhagat Singh
(c) Sukhdev (d) Chandra Sekhar.

32. Chandra Sekhar Azad while fighting was shot dead in February, 1931 at
(a) Allahabad (b) Delhi
(c) Amritsar (d) Lucknow.

33. Which of the following was responsible for changing the name of the Hindustan Republican Association to the Hindustan Socialist Republican Association?
    (a) Rajguru
    (b) Bhagat Singh
    (c) Chandra Shekhar 'Azad'
    (d) Sukhdev.

34. Who remained inactive in politics during 1923-1927?
    (a) Mahatma Gandhi
    (b) Lala Lajpat Rai
    (c) Motilal Nehru
    (d) J.L. Nehru.

35. Gandhiji started the Dandi March
    (a) For Purna Swaraj
    (b) For home rule
    (c) As a protest against the imposition of salt tax
    (d) All are correct.

36. The signing of the Poona Pact resulted in the number of seats reserved for Depressed classes being
    (a) Increased
    (b) Decreased
    (c) Retained at the same level
    (d) Abolished.

37. At the time of the First Round Table Conference the Governor General of India was
    (a) Irwin (b) Willington
    (c) Reading (d) Linlithgow.

38. At the time of the First Round Table Conference Mr. MacDonald, the British Prime Minister, headed the
    (a) Labour Government
    (b) Conservative National Government
    (c) Liberal Government
    (d) Coalition of Labour and Liberals.

39. At the time of Second Round Table Conference the Governor-General of India was

(a) Irwin (b) Willingdon
(c) Reading (d) Minto.

40. Which of the following Indian Leader attended only the three Round Table Conferences

(a) M.N. Joshi
(b) B.R. Ambedkar
(c) Jai Prakash Narayan
(d) Mahtama Gandhi.

41. On the basis of the elections held in 1937, the Congress secured a majority in

(a) Five Provinces (b) Seven Provinces
(c) Ten Provinces (d) None of the above.

42. After which Congress session Mr. Jinnah left the Congress?

(a) Calcutta Session (b) Nagpur Session
(c) Gaya Session (d) Lahore Session.

43. The decision to start civil disobedience was taken at the

(a) Lucknow session (1916)
(b) Ahmedabad session (1921)
(c) Calcutta session (1920)
(d) Nagpur session (1920).

44. Muddiman commitee was appointed to report on the working of the

(a) Dyarchy
(b) Communal representation
(c) Federalism
(d) None of the above.

45. Who was not the member of the Muddiman committee?

(a) Sir Tej Bahadur Sapru
(b) Pt. Motilal Nehru
(c) Mr. M.A. Jinnah
(d) Sir Alexander Muddiman.

46. Who founded the Forward Bloc, a wing within the Congress?
(a) Sardar Patel
(b) J.L. Nehru
(c) Subhash Chandra Bose
(d) C. Rajagopalachari.

47. Who became the President of the All India States 'People' Conference in 1939?
(a) Subhash Chandra Bose
(b) Jawahar Lal Nehru
(c) C. Rajagopalachari
(d) Mahatma Gandhi.

48. Who described the Cripps proposals as "a post dated cheque on a crashing bank"?
(a) Jawaharlal Nehru
(b) Mahatma Gandhi
(c) Sardar Patel
(d) Maulana Abul Kalam Azad.

49. The slogan 'Do or Die' was given by
(a) Mahatma Gandhi
(b) Sardar Patel
(c) Subhash Chandra Bose
(d) Maulana Abul Kalam Azad.

50. Large Scale India naval ratings risings in Bombay and Karachi took place in
(a) 1944 (b) 1945
(c) 1946 (d) 1947.

51. The famous I.N.A. trails took place at the Red Fort, Delhi in
(a) 1944 (b) 1945
(c) 1946 (d) 1947.

52. The Partition of India was for the first time accepted by the
(a) Wavell Plan (b) Cripps Mission
(c) Cabinet Mission (d) Mountbatten Plan.

53. Who organised "Khudai Khidmatgar" in 1929?
(a) Abdul Gaffar Khan (b) Fakir of Ipi
(c) Ansari Brothers (d) None of the above.

54. Which of the following urdu newspapers was started by Lala Lajpat Rai from Lahore in 1920 A.D.?
(a) Qaumi Awaz (b) Milap
(c) Vir Nehru (d) Bande Matram.

55. Hindu Mahasabha was founded in
(a) 1927 (b) 1917
(c) 1925 (d) 1934.

56. Who insisted that his Fourteen points be accommodated in the all-party Reports?
(a) C. Rajagopalachari (b) M.A. Jinnah
(c) Muhammad Iqbal (d) Dr. Ambedkar.

57. Who founded Visva Bharti?
(a) Gandhiji (b) Rabindranath Tagore
(c) Gokhale (d) Tilak.

58. Which Congress session ratified the Gandhi-Irwin pact?
(a) Karachi Session (b) Lahore Session
(c) Calcutta Session (d) Tripura Session.

59. Who was not the member of the Cabinet Mission?
(a) Lord Pethick Lawrence
(b) A.V. Alexandar
(c) Sir Stafford Cripps
(d) Lord Wavell.

60. Who killed General O' Dwyer in London?
(a) Bhagat Singh (b) Madan Lal Dhingra
(c) Udham Singh (d) Veer Sarvarkar.

61. Who founded 'Abhinav Bharati'?
(a) Azad (b) Veer Sarvarkar
(c) Sardar Patel (d) M.N. Roy.

62. Where was the first Round Table Conference held?
    (a) James Palace (London)
    (b) Buckingham Palace (London)
    (c) Ilbert Hall (London)
    (d) Windsor Palace (London).

63. Under whose leadership was Chittagong Armoury Raid organised?
    (a) Jatin Das (b) Surya Sen
    (c) Rajguru (d) Sukhdev.

64. Under whose leadership was the name of the Hindustan Republican Association (H.R.A) changed to Hindustan Socialist Republican Association (H.S. R.A) on account of influence of Socialist ideas?
    (a) Rajguru
    (b) Bhagat Singh
    (c) Chandra Shekhar Azad
    (d) Ambika Chakraborty.

65. The slogan "political freedom is the breath of a nation" was given by
    (a) Jawahar Lal Nehru
    (b) Aurobindo Ghosh
    (c) Mahatama Gandhi
    (d) Bal Gangadhar Tilak.

66. The object of the Butler Committee of 1927 was to
    (a) Modernise the Indian Army
    (b) Modernise Indian Agriculture
    (c) Suppress National Movement
    (d) Improve the relationship between the Government of India and the Indian States.

67. When Turkey was fighting the Balkan powers, who headed the medical mission sent from India to Turkey?
    (a) Dr. Ansari (b) Dr. Kitchlev
    (c) Dr. Wacha (d) None of the above.

68. The newspaper 'Comrade', was published by
   (a) Bal Gangadhar Tilak
   (b) Aurobindo Ghosh
   (c) Azad
   (d) Maulana Abul Kalam Azad.

69. Which one of the following was no in a "no changer"?
   (a) T.B. Sapru (b) Dr. Ansari
   (c) Sardar Patel (d) Rajendra Prasad.

70. Who said "My only hope lies in prayer and answer to prayer"?
   (a) Mahatma Gandhi
   (b) Motilal Nehru
   (c) Subhash Chandra Bose
   (d) Jawahar Lal Nehru.

71. Who accompanied Netaji on his last known flight?
   (a) Col. Habibur Rehman
   (b) S.A. Iyer
   (c) Col Pritam Singh
   (d) Col. Glzara Singh.

72. Who raised the cry "Divide and Quit"?
   (a) Jinnah (b) Poet Iqbal
   (c) Dr. Ansari (d) C.R. Das

73. Who resigned his membership of the Viceroy's Executive Council after the Jallianwala Bagh incident?
   (a) Rabindranath Tagore
   (b) Sir Shankaran Nair
   (c) Lord Hunter
   (d) Pandit Malviya.

74. Which of the following newspapers did not advocated revolutionary terrorism after 1905?
   (a) The Kesari (b) The Kal
   (c) The Yugantar (d) The Sandhya.

75. The 'Ahrar' movement was founded by
    (a) Badruddin Tyabji
    (b) Maulan Abul Kalam Azad
    (c) Maulana Zafar Ali Khan
    (d) M.A. Jinnah.

76. When did the third split occur in the All India Trade Union Congress?
    (a) 1929 (b) 1931
    (c) 1940 (d) 1945.

77. In which year was the Indian National Congress founded at the initiative of Sardar Vallabh Bhai Patel?
    (a) 1929 (b) 1931
    (c) 1940 (d) 1945.

78. What do you understand by the Tinkathiya System?
    (a) Compulsory cultivation of tea
    (b) Compulsory cultivation of jute
    (c) a form of bounded labour
    (d) compulsory cultivation of indigo.

79. Which of the dominions directly influenced the rising tide of nationalism?
    (a) Canada (b) Ireland
    (c) Australia (d) New Zealand.

80. Who among the following first announced the word "Pakistan"?
    (a) Chaudhari Rahmat Ali
    (b) Sir, Muhammad Iqbal
    (c) Sir Agha Khan
    (d) M.A. Jinnah.

81. Who declared, 'The only hope for the India is from the masses, the upper classes are physically and morally dead'?
    (a) Gopal Krishna Gokhale
    (b) Bal Gangadhar Tilak
    (c) Mahatma Gandhi
    (d) Swami Vivekanand.

82. Who was the advocate at the famous INA trials?
(a) Bhulabhai Desai
(b) Asaf Ali
(c) Subhash Chandra Bose
(d) C. Rajagopalachari.

83. The British Cabinet Mission which came to India in March 1946 did not have as its member?
(a) Lord Pethick Lawrence
(b) Sir Stafford Cripps
(c) A.V. Alexander
(d) Campbell Johanson.

84. Who was referred to as the 'Ambasador of Hindu Muslim unity' by Sarojini Naidu in the early year of Gandhian period?
(a) Muhammad Ali Jinnah
(b) Shaukat Ali
(c) Maulana Azad
(d) Abdul Ghaffar Khan.

85. Who has been referred to as the 'Conscience-keeper' of Gandhiji?
(a) C.Raja Gopalachari (b) R. Tagore
(c) V. Patel (d) G.K. Gokhale.

86. In November 1945 three former INA officers were charged with waging war against the King emperor. Point the odd man out:
(a) Col. Sah Nawaz (b) Captain Sehgal
(c) Lt. Dhillon (d) Damodar Chapekar.

87. In the following, who was not among the first speaker at the India National Congress Session of 1885, December 28?
(a) A.O Hume
(b) A Subrahmania Aiyar
(c) K.T. Telang
(d) Surendra Nath Banerjee.

88. The partition of Bengal was revoked by the British Government in the year?

(a) 1919 (b) 1917

(c) 1914 (d) 1911.

89. The Rowlatt Act was passed in the year

(a) 1931 (b) 1919

(c) 1920 (d) 1942.

90. Initially an associate of Gandhi, he left the Congress, broke off with Gandhi and launched a radical social movement called the 'Self Respect Movement". The reference were is to

(a) Chhatrapati Maharaj (b) EVR Naicker

(c) P Tyagaraya Chetti (d) Jyotirao Govindrao.

91. What was the chief programme of the Swaraj Party?

(a) Council entry

(b) Constitutional opposition

(c) Rural Reconstruction programme

(d) None of the above.

92. Swaraj Party took part in the election in

(a) 1923, 1926 (b) 1919, 1923

(c) 1920, 1926 (d) 1919, 1920.

93. In 1923, Swaraj Party gained absolute majority in

(a) Legislative Assembly (b) U.P. Council

(c) Bengal Council (d) C.P. Council.

94. Who was the Chairman of the drafting committee of the constitution?

(a) J.B. Kriplani (b) Rajendra Prasad

(c) J.L..Nehru (d) B.R. Ambedkar.

95. M.A. Jinnah and a section of the Muslim League was willing to gave up seprarate electorte in favour of a joint electorate (with cerain conditions) at the time of the

(a) Cabinet Mission (b) Simon Commission

(c) Wavell plan (d) None of the above.

96. It led to the estrangement of M.A. Jinnah, who called it a 'parting of the ways' with the Congress, went back to the separate electorates and formulated his famous fourteen points. The reference here is to

(a) Failure, of the Round Table Conference
(b) Nehru Report
(c) The failure of non co-operation movement
(d) None of the above.

97. Which year did Bankim Chandra Chattopadhyay write Anandmath?

(a) 1858 (b) 1892
(c) 1882 (d) None of the above.

98. Who is remembered as the pioneer of economic nationalism?

(a) Bipin Chandra Pal
(b) Gokhale
(c) R.C. Dutt
(d) Madan Mohan Malviya.

99. Who wrote the play 'Andher Nagari Chaupata Raja"?

(a) Govardhanram M Tripathi
(b) Munshi Prem Chand
(c) Fakirmohan Senapati
(d) Bhartendu Harish Chandra.

100. Who proposed the preamble before the drafting committee of the constitution?

(a) Jawahar Lal Nehru (b) B.R. Ambedkar
(c) B.N. Rau (d) Mahatma Gandhi.

101. The Moplah rebellion of 1921 broken out in?

(a) Assam (b) Kerala
(c) Punjab (d) Bengal.

102. Who was the Congress president when India became free?

(a) Mahatma Gandhi (b) Jawaharlal Nehru
(c) J.B. Kripalani (d) Sardar Patel

103. In which year did the British Government announce for the first time dominion status as the goal of British policy in India?
   (a) 1922 (b) 1929
   (c) 1932 (d) 1935.

104. The formation of an interim Government set up on September 2, 1946 was first envisaged by
   (a) Cripps Mission (b) Wavell Plan
   (c) Cabinet Mission Plan (d) None of the above.

105. The main leader of the Swarajist party were
   (a) Vittalbhai, J Patel and Dr. Ansari
   (b) M.N. Roy and Muzaffer Ahmed
   (c) Motilal Nehru and C.R. Das
   (d) B.R. Ambedkar and P.C. Joshi.

106. The boundary between India and Pakistan was demarcated by
   (a) Lord Mountbatten (b) Sir Cyril Radcliffe
   (c) Sir Straffor Cripps (d) Lawrence.

107. Who was made the Home Minister when Jawaharlal Nehru formed the interim Government in 1946?
   (a) Mohammad Ali Jinnah
   (b) Baldev Singh
   (c) Liaqat Ali Khan
   (d) Sardar Patel.

108. Some of the native states refused to join the Indian Union till the last minute point the odd one out.
   (a) Travancore (b) Hyderabad
   (c) Junagadh (d) Rajkot.

109. The most important pre-Congress nationalist organisation was the Indian Association of Calcutta which was founded by S.N. Banerjee and Anand Mohan Bose in
   (a) 1875 (b) 1876
   (c) 1879 (d) 1880.

110. In 1890, the first woman graduate of the Calcutta University addressed the Congress session. Who was she ?

(a) Kadambini Ganguly (b) Pandita Rama Bai
(c) Malvika Mukerjee (d) None of the above.

111. In 1905, who among the following raised the demand for Swarajya or self government within the British Empire, from the Congress platform?

(a) B.G. Tilak (b) G.K. Gokhale
(c) Dadabhai Nauroji (d) Pherozeshah Mehta

112. The Muhammedan Anglo Oriental Defence Association (1893) wás started by

(a) Sayed Ahmad Khan (b) T. Beck
(c) A. S. Samuelson (d) None of these.

113. When did the Congress adopt the principle that it would not take up any proposal which was considered harmful to the muslims by a majority of the muslim delegates in the Congress?

(a) 1885 (b) 1887
(c) 1889 (d) 1891.

114. Who was the most prominent of the traditional muslim scholars of the Deoband school who held the view that there was no conflict between muslims and Nationalism?

(a) Badruddin Tyabji
(b) Maulana Abul Kalam Azad
(c) Maulana Mohammad Ali
(d) Maulana Zafar Ali Khan.

115. Who played an important role in bringing together the Muslim League and the Congress in 1916?

(a) B.G. Tilak (b) Maulana Azad
(c) Lala Lajpat Rai (d) Madan Mohan Malviya.

116. The Rowlatt Act was passed during the Viceroyalty of

(a) Hardinge II (b) Chelmsford
(c) Reading (d) Minto II.

117. When Congress ministries resigned in 1939, what day was celebrated by Jinnah as the "Day of Deliverance"?
    (a) 2nd September, 1939
    (b) 2nd October, 1939
    (c) 2nd November, 1939
    (d) 2nd December, 1939.

118. Subhash Chandra Bose resigned from the presidentship of the Congress in
    (a) 1938 (b) 1939
    (c) 1940 (d) None of the above.

119. The Head Quarters of the Ghadar Party was at
    (a) Moscow (b) Berlin
    (c) San Francisco (d) Karachi.

120. The Viceroy to be assassinated in India was
    (a) Lord Hardinge
    (b) Lord North Brooke
    (c) Lord Ellenborough
    (d) Lord Mayo.

121. The Federation of India Chambers of Commerce and Industry (FICCI) was founded in 1927 by
    (a) Birla and Tata (b) Birla and Thakurdas
    (c) Tata and Thakurdas (d) None of the above.

122. The Twin principles of Gandhi's Ram Rajya were
    (a) Truth and Noni-violence
    (b) Right means and Right end
    (c) Khadi and Ahinsa
    (d) None of the above.

123. Who of the following attended all the three Round Table Conference?
    (a) B.R. Ambedkar
    (b) M.M. Malviya
    (c) Vallabha Bhai Patel
    (d) None of the above.

124. On 17th October, 1940, the individual satyagraha was inaugurated by
    (a) Sardar Vallabh Bhai Patel
    (b) Jawaharlal Nehru
    (c) M.K. Gandhi
    (d) Acharya Vinobha Bhave.

125. The Rating of RIN (Royal Indian Navy) went on a strike on 18 Feb. 1946. The strike raised the ------------- flag.
    (a) The National Congress
    (b) The League's
    (c) The Red
    (d) All of the above.

126. The most enduring as well as the most militant of the agitations originating in the period 1945-47 was the
    (a) Tebhaga movement
    (b) Telengana movement
    (c) The Travancore agitation
    (d) Peasants agitation.

127. Strafford Cripps was a member of the
    (a) Conservative party (b) Labour party
    (c) Liberal party (d) Official hierarchy.

128. 'Do or Die' was one of the most powerful slogans of India's freedom struggle? who gave it?
    (a) Gandhi
    (b) J.L. Nehru
    (c) B.G. Tilak
    (d) Subhash Chandra Bose.

129. Hunter Commission was appointed by the British to probe into the
    (a) Bardoli Satyagraha
    (b) Khilafat agitation
    (c) Jallianwala Bagh tragedy
    (d) Chauri Chaura incident.

130. Which of the following proved to be the most short-lived of all the British constitutional experiments in India?
(a) Government of India Act, 1919
(b) The Indian Councils Act, 1909
(c) Pitt's India Act, 1984
(d) Government of India Act, 1935.

131 Some of the regional bases of millitant nationalism down to 1907-19 are given below. Find out the odd one out
(a) Bengal (b) Punjab
(c) Gujarat (d) Maharastra.

132. In March 1908, who was elected as the 'permanent' president of the Muslim league?
(a) Nawab Salimullah (b) Syed Ahmad Khan
(c) Aga Khan (d) Syed Amir Ali.

133. Gokhale's Servants of India Society launched in June 1905 did not have one of the following as its aim
(a) Moral purity
(b) Self sacrifice
(c) Swadeshi and boycott
(d) Full time national work on a salary of Rs. 65/- per month.

134. Which of the following was the president of the Congress at the time of Moderate-Extremist split?
(a) Pherozeshah Mehta
(b) Rashbehari Ghosh
(c) Madan Mohan Malaviya
(d) Dinshaw Wacha.

135. Who of the following Acts formally introduced the principle of elections for the first time?
(a) The Indian Counil Act, 1909
(b) Government of India Act, 1919
(c) The 1935, Act
(d) India Independance Act, 1949.

136. When did Muslim league adopt self-government as one of its objectives?
(a) 1919 (b) 1911
(c) 1912 (d) 1920.

137. On September 20, 1932 Mahatma Gandhi began a fast unto death in Yervada jail against
(a) British repression of the Satyagrahis
(b) Violation of the Gandhi Irwin Pact
(c) Communal Award of Ramsay Mac Donald
(d) Communal riots in Calcutta.

138. On the Direct Action Day unprecedented bloodshed took place as a result of Hindu-Muslim riots in
(a) Bombay (b) Dhaka
(c) Calcutta (d) Delhi.

139. On February 20, 1947, Prime Minister Attslee announced the British Government decision to withdraw from India latest by
(a) August 1947 (b) January 1948
(c) June 1948 (d) August 1948.

140. During the first world war, assistance was organised through few centres abroad which of the following was not such a centre?
(a) Kabul (b) New York
(c) London (d) Berlin.

141. In which of the following movement did Mahatma Gandhi make the first use of hunger strike as a weapon?
(a) Non-co-operation movement, 1920-22
(b) Rowlatt Satyagraha, 1919
(c) Ahmedabad Strike, 1918
(d) Bardoli Satyagraha.

142. The organisational change to trun the Congress party into a real mass political party was made for the first time in
(a) 1916 (b) 1918
(c) 1920 (d) 1930.

143. The first definitely communist journal to be published in India was
   (a) Vanguard of India Indepedence
   (b) Socialist
   (c) Atmashakti
   (d) Dhumketu.

144. In 1939, Gandhi for the first time tried out his specific techniques of controlled mass struggle in a native state. He allowed a close adjutant of his to lead a satyagraha who was he?
   (a) Mysore, K.T. Bhashyam
   (b) Jaipur, Jamnalal Bajaj
   (c) Rajkot, Vallabh Bhai Patel
   (d) Dhenkanal, Nebakrishna.

145. The governor-general of India who initiated the introduction of English in India was
   (a) Lord Curzon (b) Lord Macaulay
   (c) Lord Beatick (d) Lord Bastings.

146. Quit India Movement was adopted by the INC at
   (a) Bombay (b) Ahmedabad
   (c) Pune (d) Calcutta.

147. King George V visited India during the viceroyalty of
   (a) Lord Ripon (b) Lord Curzon
   (c) Lord Harding (d) Lord Hastings.

148. Which of the following Acts gave representation to Indians for the first time in the legislature?
   (a) Indian Council Act, 1909
   (b) Indian Council Act, 1919
   (c) Government of India Act, 1935
   (d) None of the above.

149. The First Satyagraha campaign of Gandhiji was started in
   (a) Champaran (b) Bardoli
   (c) Dandi (d) Baroda.

150. The first Muslim president of the INC was
(a) Ajmal Khan (b) M.A. Jinnah
(c) Abul Kalam Azad (d) Rahimulla Sayani.

151. Who among the following communist of India played a notable role in the world communist movement?
(a) A.K. Gopalan (b) S.A Dange
(c) M.N Roy (d) EMS Namboodiripad.

152. Gandhiji founded Satyagraha Sabha in 1919 to protest against the
(a) Salt law
(b) Rowlatt Act
(c) Government of India Act, 1919
(d) Jallianwala Bagh massacre.

153. A systematic critique of Moderate politics was emerging in the 1890 in
(a) Maharashtra, Gujarat, Andhra Pradesh
(b) Maharashtra, Bengal, Punjab
(c) Bengal, Gujarat, Maharashtra
(d) Maharashtra, Bengal, Tamil Nadu.

154. Who set up the famous Bengal Chemical Swadeshi Stores during the swadesh movement?
(a) PC Roy
(b) Rabindra Nath Tagore
(c) Ashwini Kumar Dutt
(d) Anandamohan Bose.

155. Who committed the most daring murder in 1907 of Sir Curzon Wyllie at a public meeting in London?
(a) B.N. Datta (b) M.L. Dhingra
(c) Sardar Ajit Singh (d) S.C. Chatterjee.

156. Which was the only province where muslims had taken to commerce and education quite early?
(a) Calcutta (b) Punjab
(c) Madras (d) Bombay.

157. Under whose presidentship did the INC meet in August 1918 at Bombay to consider the proposals of Montague Chelmsford?

(a) Hasan Imam (b) Annie Besant
(c) Badruddin Tayabji (d) B.G. Tilak.

158. An all parties conference appointed a sub-committee (1928) whose member included Ali Imam, T B Sapru and S C Bose. Who headed this sub-committee?

(a) Motilal Nehru
(b) Maulana Azad
(c) Vallabh Bhai Patel
(d) Madan Mohan Malviya.

159. Who was the Viceroy of India when the Quit India Movement started in 1942?

(a) Linlithgow (b) Willingdon
(c) Wavell (d) None of the above.

160. Point the odd out

(a) Max Mullar (b) Fergusson
(c) Todd (d) Cunningham.

161. Mahadev Govind Ranade was a member of the

(a) Arya Samaj (b) Prarthana Samaj
(c) India League (d) Theosophical society.

162. Annie Besant

(a) Founded the Theosophical society
(b) Became president of the INC
(c) Was a disciple of Swami Vivekananada
(d) Was a member of Prathana Samaj.

163. One Act of the Government that gave the nationalist movement the final puch to acquire an organisation form was

(a) The Vernacular Press Act
(b) The Arms Act
(c) The Ilbert Bill
(d) Lowering the age for Indian Civil Service Examination.

164. The civil disobedience movement caught the imagination of the people in the states. In many places, significant popular movement came into being point out where it did not?

(a) Rajkot (b) Hyderabad
(c) Travancore (d) Rampur.

165. How many times J.L. Nehru became the president of INC

(a) 2 (b) 3
(c) 4 (d) 5.

166. In the Allahabad district in 1929, at a time of the world wide economic depression; a 'No-tax' campaign on behalf a peasant was led by

(a) J.L. Nehru (b) Sahjanand Saraswati
(c) M.N. Roy (d) P. C. Joshi.

167. Protesting againsts Simon Commission in a demonstration, Lala Lajpat Rai sustained fatal injuries. Where did the incident occur?

(a) Amritsar (b) Meerut
(c) Lahore (d) Jallandhar.

168. Individual Civil Disobedience movement was launched in

(a) 1942 (b) 1940
(c) 1945 (d) 1947.

169. Who gave Vallabh Bhai Patel the title of 'Sardar'

(a) C. Rajagopalachari (b) M.K. Gandhi
(c) J.L.Nehru (d) M.A. Jinnah.

170. Who was the heroine of the 1942 Quit India movement?

(a) Dr. Annie Besant (b) Suchitra Kriplani
(c) Aruna Asaf Ali (d) Sarojini Naidu.

171. Who among the early nationalists worked in England to mobilise public opinion in favour the Indian National movement?

(a) Gopal Krishna Gokhale
(b) Lala Lajpat Rai
(c) Dahabhai Naoroji
(d) D.E. Wacha.

172. The three states which had not acceeded to either Dominion by August 15, 1947, were all ruled by princes whose own religion was different from that of the majority of their subjects point the odd one out?

(a) Bhopal (b) Junagarh
(c) Hyderabad (d) Kashmir.

173. He was the most passionate exponent of the extremists point of view and the programme spelled out by him anticipated the one adopted by Gandhi some year's later. The reference here is to

(a) Lal Lajpat Rai
(b) Aurobindo Ghosh
(c) B.G. Tilak
(d) None of the above.

174. To counteract unfavourable articles on India in the British press and to supply authentic information, a journal was started in 1890 name it.

(a) Dawn (b) News chronicle
(c) India (d) Wheel of History.

175. In which year five districts and the tribal area were taken away from Punjab to create the North west Frontier province?

(a) 1904 (b) 1935
(c) 1901 (d) 1911.

176. Who was the Governor General of India who proposed the charge of capital from Calcuta to Delhi?

(a) Lansdowne (b) Lord Curzon
(c) Lord Hardings II (d) Dufferin.

177. He wanted to become a 'Muslim Gokhale', while Gokhale returning the Compliment said, he has true stuff in him and that freedom from all sectarian prejudice will make him the best ambassador of a Hindu Muslim unity. The reference here is to

(a) Syed Ahmad Khan (b) Aga Khan
(c) M.A. Jinnah (d) Maulana Azad.

178. The last two years of British rule were marked by several movement. Mark the odd one out.
    (a) Punnapra Vayalar in Travancore
    (b) Tebhaga in Bengal
    (c) Telengana movement in Hyderabad
    (d) Eka movement in Avadh.

179. The Communist Party was legalise in the year
    (a) 1944 (b) 1942
    (c) 1945 (d) 1940.

180. Name the first major issue that the Indian Association the precursor of the Congress, took up for agitation.
    (a) Protection of the tenants from oppression by the Zamindars
    (b) Agitation againsts the Arms Act
    (c) Agitation againsts the vernacular press Act
    (d) Reform of the civil service regulations.

181. Identify one of the following which was not the aims and objectives of the Indian National Congress founded in 1865?
    (a) To promote friendly relations between nationalist political workers from different part of the country
    (b) To organised political education of the masses in order to prepare them for self government
    (c) To develop and consolidate the feeling of nation unity irrespective of caste, religion or province
    (d) To formulate popular demands and present them before the government.

182. What was the principal reason for the extremists insisting on the two tactics of the Swadeshi and Boycott as the right means to bring pressure on the British Government?
    (a) They wanted to appear like westerners since boycott was used as weapon in the Irish freedom struggle, and the idea of swadeshi was the bulwark of the American War of Independence
    (b) The extremists wanted to edge out the moderates
    (c) The extremits knew that they would be hitting manchester and Brimingham

(d) The extremists owed more to the traditions and legacy of India than to message that came through the English language.

183. The split in the Congress in 1907 was due to the
(a) Difference of ideology
(b) Difference in objectives
(c) Difference in methods employed to attain the goals
(d) Terrorist activities that quickly spread over Bengal.

184. What offence were Tilak and other charged with the jailed in 1897?
(a) For carrying arms in violation of provisions of the Arms Act
(b) For their refusal to appear before the court president over by a British judge
(c) For breaking the salt tax law
(d) For spreading disaffection againsts the Government through their speeches and writings.

185. The salt satyagraha of Gandhiji was momentous because of various happening except one, which one is that
(a) Woman started picketing shops sellings foreign goods, and also foreign institutions
(b) In Peshawar when the Government ordered Royal Garhwal Rifles to fire on peasants, they refuses to do so
(c) South India was not involved
(d) The Akalis sent detachments to support a revolt of the tribes in the North West.

186. Which pair of traders opposed any kinds of compromise with the extremists, but death cut them short?
(a) Gopal Krishna Gokhale and Dada Bhai Naoroji
(b) Gopal Krishna Gokhale and Pheroze Shah Mehta
(c) M.G. Ranade and Gopal Krishan Gokhale
(d) Gopal Krishan Gokhale and Surendarnath Banerjee.

187. What is the most significant thing about the Ghadar party in view of the later days developments?
   (a) It was organised by the U.S.A.
   (b) Ordinary people, both Hindu and Muslim, contributed to its funds
   (c) It tried to incite the Indian Regiment in the British army to mutiny
   (d) A regiment revolted in Singapore as a result of its activities.

188. The Rowlatt Act of 1919, were enacted by the government with a view to
   (a) Deal with anti-national activities of the terrorists
   (b) Dispense with the procedure of a trail of the accused person and to secure their arbitray confinement
   (c) Deal with political criminals
   (d) Check the rising tide of nationalism.

189. Which of the traits of peasants revolt is the most significant in the Champaran struggle from 1917 to 1918?
   (a) Led and organised by the intelligentsia-Gandhiji, Dr. Rajendra Prasad, Brij Kishore Prasad, Mazhar-ul-Haq
   (b) In 1916 the Lucknow session of the Congress took up the cause of peasant for the first time in its history
   (c) Gandhiji recorded the statements of 8000 peasant againsts to indigo factories
   (d) The indigo cultivators were tortured and they were tied to trees so that red ants could bite them.

190. Which point relating to the struggle of Kheda peasantry is the most significant?
   (a) The authorities refused to accept the demands of the peasants
   (b) Leadership of Ghandhiji, Vallabh Bhai Patel and Indulal yognik
   (c) The authorities confiscated cattle and all moveable property, but they had ultimately to accept the demands of the peasants
   (d) A peasant leader, Chaudhary Perru Singh, attended the Congress in the 1918 and demanded swaraj.

191. The Ghadar movement had distinct revolutionary peasant traits. Which out of them is the most significant?

(a) A sikh peasant, Thakur Singh, living in canton was one of its leaders

(b) Some members, after returning to India, decided that property should be held in common—one hour's work in the morning and one hour's in the evening would suffice for the cultivation of the common village land

(c) They looted 50 money lenders in 1919, but no government servant was attacked and no official property was looted

(d) Four thousand were arrested and some 500 were sentenced.

192. The first public act of Gandhiji in India was

(a) The Bordoli Satyagraha

(b) The call for passive resistance against Rowlatt Acts

(c) Championing the cause of the indigo farmers in the Champaran

(d) Making the textile mill owners of Ahmedabad increased the wages of workers by 35 percent.

193. What were the reason for the Congress leaders supporting the Khilafat agitation?

(a) Because in dismembering the Ottoman empire, Britain had violated its earlier pledge

(b) Because it was part of Lucknow pact of 1916

(c) Because the Muslim League asked for twin support

(d) Because in it they found a golden opportunity for cementing Hindu Muslim unity and bringing the muslim masses into the nation movement.

194. The non-violent, non co-operation movement in 1920 was launched with a view of

(a) To restore communal harmony

(b) To protest against the Indian Government's failure to restore the authority of Khalifa?

(c) To protest against the Indian government for not taking action against the persons involved in the Jallianwala Bagh Massacre

(d) Both (b) and (c).

195. Which happening in the 20's of the 20th century was responsible for widening the gulf between Muslims and Hindus?

(a) The Khilafat movement fell through when Turkey abolished the Caliphate and, with it a good opportunity was lost to build bridges of understanding between the two communities

(b) Communal colouring was given for certain agrarian troubles like Moplah Revolution Kerala

(c) The Militant Shudhhi and Sanghathan movements of Hindu Mahasabha

(d) Jinnah broke off from the All parties conference and attended the All India Muslim conference in 1929.

196. What was the most important significance of Komagatamaru incident (handful of Panjabis wanted to land at Vancouver in Canada but they were not permitted)?

(a) After their return from their unsuccessful bid to enter Canada they clashed with the police and a few were killed

(b) Emerged by this news, some Panjabis returned to India to launch an armed campaign against British rule

(c) Unable to procure German arms they contacted the Bengali Reuolutionaries

(d) These incidents helped the Ghadar party.

197. In which way the terrorist movement contributed to the emancipation of the country?

(a) It goaded the Congress whenever it fumbled for direction

(b) It revealed to the British the extent to which India could go in its struggle

(c) It inspired and enthused students and the young recruits of the Congress

(d) It gave a punched to the nationalist movement.

198. Which one of the following hurt the sentiments of muslims the most?
   (a) Shivaji and Ganapati festivals organised by Tilak
   (b) Mystical approach of Aurobindo in India as the mother and nationalism as the religion
   (c) The terrorists taking oaths before Goddess Kali
   (d) Purificatory baths in the Ganga before starting the anti-partition campaign.

199. Which one was the most important reason for the separate muslim nationalist movement?
   (a) Upper class amongst the Muslim consisted mostly of Zamindars and aristocrats
   (b) Backwardness of Muslims in education and trade and Industry
   (c) The number of educated muslims was very small
   (d) Muslims reformers turning to the history of west Asia for their traditions and moments of pride.

200. Bhagat Singh, Rajguru and Sukhdev were hanged in March 1931 on the charge of
   (a) An attempt to blow up the Central Legislative assembly
   (b) An attempt on the life of the prince of Wales
   (c) An attempt on the life of Lord Hardinge
   (d) Murder of Saunders at Lahore.

201. How did the government reach to the Salt Satyagraha and the Dandi march?
   (a) The Congress was banned
   (b) The government resorted to repressive measures.
   (c) They did not take them seriously
   (d) They were no there guard and took measures to prevent the mischief from spreading.

202. What were the main objectives and programmes of the Red shirts under the leadership of Khan Abdul Ghaffar Khan?
   (a) To offer resistance to the military operations of the government in the north-western frontier portion.

(b) To carry on revolutionary and terrorist activities.
(c) To propagate the Congress programme.
(d) To build up a para-military organisation.

203. Show which one of the following was not the reason why the third Round Table Conference has been described as a piece of window dressing?
(a) Its composition was changed
(b) Most of the preliminary work of the conference had been done by the committees of second conference
(c) As there was no fundamental issue before the conference, it was had to deal mostly with details
(d) From India only the princes attended the conference.

204. Which one of the following was not a feature of the government of India Act 1935?
(a) All India Federation was composed of British provinces and princely states
(b) There was autonomy at the provincial level
(c) A bicameral legislature with disproportionate weightage for the state was set up
(d) System of dyarchy both at the centre as well as in the provinces was established.

205. The Congress tendered their resignation in 1939 due to
(a) British decision to make India a party to war without consulting the Congress
(b) Internal bickerings of various ministers
(c) Undue interference by the central government in their affairs
(d) All of the above.

206. Identify one of the following which was not one of the important political happenings during 1935-39?
(a) Rapid growth of socialist ideas within and outside the Congress
(b) The spread of national movement to the princely states
(c) The increasing interest of Congress in world affairs
(d) Co-operation between the Congress and the Muslim league on all important issues.

207. The main factor responsible for the growth of socialist ideas in India was
   (a) Disillusionment with the policies of the British government
   (b) Socialist propaganda by the Soviet government
   (c) The progress achieved by the Soviet Union even in the face of world wide economic depression
   (d) The diffusion of marxist ideologies among the working classes by the communists.

208. One of the followings false with regard to the 'August offer'.
   (a) The setting up of a provisional National Government after the second world war
   (b) A war advising council consisting of the representative of British India and Indian state
   (c) To enlarge the Viceroy's Executive Council by nominating additional Indian member
   (d) After the war, a new body was to be constituted to draft a new constitution for India.

209. In 1942 Cripps Mission conducted negotiations with the Congress to find a solution for the India problem. The sticking points which resulted in rejection of these proposals by the Congress was
   (a) Refusal to set up a constitution making body immediately
   (b) Refusal to accept the Congress demand for the immediate transfer of effective power to Indians
   (c) Broken promises of the past
   (d) The proposal of Sir Cripps regarding partitioning of India.

210. The immediate cause for launching the 'Quit India' Resolution in 1942 was
   (a) The failure of the Cripps Mission
   (b) Arrest of national leaders upon departure of Sir Stafford Cripps
   (c) The failure of the British Government to take effective steps to protect India from the imminent Japanese invasion

(d) Repressive measures adopted by the Government.

211. The Provisionsal Government of Free India was announced by
(a) Veer Savarkar in U.S.A. in 1944
(b) Subhash Chandra Bose in Singapore in 1943
(c) Rash Behari Bose in Singapore in 1942
(d) None of the above.

212. The 'Quit India' movement was different from the earlier movement because
(a) It was a violent movement
(b) It was led by young militant leaders
(c) It was widespread and draw support from almost all the section of society
(d) It started spontaneously in all parts of the country.

213. In 1945 Lord Wavell suggested a plan for resolving the constitutional tangle of India but it fell through because
(a) The Congress and the muslim leagure could not come to an agreement
(b) The Congress was not in favour of the continuance of the Governor-General's veto
(c) The league wanted to extract a promise for an independent state of Pakistan
(d) The proposal was not backed by the Government of Britain.

214. Name one of the following which was fundamental point of difference between the Congress and Muslim league with regard to the Cabinet mission?.
(a) Creation of Pakistan
(b) Framing of the Union constitution by a constituent assembly to be elected on a communal basis
(c) The plan for an interim government which would convene a constituent assembly to frame the constitution
(d) The option to be given to the individual provinces to form regional unions to which they could surrender, by mutual agreement, some of their powers.

215. Cite one of the following which did not lead to the Muslim league with drawing its acceptance of the cabinet mission's plan deciding on August 16, 1946 as Direct Action Day?

(a) Muslim League accepted the Cabinet Mission's proposal, but the Congress rejected the Viceroy's proposal for an Interim Government, although it agree to participate in the constituent assembly

(b) The Muslim League demanded that the Viceroy should proceed with his scheme for an interm government, even though the Congress would not take part in it but the Viceroy did not agree to do

(c) In the meeting of the All India Muslim League council held on July 27, 1946, a resolution was passed formally with drawing the Muslim League acceptance of the Cabinet Mission proposal

(d) Nehru accepted the viceroy's invitation, but when he invited Jinnah to join, the latter not only refused to join but also gave a call for the 'Direct Action Day'.

216. Match the following:

A.	1833	1.	Full condification of the Indian system of law and procedure
B.	Ilbert Bill	2.	Imperial darbar at Delhi
C.	1877	3.	Partition of Bengal
D.	1905	4.	Gave Indian magistrate the right to try Europeans in criminal cases

	A	B	C	D
(a)	2	4	1	3
(b)	1	4	2	3
(c)	1	4	3	2
(d)	4	2	1	3.

217. Match the following:

A.	The Justice Party	1.	Jotirao Phule
B.	Self Respect Movement	2.	Chhatrapati Shahu Maharaj

C.	Satya Shodhak movement	3.	EV Ramasami Naicker
D.	Satya Shodhak Samaj	4.	TN Nair, RT Chetti, CN Mudaliar

(a) A-4, B-3, C-1, D-2 (b) A-3, B-4, C-1, D-2
(c) A-4, B-3, C-4, D-1 (d) A-4, B-3, C-2, D-1.

218. Many of Gandhiji associates joined him in political carrier during the course of several activities under taken by him. Match

A.	Champaran Indigo Cultivators	1.	Anasuya Behn
B.	Ahmedabad textile worker	2.	Vallabha Bhai Patel and Indulal Yagnik
C.	Kheda Peasants	3.	Rajendra Prasad, Brij Kishore Prasad, and J B Kriplani
D.	South Africa	4.	Gokhale

(a) A-3, B-4, C-1, D-4 (b) A-3, B-1, C-2, D-4
(c) A-1, B-3, C-2, D-4 (d) A-4, B-1, C-2, D-3.

219. Match the authors with their books

A.	Bankim Chandra Chattopadhyay	1.	Bharat Durdashan
B.	Goverdhanram M. Tripathi	2.	Nibandh mela
C.	Bhartendu Harish Chandra	3.	Bangadarshan
D.	Vishnu Krishna Chiplunkar	4.	Saraswati Chandra

(a) A-3, B-4, C-1, D-2 (b) A-1, B-4, C-2, D-3
(c) A-4, B-3, C-2, D-2 (d) A-3, B-4, C-2, D-1.

220. Match the following and select the correct code

A.	Chhaman Atha Guntha	1.	Sarat Chandra Chattopadhyay
B.	Karambhumi	2.	Tarashankar Bandopadhyay

C Bipradas 3. Fakirmohan Senapati
D. Ganadevate 4. Prem Chand
(a) A-4, B-3, C-1, D-2 (b) A-3, B-1, C-3, D-2
(c) A-3, B-4, C-1, D-3 (d) A-2, B-4, C-1, D-3.

221. Match the following leaders with the movement they were connected with

A. Chakra Bisai 1. Pabna Uprising
B. Sido and Kanhu 2. Khonds of Ghumsar
C. Radhakrishna Dandasena 3. Savara rebellions
D. Kesab Chandra Roy 4. Santhal rebellions
(a) A-4, B-2, C-1, D-3 (b) A-2, B-3, C-4, D-1
(c) A-2, B-4, C-3, D-1 (d) A-2, B-3, C-1, D-4.

222. Match the strikes with the year in which they took place

A. Nagpur Empres Mills 1. 1853
B. River Transporters 2. 1862
C. Railways 3. 1877
(a) A-2, B-3, C-1 (b) A-2, B-1, C-3
(c) A-3, B-2, C-1 (d) A-1, B-2, C-3.

223. Match the following leaders with the movement they led

A. Tomma Dora 1. Savara Rebellion
B. Shambunath Pal 2. Munda Revolt
C. Birsa Munda 3. Koya rebellion
D. Radha Krishna Sena 4. Pabna uprising
(a) A-3, B-4, C-2, D-1 (b) A-4, B-1, C-2, D-3
(c) A-4, B-2, C-3, D-1 (d) A-3, B-1, C-2, D-4.

224. Match the revolt with his its respective area

A. Kuki Revolt 1. Punjab
B. Kuka Revolt 2. Bengal
C. Pabna Peasant Revolt 3. Bihar
D. Birsa Munda's Revolt 4. Tripura
(a) A-4, B-1, C-2, D-3 (b) A-4, B-2, C-1, D-3
(c) A-2, B-3, C-1, D-4 (d) D-4, B-1, C-3, A-4.

225. Match the following association with the year in which they were organised

A.	Madras Native Association	1.	1843
B.	British Indian Association	2.	1948
C.	Bombay Association	3.	1851
D.	Bengal British Indian Association	4.	1852
		5.	1855

(a) A-5, B-4, C-1, D-3 (b) A-4, B-3, C-4, D-1
(c) A-3, B-2, C-4, D-1 (d) A-2, B-1, C-5, D-4.

226. Match the following viceroys with the event that occurred during their respective tenures

A.	Wavell	1.	First demand for Pakistan
B.	Reading	2.	The Moplah Revolt
C.	Willingdon	3.	Simla Conference
D.	Linlithgow	4.	Communal Award

(a) A-3, B-2, C-4, D-1 (b) A-4, B-1, C-3, D-2
(c) A-3, B-4, C-2, D-1 (d) A-1, B-2, C-4, D-3.

227. Match the following Governors General with their respective achievements

A.	William Bentick	1.	Establishment of Public Works Deptt.
B.	Charles Matcalf	2.	Annexation of Sind
C.	Ellenborough	3.	Abolition of persion as the court language
D.	Dalhousie	4.	Signing of treaty with Ranjit Singh

(a) A-2, B-4, C-3, D-1 (b) A-1, B-2, C-3, D-4
(c) A-3, B-4, C-2, D-1 (d) A-2, B-3, C-4, D-1.

228. Between 1945 and 1947, several peasant agitations took place in different parts of the country. The leadership was provided by different organisations. Match.

A.	The Worlis Tribal Peasant Agitation	1.	The Bengal Provincial Kisan Sabha

B.	Bakasht peasant Agitation	2.	The Communists
C.	Travancore Agitation	3.	Maharastra Kisan Sabha
D.	Tebhaga movement	4.	The Bihar Kisan Sabbha

(a) A-3, B-4, C-2, D-1 (b) A-3, B-2, C-1, D-4

(c) A-2, B-4, C-3, D-1 (d) A-2, B-4, C-1, D-3.

229. Match the following:

A.	G.V. Joshi	1.	Calcutta
B.	Anand Charlu	2.	Poona
C.	K.T. Telang	3.	Madras
D.	Dwarkanath Ganguli	4.	Bombay

	A	B	C	D
(a)	2	3	4	1
(b)	3	2	4	1
(c)	4	3	2	1
(d)	2	1	3	4.

230 The end of the Shiwadesh movement saw most of its established leadership disappear from the scene. Match the following in this context

A.	B.G. Tilak	1.	Went abroad
B.	Aurobindo Ghosh	2.	Temproary retirement from politics
C.	B.C Pal	3.	Revolutionary conspiracy case
D.	Lajpat Rai	4.	Mandalay Jail

	A	B	C	D
(a)	2	4	3	1
(b)	4	3	2	1
(c)	1	3	4	2
(d)	2	3	1	4.

231. Match the following:

A.	Mahatma Gandhi	1.	Dandi March
B.	Jawaharlal Nehru	2.	Red Shirts movement

C. Abdul Gaffar Khan — 3. Bardoli Andolan
D. Sardar Patel — 4. Poorna Swaraj resolution at Lahore session of Congress

	A	B	C	D
(a)	4	1	3	2
(b)	1	4	2	3
(c)	4	3	1	2
(d)	2	1	4	3.

232. Match the following:

A. Sachin Sanyal — 1. Why am I atheist
B. Sharat Chandra Chatterjee — 2. Pather Dabi
C. Bhagat Singh — 3. Bandi Jivan
D. Jyotiba Phule — 4. Ghulam Giri

	A	B	C	D
(a)	2	3	1	4
(b)	3	2	1	4
(c)	3	2	4	1
(d)	2	3	4	1.

233. Match the following revolutionaries with the short of end they met

A. Jatin Das — 1. Life Sentence
B. Chandra Shekhar Azad — 2. Died on a Hunger strike
C. Bhagat Singh — 3. Killed in an encounter
D. Kalpana Dutt — 4. Hanged

	A	B	C	D
(a)	2	3	1	4
(b)	3	2	4	1
(c)	2	3	4	1
(d)	3	4	1	2.

234. Match the newspaper/weekly with its founder

A. New India Common Wealth — 1. Maulana Mohammad Ali

B.	Comrade	2.	K.K. Mitra
C.	Sanjivani	3.	M.N. Roy
D.	Vanguard of Indian Independence	4.	Annie Besant

(a) A-4, B-2, C-3, D-1 (b) A-2, B-3, C-4, D-1
(c) A-4, B-1, C-2, D-3 (d) A-1, B-2, C-4, D-3.

235. Match the following Viceroy with the events that occurred during their respective tenures:

A.	Hardinge II	1.	Coronation Durbar at Delhi
B.	Chelmsford	2.	Visit of the Prince of Wales
C.	Reading	3.	The Rowlatt Act
D.	Willingdon	4.	Second Round Table Conference

(a) A-1, B-3, C-2, D-4 (b) A-2, B-3, C-1, D-4
(c) A-1, B-3, C-4, D-2 (d) A-3, B-1, C-2, D-4.

236. Match the following:

A.	Dinabandhu Mitra	1.	Widow Remarriages Association
B.	Keshab Chandra Sen	2.	Neel Darpan
C.	Aurobindo Ghose	3.	Native (Civil) Marriages Act
D.	Justice Ranade	4.	Bomb Attack at Mazaffarpur

(a) A-2, B-3, C-4, D-1 (b) A-2, B-4, C-3, D-1
(c) A-1, B-3, C-4, D-2 (d) A-2, B-3, C-1, D-4.

237. Match the following

A.	The Rowlatt Act	1.	Indian magistrates could also judge cases incolving British subjects
B.	Montford Reforms	2.	Gave judges the power to try political cases without Juries

C.	Ilbert Bill	3.	Made a clear division between the functions of the central and the provincial governments
D.	The India Council Act of 1892	4.	The principle of election, though indirect was granted in practice

(a) A-2, B-3, C-1, D-4 (b) A-1, B-4, C-3, D-2
(c) A-1, B-3, C-2, D-4 (d) A-2, B-4, C-1, D-3.

238. Match the following:

A.	1881	1.	Abolition of Import duty on cotton goods
B.	1883.	2.	The Factories Act
C.	1878	3.	The Statutory Civil Service
D.	1879	4.	The Famine code

(a) A-1, B-2, C-3, D-4 (b) A-2, B-4, C-1, D-3
(c) A-4, B-2, C-3, D-1 (d) A-2, B-1, C-4, D-3.

239. Match the following:

A.	Such an opportunity for uniting Hindus and Mohammedans would not arise in a hundred years.	1.	J.L.Nehru
B.	A Curious knack for doing the right thing at the right psychological moment	2.	S.C. Bose
C.	Must we train the three hundred and odd millions of Indians in the theory and practice of non-violent action before we could go forward	3.	Gandhi

D. Uniform consistent and continuous obstruction of legislation — 4. C.R. Das

(a) A-1, B-3, C-2, D-4 (b) A-3, B-1, C-2, D-4
(c) A-3, B-2, C-4, D-1 (d) A-1, B-2, C-3, D-4.

240. Match the following methods of protest against the British with its propounder

A. Method of direct action — 1. Gokhale
B. Non-constitutional means — 2. Bhagat Singh
C. Method of petitions and resolutions — 3. Tilak
D. Acts of courage to rouse masses; revolt by masses; for the masses — 4. Gandhi

(a) A-3, B-4, C-1, D-2 (b) A-2, B-4, C-1, D-3
(c) A-4, B-2, C-3, D-1 (d) A-3, B- 4, C-2, D-1.

241. Match the following:

A. C.R. Das — 1. Bardoli Satyagraha
B. Vallabh Bhai Patel — 2. Swarajist
C. Abdul Ghaffar Khan — 3. Khilafatist
D. Maulana A.K. Azad — 4. Khudai Khidmatgar

(a) A-2, B-1, C-4, D-3 (b) A-2, B-4, C-1, D-3
(c) A-4, B-1, C-3, D-2 (d) A-2, B-1, C-3, D-4

242. Match the following:

A. Announcement of Dominion status as the goal of British policy in India — 1. 1930
B. Civil Disobedience movement — 2. 1929
C. Poona Pact — 3. 1931
D. Gandhi-Irwin pact — 4. 1932

(a) A-1, B-2, C-4, D-3 (b) A-2, B-1, C-4, D-3.
(c) A-2, B-1, C-3, D-4 (d) A-3, B-1, C-4, D-2

243. Match the following in a chronological manner:

A.	All India States People Conference was formed	1.	1924
B.	The Turks abolished the caliphate	2.	1929
C.	Execution of Bhagat Singh and his collegues	3.	1927
D.	J.L. Nehru became the president of the Congress	4.	1930

(a) A-2, B-1, C-4, D-3 (b) A-3, B-1, C-4, D-2
(c) A-3, B-4, C-2, D-1 (d) A-4, B-1, C-2, D-4

244. Match the following:

A.	Surya Sen	1.	Communist Party of India
B.	N M Joshi	2.	Indian Republican Army
C.	P C Joshi	3.	Radical President of Congress
D.	S.C. Bose	4.	All India Trade Union Federation

(a) A-2, B-4, C-1, D-3 (b) A-2, B-3, C-4, D-1
(c) A-2, B-1, C-3, D-4 (d) A-2, B-4, C-3, D-1.

245. Match the following:

A.	Gandhiji was taken to the Yeravada Perison	1.	for endorsing the Delhi Pact
B.	Gandhiji undertook a fast unto death	2.	the civil disobedience movement
C.	Gandhiji was greeted with black flag demostration all among his route to Karachi	3.	The Congress crises of 1939
D.	Gandhiji called the defeat, "More mine than his"	4.	The communal award

(a) A-2, B-4, C-1, D-3 (b) A-2, B-3, C-4, D-1
(c) A-1, B-4, C-2, D-3) A-2, B-4, C-3, D-1.

246. Match the following:

A.	Individual Satyagrah	1.	1939
B.	Forward Formula	2.	1940
C.	Rajaji Formula	3.	1945
D.	INA Trials	4.	1944

(a) A-2, B-1, C-4, D-3 (b) A-3, B-1, C-4, D-2
(c) A-2, B-1, C-3, D-4 (d) A-3, B-4, C-2, D-1

247. Match the following:

A.	Abhinav Bharat	1.	1905
B.	All India Muslim League	2.	1904
C.	The Congress split	3.	1907
D.	Partition of Bengal	4.	1906

(a) A-2, B-4, C-1, D-3 (b) A-4, B-1, C-2, D-3
(c) A-3, B-4, C-2, D-3 (d) A-2, B-3, C-1, D-4.

248. Match the following:

A.	"The elections have well established the Muslim league as the only mouth piece of the Muslims. They are decided upon a divided India and this question must be tackled first...."	1.	M.A. Jinnah, 1945
B.	"Pakistan is our irrevocable and unalterable National demand...."	2.	M.A. Jinnah, 1944
C.	"India is a multilingual and therefore a multinational country......"	3.	Adhikari Thesis, 1942

D. Rajaji formula offers only a shadow and husk, a maimed, multilated and moth-eaten Pakistan	4. B.R. Ambedkar, 1946

(a) A-4, B-2, C-1, D-4 (b) A-3, B-2, C-1, D-4
(c) A-4, B-1, C-3, D-2 (d) A-3, B-1, C-2, D-4.

249. Match the following:

A. Failure of Cripps Mission	1. The Government India declared India to be at war with Germany
B. Resignation of Congress Ministries in the provinces	2. Individual Satyagraha
C. August offer	3. Quit India Movement
D. Cabinet Mission Plan	4. Direct Action Day

(a) A-3, B-1, C-2, D-4 (b) A-3, B-4, C-2, D-1
(c) A-4, B-1, C-2, D-3 (d) A-4, B-2, C-3, D-1.

250. The rise of nationalism was due to many factors, which one is wrongly listed?
(a) Unification of the country under the British
(b) Western education and thought
(c) Economic exploitation of India
(d) None of the above.

251. One of the following statement is wrong with regard to the moderate nationalists.
(a) They try to persuade other friendly countries to xrert pressure on Britain to concede their genuine demands
(b) They sought greater share for the Indians in the governance of the country
(c) They sought to secure concessional through appeals, petitions and memoranda to the Britishers
(d) They tried to educate British masses about the genuineness of India demand.

252. Although the nationalists sought primarily concessions and constitutional changes till 1905, their efforts bore fruit in many ways except one, which was that?
   (a) Some English leaders like Charles Bradlaugh took up the cause of India
   (b) The Indian Council Act of 1892 came up to the expectations of the Congress
   (c) Revealed the liberal traditions underneath the colonial and exploitive layer of the British rule
   (d) Women and students got activated.

253. The partition of Bengal reveals many facts of significance except for one. Which one is that?
   (a) It was aimed at cutting the Bengali nationalists to size
   (b) The people of Calcutta celebrated Raksha Bandhan ceremony as a mark of protest against partition
   (c) Tagore too participated in it, and for the first time Vande Matram was sung by the people
   (d) It became administratively convenient to govern Bengal, for before the partition it was too big and unwidely.

254. Which statement about Gokhale is incorrect?
   (a) He was nominated to the imperial legislative council in 1902
   (b) He visited South Africa in 1912, and helped Gandhiji in his fight against aparotheid
   (c) At principal of Poona college, he received a salary of Rs. 70/- per month
   (d) He wanted Tilak to become President of Indian National Congress in 1907.

255. Which statement about Gopal Krishna Gokhale (1866-1915) is incorrect?
   (a) Born at Kolhapur, role to the office of the principle of Ferguson college, Poona; Tilak called him the 'diamond of India.' 'The Jewel of Maharashtra' and 'The prince of workers'
   (b) He presided over the Banaras Congress

(c) He was invited to England in 1897 to give evidence on India's expenditure before Welby commission
(d) He was an extremist.

256. Which statement about Surendra Nath Banerjee (1848-1925) is incorrect?
(a) He was the Indian ICS officer; he founded the Ripon college which was later renamed after him
(b) He founded Indian Association in 1876; he was the founder member of Indian National Congress over the sessions of which he presided in 1898 and 1902
(c) He was elected to the Imperial Legislative Council
(d) No statement is incorrect.

257. Which statement about Lala Lajpat Rai (1865-1928) is incorrect?
(a) An Arya Samaji, he became famous as the 'lion of Punjab', he wrote the biography of Swami Dayanand
(b) He was the member of Indian National Congress (1885)
(c) A recognised fiery orator, he along with Gokhale toured England to enlighten the English people regarding Indian problems; he belonged to extremist section of the Congress
(d) He was deported to mandalay in 1907, where he wrote his famous book, 'The story of my Deportation'.

258. Which statement about Bipin Chandra Pal is incorrect?
(a) He joined Brahma Samaj and was editor of New India
(b) He played a great part in the development of the extremist movement in the country
(c) He was chosen Congress president in 1907
(d) Once he wrote an articel Anthology of the Bomb for which he ws tried but be apologised.

259. The spirit of unrest and discontent voiced by Tilak was caused by the following except one. Identify it.
(a) The spread of nationalist sentiment because of western democratic ideas

(b) Shabby treatment meted out to Indians in South Africa
(c) Autocratic rule of Curzon and the partition of Bengal
(d) The government ban on the public recital of 'Bande Matram' in Bengal.

260. Which statement on Tilak is incorrect?
(a) opposed interference in orthodox ways of life
(b) Attacked the age of consent Bill for bidding consummation of marriage till a girl was 12 years old
(c) Never went to England to influence British politicians
(d) None of these.

261. Which of the differences mentioned below was not true of the extremists and the moderates respectively?
(a) Hindu resurgence and reorientation of Hinduism
(b) Inspiration from vedants and Gita and philosophy of the liberals
(c) Political strategy of Shivaji and Guru Govind Singh along with the Gandhi cap and the Khaddar Kurta in place of gradualness and the interjacket
(d) Sophisticated oxford accent and the rhetoric of Burke and Fox.

262. Regarding the differences in the methods advocated by the extremists and the moderates respectively which statement is not correct?
(a) No need for benevolent guidance of the British and slow changes towards constitutionalism
(b) Boycott and Swadeshi and avoid things leading to violence
(c) Do not respect British ideas and trust British liberalism
(d) Aggressive demand for independence, and promotion of education to enable the people to ultimately have a say in the government.

263. Which statement on India's contribution to the war effort of Britain in the first world war is incorrect?
(a) Indian troops repulsed the Turkish attack on the Suez canal

(b) They participated in the campaign against Macedonia and captures Baghdad, Jerusalem, Danascus and Steppo

(c) Indian troops fought in France to repulse German attacks successfully

(d) One and a quarter million Indian troops were recruited.

264. Which point regarding the events during the First World War is incorrect?

(a) Fourteen points of Wilson was a short in the arm of the nationalists

(b) Tilak went to London and pleaded that the word 'boycott' was the same as the word 'opposition'

(c) The house of Lords and a minority of the House of commons condemmed the Jallianwala Bagh incident

(d) Gandhiji called the British Raj Satanic.

265. Which of the consequences mentioned below after the Congress approved the tactics of swadeshi and boycott, is incorrect?

(a) Some merchants voluntarily handed over salt and cloth for destruction

(b) Swadeshi factories and Swadeshi stores came up

(c) An impetus to large scale industries

(d) An impetus to cottage industries.

266. Regarding the goals of extremists and the moderates which statement is incorrect?

(a) Extremists wanted Swaraj and Aurobindo claimed that it was the mantra

(b) Gokhale believed that only mad man think such things as swaraj

(c) The extremists preferred swaraj to social reform

(d) Although moderates thought that there was no alternative to British rule, they aimed at dominion status.

267. Which statement regarding the British expliotation of India is incorrect?

(a) No governor-general and leading statesman protested against the harm done to Indian economy

(b) The economic exploitation during the Diwani period was the most heinous

(c) The policy of 'Free Trade' while Britain advanced industrially caused immense damage to Indian economy

(d) A regiment revolted in Singapore as a result of its activities.

268. Which statement on the 1922 mass civil disobedience is incorrect?

(a) It called for not payment of taxes unless political prisoners were released within seven days

(b) At Chauri Chaura 22 policemen were killed

(c) At Chauri Chaura 37 policemen were killed

(d) Gandhi doubted the correctness of his own decision.

269. Which statement on the terrorists is incorrect?

(a) Tilak wanted responsive cooperation and only gave moral support to Russian methods

(b) Russian Ninilists, who resorted to bombs influenced the terrorists

(c) V.D Savarkar organised the secret society for revolution

(d) There were a dozen such secret organisations.

270. Which statement on the Nagpur session by the Congres is correct?

(a) The old 'Constitutional' means to secure political concessions were abandoned and all the peaceful and legitimate means were now to be adopted

(b) The old aim of self government within the British Empire was renounced and Swaraj within the British empire was declared the necessary goal

(c) Gandhiji became an undisputed leader of the Congress

(d) All the above.

271. The 'Pakistan resolution' (1940), had many defects which one was not one of them?
   (a) It was quite indefinite and ambiguous about the goal
   (b) The resolution was equally vague in defining the areas in which the Muslims were numerically in a majority
   (c) It failed to take into account the Muslims residing in the mainland of India
   (d) It did not mention the nature of the state of Pakistan.

272. When Radcliffee demarcated the boundaries between India and Pakistan, he did certain things but one of them is incorrect. Identify it.
   (a) Turned down the request of the sikhs for Nankana sahib and the city of Lahore
   (b) Gave the Muslim majority district of Gurdaspur of India
   (c) A number of enclaues were left in the former East Pakistan and West Bengal where India and Pakistan exercised sovereign rights
   (d) Recommended the transfer of Berubari enclave to Pakistan.

273. Which statement about Sardar Patel is true?
   (a) He was home minister in interim government formed by Jawaharlal Nehru in 1946
   (b) He was the first Deputy Prime Minister of free India
   (c) He known as 'Iron Man' of India.
   (d) All statements are true.

274. Whcih statement about Subhash Chandra Bose (1897-1945) is incorrect?
   (a) Select into ICS, but he refused to take an oath of allegiance to the crown and left the service in 1921.
   (b) He was deported to Mandalay
   (c) He was elected President of the Congress twice in 1938 and 1939; in the second case he defeated Gandhiji's candidate Pattabhi Sitaramayya in 1939 he resigned from the presidency
   (d) never criticised Gandhiji.

275. Which statement about Maulana Abul Kalam Azad (1888-1958) is incorrect?
   (a) Born at Mecca, he came to India in 1898; was a great scholar of Arabic
   (b) He started his weekly 'Alhilai' in 1912
   (c) He was the Congress president during world war II
   (d) All statements are true.

276. Put the following events in the correct chronological sequence.
   A. March from Sabarmati Ashram to Dandi Beach.
   B. The Lahore Congress.
   C. Gandhi attended the second Round Table Conference.
   D. The Gandhi Irwin pact.
   (a) B,C,D,A (b) A,C,D,B
   (c) B,A,D,C (d) A,B,D,C.

277. Give the correct Chronological order
   1. Communal Award
   2. Simon Commission
   3. First Round Table Conference
   4. Gandhi Irwin pact
   (a) 1,2,3,4 (b) 2,1,3,4
   (c) 2,3,1,4 (d) 2,3,4,1.

278. Put the following in chronological order
   1. Formation of an interim government
   2. The arrival of a cabinet mission
   3. League launched direct action
   4. Jinnah's wrecking of the Simla conference
   (a) 4,2,3,1 (b) 2,4,3,1
   (c) 1,2,4,3 (d) 4,2,1,3.

279. Put in a chronological manner
   A. Split in the trade union movement between the communists and the moderate trade unionists.
   B. Vallabh Bhai Patel led a 'No tax' campaign in Bardoli district of Gujarat.

C. Chamber of Prince was created.

D. Establishment of the Communist party.

(a) D,B,C,A (b) D,C,B,A

(c) C,D,B,A (d) B,D,C,A.

280. 'The sleeping giant of Asia has waken up and no power on earth can stop him now', who said it and for whom?

(a) Lenin, for the textile workers who came out on the streets in protest against Tilak is transportation in July, 1908

(b) M.K. Gandhi, for the poor peasant when they participated in the Bardoli satyagraha

(c) Subhash Cnandra Bose for INA soliders

(d) None of the above.

281. Moderate politics was criticised in 1893-94 in a series of an articles entitled "New Lamps for old" written by

(a) Bipin Chandra Pal

(b) B.G. Tilak

(c) Ashwini Kumar

(d) Aurobindo Ghosh.

282. Which extremist leader opined "We will not achieve any success in our labours if we croak once a year like a frog "?

(a) B.G. Tilak

(b) Lala Lajpat Rai

(c) Bipin Chandra Pal

(d) None of the above.

283. Who looked upon the Khilafat agitation as "an opportunity for uniting Hindu and Mohammedens as would not arise in a hundred years?

(a) Gandhi (b) Maulana Azad

(c) B.G Tilak (d) None of the above.

284. Who persuaded the rating of RIN to surrender on 23rd February 1946?

A Vallabhbhai Patel B Jawaharlal Nehru

C M.A. Jinnah D S. C. Bose

(a) Only B (b) B and C
(c) A and C (d) Only D.

285. The Cabinet mission was sent to India

A. To establish a national government.
B. To work out a constitutional arrangement for the transfer of power.
C. To accede to Jinnah demand for Pakistan and work out its detail.
D. None of the above.

(a) B (b) A and B
(c) C (d) D.

286. Which of the following is correctly matched

A. Swaraj is my birth right and I shall have it B.G. Tilak
B. Give me blood and I will give you freedom J.L. Nehru
C. Karenge ya marenge S.C. Bose
D. A new star arises, the star of fredom in the East M. Gandhi.

287. "To sound the order of retreat just when public enthusiam was reaching the boiling point was nothing short of a national calamity". Who said it regarding the unilateral with drawal of the non-cooperation movement by Gandhi on February, 1922?

(a) S.C. Bose
(b) J.L. Nehru
(c) Mohammad Ali
(d) C.R. Das.

288. "A Sanyasi who came to that district after a spell as an indentured labourer in Fiji carrying a copy of Tulsidas Ramayana on his back from which he would recite verses to rural audience". The peasant leader referred to here is

(a) Jhinguri Singh
(b) Jadunandan Sharma
(c) Baba Ram Chamdra
(d) Sahajananda Saraswati.

289. While referring to the Morley-Minto reforms, who remarked "if it could be said that this chapter of reforms led directly or necessarily to the establishment of a parliamentary system in India, I for one would have nothing at all to do with it"?

(a) Morley (b) Minto
(c) Crewe (d) Curzon.

290. "My own belief is that the Congress is toltering and one of my great ambition is to assist it to a peaceful dath". Who said it?

(a) Winston Churchill (b) Lord Canning
(c) Lord Curzon (d) M.A. Jinnah.

291. "Nauseating and humiliating spectacle of Gandhiji striding half naked up the step of the viceroy's palace to negotiate one equal terms with the representative of the king emperor". Who said this?

(a) Clement Atllee
(b) William Digby
(c) Winston Churchill
(d) Strafford Cripps.

292. Who said, "Cowardice and ahimsa do not go together any more than,water and fire?

(a) Acharya Vinobha Bhave
(b) Acharya Narendra Dev
(c) Jaya Prakash Narayan
(d) M. Gandhi.

293. Which one of the following is not correctly matched?

A.	Bal Gangadhar Tilak	Bombay Association
B.	Mary Carpenter	National Indian Association
C.	Surendra Nath Bannerjee	Indian National Conference
D.	Anand Mohan Bose	Indian Society

(a) C (b) B
(c) D (d) A.

294. The movement that came to an abrupt end due to the Charurichaura incident was the
(a) Wahabi movement
(b) Home rule movement
(c) Non-cooperation movement
(d) Civil disobedience movement

295. The Quit India Campaign was launched by the National Congress after the failure of the
A. Cripps Mission
B. Simla Conference held at the instance of the Governor General, Lord Wavell
C. Cabinet Mission
D. None of the above
(a) a (b) b
(c) c (d) d.

296. The first attempt at introducing a representative and popular element in a governance of India was made through the
A. Indian Council Act, 1861
B. Indian Council Act, 1892
C. Indian Council Act., 1909
D. Government of India Act, 1919
(a) D (b) C
(c) A (d) B.

297. Who led the revolutionary Yugantar Party which tried to conserve its resource and build international contacts so as to organise a real military conspiracy at an appropriate time?
(a) Jatindranath Mukherjee (b) Sachindranath Sanyal
(c) Rashbehari Bose (d) None of the above.

298. Who strongly objected to the British government negotiating on terms of equality with the "Seditious Fakir", i.e. Mahatma Gandhi in February-March, 1931.
(a) Ramsay MacDonald (b) Lord Linlithgow
(c) Winston Churchill (d) Lord Wavell.

299. Which pair threw a bomb at a carriage that they believed was occupied by Kingsford, the unpopular judge at Muzzafarpur.
(a) Ramprasad Bismil, Surya Sen (1906)
(b) Khudiram Bose, Prafulla Chaki (1908)
(c) Jatindra Nath Das, Ashfaqullah Khan (1910)
(d) None of the above.

300. Cooperation in any shape or form with this satanic government is sinful, Gandhiji declared after
(a) The passing of Rowlatt Act
(b) The Punjab tragedy
(c) Failure of the Round Table Conference
(d) None of the above.

301. In Hyderabad, a movement based on Gandhian principle became very popular in the rural areas. It provided vital support to the local Congress party during the struggle for inter-gration of Hyderabad with the Indian Union in 1947. Who led the movement.
(a) N.M. Joshi
(b) Swami Ramanand Tirth
(c) P.C. Joshi
(d) None of the above.

302. Linlithgow described it as "by far the most serious rebellion since that of 1851, the gravity and extent of which we have so far concealed from the world for reasons of military security which is the movement referred here.
(a) Khilafat movement
(b) Civil disobedience movement
(c) Tebhage movement
(d) Quit India movement.

303. Who of the following did not belong to what popularly was known as the Bombay Triumvirate?
(a) B.G. Tilak (b) Ferozshah Mehta
(c) K.T. Telang (d) Badruddin Tyabji.

ANSWERS

1.	(c)	2.	(b)	3.	(b)	4.	(c)
5.	(a)	6.	(a)	7.	(a)	8.	(c)
9.	(a)	10.	(a)	11.	(b)	12.	(b)
13.	(c)	14.	(c)	15.	(c)	16.	(b)
17.	(a)	18.	(b)	19.	(a)	20.	(a)
21	(d)	22.	(b)	23.	(d)	24.	(a)
25.	(b)	26.	(a)	27.	(a)	28.	(a)
29.	(c)	30.	(c)	31.	(d)	32.	(a)
33.	(c)	34.	(a)	35.	(c)	36.	(a)
37.	(a)	38.	(a)	39.	(b)	40.	(b)
41.	(b)	42.	(b)	43.	(b)	44.	(a)
45.	(b)	46.	(c)	47.	(b)	48.	(b)
49.	(a)	50.	(c)	51.	(b)	52.	(d)
53.	(a)	54.	(a)	55.	(b)	56.	(b)
57.	(b)	58.	(a)	59.	(d)	60.	(c)
61.	(b)	62.	(a)	63.	(b)	64.	(c)
65.	(b)	66.	(d)	67.	(a)	68.	(a)
69.	(a)	70.	(a)	71.	(c)	72.	(a)
73.	(a)	74.	(a)	75.	(b)	76.	(c)
77.	(d)	78.	(d)	79.	(b)	80.	(a)
81.	(d)	82.	(a)	83.	(d)	84.	(a)
85.	(a)	86.	(d)	87.	(d)	88.	(d)
89.	(b)	90.	(b)	91.	(a)	92.	(a)
93.	(d)	94.	(d)	95.	(b)	96	(b)
97.	(c)	98.	(c)	99.	(d)	100	(a)
101.	(b)	102.	(c)	103.	(b)	104.	(c)
105.	(c)	106.	(b)	107.	(d)	108.	(d)
109.	(b)	110.	(a)	111.	(b)	112.	(b)
113.	(c)	114.	(b)	115.	(a)	116.	(b)
117.	(d)	118.	(b)	119.	(c)	120.	(d)
121	(b)	122	(b)	123.	(a)	124.	(d)
125.	(d)	126.	(b)	127.	(b)	128.	(d)
129.	(c)	130.	(b)	131.	(c)	132.	(c)
133.	(c)	134.	(b)	135.	(a)	136.	(c)
137.	(c)	138.	(c)	139.	(c)	140.	(c)
141.	(c)	142.	(c)	143.	(b)	144.	(b)
145.	(c)	146.	(a)	147.	(c)	148.	(c)
149.	(a)	150.	(d)	151.	(c)	152.	(b)
153.	(b)	154.	(a)	155.	(b)	156.	(d)

157. (a)	158. (a)	159. (a)	160. (d)
161. (b)	162. (b)	163. (c)	164. (d)
165. (b)	166. (c)	167. (c)	168. (b)
169. (b)	170. (d)	171. (c)	172. (a)
173. (b)	174. (c)	175. (c)	176. (c)
177. (c)	178. (d)	179. (b)	180. (d)
181. (b)	182. (d)	183. (c)	184. (d)
185. (c)	186. (b)	187. (d)	188. (b)
189. (a)	190. (d)	191. (b)	192. (b)
193. (d)	194. (d)	195. (d)	196 (d)
197. (c)	198. (d)	199. (b)	200 (d)
201. (c)	202. (b)	203. (d)	204. (d)
205. (a)	206. (d)	207. (c)	208. (a)
209. (c)	210. (a)	211. (b)	212. (a)
213. (a)	214. (c)	215. (d)	216. (b)
217. (a)	218. (a)	219. (a)	220. (b)
221 (a)	222. (c)	223. (c)	224. (d)
225. (d)	226. (d)	227. (a)	228. (b)
229. (b)	230. (c)	231. (d)	232. (d)
233. (c)	234. (d)	235. (d)	236. (d)
237. (a)	238. (a)	239. (b)	240. (a)
241. (c)	242. (b)	243. (c)	244. (b)
245. (d)	246. (a)	247. (a)	248. (d)
249. (d)	250. (b)	251. (b)	252. (c)
253. (c)	254. (d)	255. (a)	256. (d)
257. (d)	258. (c)	259. (d)	260. (d)
261. (c)	262. (d)	263. (d)	264. (b)
265. (c)	266. (d)	267. (c)	268. (c)
269. (d)	270. (d)	271. (c)	272. (d)
273. (d)	274. (a)	275. (d)	276. (c)
277. (a)	278. (c)	279. (c)	280. (b)
281. (d)	282. (c)	283. (b)	284 (b)
285. (a)	286. (a)	287. (d)	288. (d)
289. (a)	290. (a)	291. (c)	292. (d)
293. (b)	294. (d)	295. (a)	296 (d)
297. (c)	298. (b)	299. (b)	300 (a)
301. (c)	302 (c)	303 (b)	

SET I
ASSESS YOURSELF

1. Arrange the various writers of Sanskrit drama in an ascending chronogical order

   A. Bhasa　　B. Asvaghosa
   C. Bhavabhuti　　D. Kalidasa
   (a) C, B, D, A　　(b) B, A, D, C
   (c) A, C, B, D　　(d) B, A, C, D.

2. Match the following

   List-1
   A. Elephanta caves and temples
   B. Ajanta
   C.. Nasik Cave Temples
   D. Ellora

   List-II
   1. Mahayana and Hinayana
   2. Shaivite
   3. Buddhist, Jain and Hindus
   4. Buddhist, Shaivite and Vaishnavite

	A	B	C	D
(a)	2	3	4	1
(b)	2	4	3	1
(c)	2	1	4	3
(d)	2	4	1	3.

3. Buddha's preachings were mainly related to

   (a) Purity of thought and conduct
   (b) Idol worship

(c) Belief in one god
(d) Practice of rituals.

4. The main historical source regarding the information about village government under the Cholas is the
(a) Jatwai Inscription
(b) Uttaranerur inscription
(c) Chandravallo inscription
(d) Halmidi inscription.

5. Harrapan people had a common burial system, which is proved by
(a) The burial of commonly used items with the dead
(b) The earth burials with head of the dead normally laid towards the north
(c) The burial of the dead body in the sitting posture
(d) Both (a) and (b) are correct.

6. Which of the following pairs of Jain religious texts and their contents is not correctly matched?
(a) Mula-Sutras deal with the basic doctrine of Jainism
(b) Dhgas-explain the Jain doctrines through big end
(c) Prakimas-deal with monastic order of the nuns
(d) Chheda- Sutras explain the rules of discipline of themonastic order.

7. There is evidence to show the Vishnu cult spread overseas in the early centuries of the Christian era. Which was the place that this cult spread to
(a) China
(b) Egypt
(c) Cambodia
(d) Thailand.

8. Buddhist literary texts attach importance to a Buddhist overseas mission. To which place was the mission sent?
(a) Cambodia (b) Java
(c) Sumatra (d) Sri Lanka.

9. The question of the granting of land and its merits or demerits are debated for the first time in the
   (a) Legend of Sudasa and Vasistha
   (b) Legend of Vedigha Mathava
   (c) Legend of Vishwakarma
   (d) None of the these.

10. Match the name of the Mahajanpadas with the name of the capital

A. Kashi	1. Vaisali
B. Dhga	2. Varanasi
C. Vajji	3. Kaushambi
D. Vatsa	4. Champa

	A	B	C	D
(a)	2	4	1	3
(b)	2	1	4	3
(c)	4	2	1	3
(d)	3	2	1	4.

11. In the context of the later Vedic period, read the following statement and point out the wrong ones
   A. Only labour intensive agriculture was practiced
   B. It is impossible to say that the Vedic society shifted eastwards
   C. People married outside their gotra
   D. Iron technology was mostly used for weapons of war
   (a) C and D are false (b) Only A is false
   (c) B and C are false (d) A, B and C are false.

12. The early kings of Magadha ascertained its stability by achieving which of the following :
   A. Expanding the frontier upto Gandhara
   B. Conquering the Anga Capital of Champa
   C. Capturing the iron mines of Avanti
   D. Incorporating the neighbouring kindoms through war and alliance
   (a) B and D only (b) A and C only
   (c) D only (d) A, B, and C only.

13. Which of the following is not characteristic of paintings of the Mughal period? The depiction of
    (a) Mythological themes
    (b) Court and cultural scenes
    (c) Scenes of battle
    (d) Religious scenes.

14. Put in ascending chronological order of construction
    (a) Mamallapuram Rathas
    (b) Puri Jagamath Temple
    (c) Qutab Minar
    (d) Meenakshi Temple.

15. The first Sultan of Delhi who initiated the policy of associating Indian Muslims with administration was
    (a) Iltutmish (b) Balban
    (c) Alauddin Khilji (d) Firoz Tughluq.

16 Match the folowing:

(A)	Abolition of Pilgrimage Tax	1.	1580
(B)	Abolition of Jaziya	2.	1579
(C)	Declaration of Mahzar Nama	3.	1579
(D)	Introduction of Dahsala System	4.	1564

	A	B	C	D
(a)	2	3	1	4
(b)	4	3	2	1
(c)	2	4	3	1
(d)	4	2	1	3.

17. Which king of Slave Dynasty was an expert calligraphist and spent his leisure time copying the Quran?
    (a) Illtutmish (b) Balban
    (c) Bahramshah (d) Iyasir-ud-din.

18. He was a Frenchman and Physician by profession. He was attached to the Court of Shah Jehan and was witness to the war of succession between Dara Shikoh and Aurangzeb. The reference here is to:
    (a) Jean Baptiste (b) Ferhao Muniz
    (c) Nicola o Manucci (d) Frahacois Bernier.

19. Who presided over the Fourth Buddhist Council when Buddhism split into two broad sects, Mahayana and Hinayana.
    (a) Nagarjuna
    (b) Nagasena
    (c) Vasumitra and Asvaghosha
    (d) Maha Kashyap.

20. Mir Qasim formed an alliance with the Nawab of Avadh and the Mughal Emperor to sight against the British. What was the name of the Nawab of Awadh?
    (a) Aziz-ud-din
    (b) Ghazi-ud-din
    (c) Shuja-ud-daula
    (d) Majib-ud-daula.

21. What is the chronological sequence in which the following places witnessed sepoy revolts?
    (A) Naushere (B) Delhi
    (C) Merrut (D) Hoti Mardan.
    (a) CBAD (b) BCAD
    (c) CBD (d) BADC.

22. Who was the author of the book `The Indian War of Independence,1857'?
    (a) R.C. Majumdar
    (b) Sir Syed Ahmad Khan
    (c) V.P. Savarkar
    (d) S.R. Sharma.

23. Which of the following areas were affected by Wahabi Movement?
    (A) Bihar (B) Bengal
    (C) Assam (D) Rajasthan.
    (a) ACDE (b) ABE
    (c) ACD (d) BCD.

24. Which tribal revolt among the following is the best example of the reaction of the tribal to the activities of the christian missionaries in their areas?

(a)	Chuar revolt of	1832
(b)	Koya revolt of	1922-24
(c)	Chenchu revolt of	1921-22
(d)	Munda revolt of	1899-1900.

25. Which code gives the correct pairing of the following?

LIST-I (ORGANISATION)

A. Mysore Praja Mitra Mandal

B. Satyasho dak Samaj

C. All India Anti-untouchability League

D. Malyali Memorial

LIST-II (FOUNDERS)

1. Jyotiba Phule
2. G.V. Raman Pillai
3. C.R. Reddy
4. M.K. Gandhi

	A	B	C	D
(a)	3	1	4	2
(b)	1	3	2	4
(c)	3	1	2	4
(d)	3	4	1	2.

26. Which of the following persons accompanied Gandhi to Champaran?

(A) Rajendra Prasad (B) Jawaharlal Nehru

(C) J.B. Kriplani (D) Mahadev Desai.

(a) ABC (b) ABD

(c) BCD (d) ACD.

27. Arrange the following events in the correct chronological order?

1. Repeal of the Vernacular Press Act
2. Appointment of the first Famine Commission

3. Passing of the Ilbert Bill
4. Passing of the First Indian Factory Act

(a) BDAC (b) BDCA
(c) DBAC (d) BADC.

28. Which of the following was/were not responsible for the failure of the revolutionary terrorists?

(A) Class and Caste limitation
(B) Lack of communication facilities
(C) Lack of central leadership and a common plan
(D) Secular beliefs of the terrorists.

(a) Only A (b) Only A and B
(c) Only D (d) Only C.

29. the Indian National Congress decided to start a non-violent Non-Cooperation Movement at its sessions at:

(a) Ahmedabad (b) Amritsar
(c) Allahabad (d) Calcutta.

30. Who made the `Deepavali Declaration' and when?

(a) Subhash Chandra Bose - 1941
(b) Lord Irwan - 1929
(c) Lord Linlithgow - 1940
(d) Mahatma Gandhi - 1919.

31. The earliest of the pre-Harappan culture in the Indus region probably is that of

(a) Amri
(b) Sothi
(c) Kot Dizi
(d) Alranji Khera.

32. The Pictographs of the bird dove appear on Harappan

(i) Seals (ii) Amulets
(iii) Pottery (iv) Beads.

(a) (i), (ii),(iii) (b) (i),(iii)
(c) (iii) (d) (i).

33. In which of the following sites of shob culture has the mother Goddess been found?
   (a) Amri (b) Mundijak
   (c) Rana Ghundi (d) Dabarkot.

34. Steatile was imported from one of these places?
   (a) Tell Asmar (b) Khora San
   (c) Susa (d) Tepe Yahya.

35. In Hindu Myth, which god is believed to have devoured his parents at birth?
   (a) Vishnu (b) Agani
   (c) Shiva (d) Vayu.

36. Which ancient city was the home of the scholar sages Kapila, Gargi and Maitreyi?
   (a) Mithila (b) Vidisha
   (c) Juuaini (d) Patliputra.

37. Which part of modern India is referred to as greak or `hill' in the Purans?
   (a) Himachal Pradesh (b) Uttar Pradesh
   (c) Kashmir (d) Assam.

38. Two of Ashoka's lion pillars built in the 3rd Century BC stands perfect preserved even today at their original location. One is at Lauriya Nadangarh. Where is the other?
   (a) Sarnath (b) Kothua
   (c) Aurangabad (d) Nalanda.

39. Which Ayurvedic Text contains an oath of honesty service to mankind similar to the Hipperatic oath?
   (a) Charaka Samhita (b) Susruta Samhita
   (c) Naveetaram (d) Upchar.

40. Match these languages to the scripts they were once written in:
   1. Tamil (a) Shikasta
   2. Magadhi (b) Kolezhurttu
   3. Kashmiri (c) Bhahmi

4. Urdu (d) Grantham.
5. Malyalam (e) Sharda
(a) 1-e, 2-d, 3-c, 4-b, 5-a
(b) 1-d, 2-c, 3-e, 4-a, 5-b
(c) 1-a, 2-b, 3-c, 4-d, 5-e
(d) 1-a, 2-e, 3-b, 4-d, 5-c.

41. Herpes in Hindu mythology carried flags with their personal emblems to batte, just like bingd Chief tains the world over. Identify the emblems of these mythical figures.

1. Arjun A. Blue lotus
2. Karna B. King Cobra
3. Duryodhana C. Monkey god with lions tail
4. Dronacharya D. Attar, Pitcher & bow.

(a) 1-C, 2-A, 3-B, 4-D.
(b) 1-A, 2-B, 3-C, 4-D
(c) 1-D, 2-C, 3-B. 4-A
(d) 1-A, 2-D, 3-B, 4-C.

42. Kaundinya, a South Indian Brahmin, founded a royal dynasty in South East Asia. What is the country dynasty now known as
(a) Thailand (b) Laos
(c) Burma (d) Kampuchea.

43. The oldest synagague in the common wealth, the Pardesi, was built in India in 1568 where?
(a) Surat (b) Bombay
(c) Cochin (d) Calcutta.

44. Ludo, the English game patented in 1880 by the British crown in actually derived from an ancient Indian board game, Name?
(a) Chaupar (b) Dhayut
(c) Pachisi (d) Kreeda.

45. Which scientific treatise did each of these ancient Indian authors wrote is not correctly matched.

(a) Sridhara | | Ganita Sara
(b) Bhaskara | | Bijaganita
(c) Aryabhatta | | Mahasidhanta
(d) Brahmagupta | | Chandra Siddhanta.

46. Members of which Indian tribe classified as `Criminal' by the British in India, were once the guardians of the Jaipur Royal Treasury?

(a) Sansis (b) Bhils
(c) Minas (d) Kanjars.

47. Which Bengali Muslim King, a vassal of Babur, had the Mahabharata translated into Bengali?

(a) Nusrat Shas (b) Shah Riza
(c) Alam (d) Sher Khan.

48. Which ancient Indian river was called Cririkarnika?

(a) Ravi (b) Sabarmati
(c) Jhelum (d) Khuba.

49. Who is hailed as the `God of Medicine" by Practitioners of Ayurveda?

(a) Charaka (b) Susruta
(c) Chayavana (d) Dhan Wantari.

50. Indian Military history features several famous cannons valued for being vital to the defence of their forth. Match these cannons to the forts to which they belong:

1. Jajiwaan A. Jhansi
2. Radak Bijli B. Daulatabad
3. Qila Shikah C. Amber
4. Malik-i-Maidan D. Bijapur.
5. Belsa E. Gwalior

(a) 1-C, 2-A, 3-B, 4-D, 5-E
(b) 1-A, 2-B, 3-C, 4-D, 5-E
(c) 1-B, 2-A, 3-D, 4-C, 4-E
(d) 1-E, 2-D, 3-C, 4-B, 5-A.

ANSWERS

1.	(b)	2.	(c)	3	(a)	4.	(b)
5.	(d)	6.	(a)	7.	(c)	8.	(d)
9.	(c)	10.	(a)	11.	(b)	12.	(a)
13.	(d)	14	(a)	15.	(c)	16.	(c)
17.	(d)	18.	(d)	19.	(c)	20.	(c)
21.	(a)	22.	(c)	23.	(b)	24.	(d)
25.	(a)	26.	(d)	27.	(a)	28.	(d)
29.	(d)	30	(b)	31.	(a)	32.	(c)
33.	(c)	34.	(d)	35.	(b)	36.	(a)
37.	(c)	38.	(b)	39.	(a)	40.	(b)
41.	(a)	42.	(d)	43.	(c)	44.	(c)
45.	(d)	46	(d)	47.	(a)	48.	(b)
49.	(d)	50.	(a)				

SET II
ASSESS YOURSELF

1. Which Greek historian besides Megasthenes wrote a book called Indica?

   (a) Herodotus (b) Theophrastas

   (c) Arrain (d) Diomedes.

2. A boatman, Nizami Sayed Humayun from drowing and was made king for half a day. Where is his tomb located ?

   (a) Lucknow (b) Kanpur

   (c) Jaipur (d) Ajmer.

3. Which sufi at the Court of the Delhi Sultanate is said to have miraculously turned water into oil?

   (a) Amir Khusro (b) Muinuddin Chisti

   (c) Nizamuddin Aulia (d) Baba Farid.

4. In which ancient Hindu scripture would you find the first account of a Primeval deluge rather like the Biblical tale of Noah?

   (a) Righ Veda

   (b) Satapatha Brahmana

   (c) Brihadaranyaka Upnishad

   (d) Vishnu Purana.

5. Which ancient Indian dynasty was also called Vindhyashakti because of its dominion over the Vindhya range?

   (a) Guptas (b) Chalukyas

   (c) Rashtrakutas (d) Vakatakos.

6. Which city displaced Madurai as the literacy centre of Tamil Nadu in the 7th century?

(a) Chidambaram (b) Tanjavur
(c) Yellore (d) Pulicat.

7. Where are these sun temple located?

1..	Martand	A. Tamil Nadu
2..	Konak	B. Kashmir
3.	Suryan Kovil	C. Orrisa
4.	Modhera	D. Gujarat.

(a)	1-A,	2-B,	3-C,	4-D
(b)	1-D,	2-C,	3-B,	4-A
(c)	1-B,	2-C,	3-A,	4-D
(d)	1-B,	2-A,	3-C,	4-D.

8. To which mortal is Indra supposed to have first revealed the secret science of Ayurveda?

(a) Bharadwraja (b) Nala
(c) Varahamihira (d) Susruta.

9. Commercial tea plantations were started in India by the British East-India Company. Which Governor General initiated this decision?

(a) Lord Bentick (b) Lord Cornwallis
(c) Lord Dalhousie (d) Lord Irwin.

10. Where on the banks of the Yamuna did Baburs wife help him create three Mughal gardens?

(a) Mathura (b) Delhi
(c) Agra (d) Allahabad.

11. The capital of central provinces in 1861 was

(a) Jabalpur (b) Bhopal
(c) Ranchi (d) Gaya.

12. Who built the fortification in the Aravallis which is some times called `The Great wall of India"?

(a) Rana Pratap (b) Rana Singh
(c) Rana Kumbha (d) Man Singh.

13. Which Buddhist monk is believed to have introduced the martial art of kalaripayattu to China and Japan?
    (a) Huein-Tsang (b) Fa-hien
    (c) Bodhi Dharma (d) Nagarjuna.

14. Just as Bhagirath is credited with bringing Ganga down from heaven. Sage Kashyapa is said to have induced another `divine' river to flow on eath. Which one?
    (a) Vitasta (b) Chandra Bhaga
    (c) Saraswati (d) Drishadwati.

15. An ancient Indian text on alchemy, the Rasa Rathnakara, has for its unlikely another a revered Buddhist Philosopher who was he?
    (a) Maibeya (b) Bodhi Dahrma
    (c) Nagarjuna (d) Anawa.

16. Who according to the vedas discovered fire for mortal use?
    (a) Angiras (b) Vishvamitra
    (c) Dhruva (d) Vasistha.

17. Match the dialect of Hindi in which these mediaeval Indian poets wrote.

1. Vidyapati	A. Awadhi
2. Kabir	B. Hindavi
3. Chand Bardai	C. Brajbhasa
4. Surdas	D. Bhojpuri
5. Tulsidas	E. Maithili.

(a)	1-A,	2-B,	3-C.	4-D,	5-E
(b)	1-E,	2-D,	3-B,	4-C,	5-A
(c)	1-A,	2-C,	3-D,	4-B,	5-E
(d)	1-E,	2-D,	3-C,	4-B,	5-A.

18. Which major Raga Tansen did not create:
    (a) Darbari Kanda
    (b) Miyan Ki Mlahar
    (c) Bharaya
    (d) Miyan Ki Todi.

19. Which Roman emperor had an Indian Cook?
    (a) Claudius (b) Trajan
    (c) Julian (d) Justinjan.

20. Who drafted the original Indian Panel Code in 1861?
    (a) Thomas Babington Macaulay
    (b) Charles Wood
    (c) Lord Mayo
    (d) Lord Canning.

21. In which scripture would you find the story of Urvashi and Puruavas?
    (a) Rig Veda (b) Ramayan
    (c) Vishnu Puran (d) Malvikagnimitram.

22. To kill which demon did Vishnu himself assume the forum of the dancer Mohini?
    (a) Ravana (b) Tarkasura
    (c) Bhasmasura (d) Triloki.

23. Which artist at Akbar court was known by the title of `Golden Pen' or Zarin Kalan?
    (a) Abul Fazal (b) Raja Birbal
    (c) Basawan (d) Mohammed Hussain.

24. Which disciple of Guru Nanak accompanied him or his wanderings and played the rabab while Nanak sang his hymns?
    (a) Arjun (b) Darshan
    (c) Mardana (d) Balak Padam.

25. Which Indian tribe began a socio-cultural reform movement in 1914, in the name of tribal god, Dharmas?
    (a) Junages (b) Apa Tanis
    (c) Oraons (d) Khasis.

26. Under what pseudonym did Rabindranath Tagore write his Vaishnava Padabhali?
    (a) Bhanu Sinha (b) Sushil Yadav
    (c) Padam Singh (d) Hari Singh.

27. A hill shrine close to the spot where Mahavira is said to have achieved enlightment is an important Jain centre of Pilgrimage where is it?
    (a) Mount Abu (b) Kamakhya
    (c) Parsvanath Hill (d) Rajgriha.

28. A legendary Maratha sea lord practically controlled the coast between Bombay and Goa forcibly levying the cauth of the seas on Portuguese, English and Sidiv Vessels, who was he?
    (a) Tulajaji Bhonsale (b) Mahadaji
    (c) Tahaji (d) Kanhoji Ahgre.

29. Which of these operatic dramas did Wajid Ali Shah, Nawab of Lucknow, compose and play the lead in?
    (a) Balmiki Pratibha
    (b) Sarabanja Bhoopala Kuravanji
    (c) Indra Sabha
    (d) Kalyana Saugandhika.

30. All recruits for the Former Indian civil service were drawn between 1809 and 1853 from one special school. Which are?
    (a) Fort William
    (b) East Indian College in Haileybury
    (c) Hastings Madarsa
    (d) Royal British College.

31. Besides Daswant and Kesavadas, whom else did Akbar regard as the leading miniature pointer of his regin?
    (a) Bisan Dad (b) Basawan
    (c) Masur (d) Mohammad Fiza.

32. Who among the following Britishers were associated with the introduction of the Mahalwari system.
    (a) R.M. Bird
    (b) Sir John Lawrence
    (c) William Carey
    (d) Sir Alexander Cuningham.

33. Who chose to live voluntarily with Shah Jahan and latter was accorded great honour by Aurangzeb?
    (a) Jahanara (b) Zebunisa
    (c) Zeenat Mahal (d) Roshanara.

34. Rajavamsaidis were
    (a) Royal grants to temples
    (b) Royal decrees to guilds of artisans
    (c) Royal places and buildings
    (d) Chronicles of dynasties.

35. Arumolivarman was the original name of which of the following Chola rulers?
    (a) Virarajendra (b) Rajendra I
    (c) Rajaraja I (d) Vikram Chola.

36. Rajasehkara, the famous poet was in the court of which Pratihara ruler
    (a) Vataraja
    (b) Nagabhatta II
    (c) Mihira Bhoja
    (d) Mahendrapala I.

37. Firuz Tugluq's chief architect who gave shape to many buildings, bridges, canals, reservoir, took tombs was
    (a) Abdul Haq
    (b) Malik Ghazi Sharma
    (c) Shaheen
    (d) Asif Jalal.

38. Which of the following statements about the officers designated as Mahamattas in Mauryan administration is correct?
    (a) These officers were charged with the responsibility of propagating Buddhism
    (b) They were appointed as viceroys of various provinces
    (c) The term was used for any senior official irrespective of the duties assigned to him
    (d) It is a Prakrit expresssion for the sanskrit word amatya.

39. Who of the following officers were charged with superintendence of women?
    (a) Dhamma mahamattas
    (b) Ithijhokha mahamattas
    (c) Anta Mahamattas
    (d) Antahpur adhyakshas.

40. Which of the following statements about antamahanatta is not correct?
    (a) These officers worked among he frontier and less civilised tribes
    (b) They were responsible for acquainting the border people with the principles of dhamma
    (c) In times of emergency they worked as wardens of Frontiers
    (d) It is quite likely that their duties included the collection of toll dues.

41. Which of the following statements about the new office of the dhamma mahamattas introduced by Asoka in his fourteen regnal year is not correct?
    (a) They alone were responsible for the propagation of dhamma
    (b) They looked into complaints of law abiding people and ensured fair treatment to them
    (c) They also attended to the welfare of prisoners and the inspection of the judiciary
    (d) They also looked after the interests of the urban men and merchants.

42. The officer of the central government, who was in-charge of the royal income or control of revenue, was :
    (a) Sannidhata (b) Karmika
    (c) Samadarta (d) Mahamatra.

43. From which of the following months did the Mauryan fiscal year use to begin?
    (a) Phalgun (March)
    (b) Asadha (July)

(c) Jyestha (June)
(d) Pausa Magha (January-February).

44. Four major provinces of the Mauryan empire were the Northern, Eastern, Western and Southern provinces, each under the viceroyalty of a prince or a member of the royal family. Which of the following privincial capitals of the Mauryan empire was the capital of the Northern province?

(a) Suvarnagiri (b) Tosali
(c) Ujjain (d) Taxila.

45. One of the following Mauryan provinces, which had a foreign Governor, was:
(a) Southern province Suvarnagiri
(b) Eastern province Tosali
(c) Western province Ujjain
(d) Saurashira Junagarh.

46. The Mauryas had a well organised civil service. The Mauryan civil servants were called by the general name of:
(a) Mahamatyas (b) Rajukas
(c) Amatyas (d) Lipikaras.

47. Match the five major Mauryan provinces with their capitals:

A.	Uttarapatha (Northern Province)	1. Ujjain
B.	Avantiratha (Western Province)	2. Suvarnagiri
C.	Dakshinapatha (Southern Province	3. Tosali
D.	Prachya (Eastern Province)	4. Pataliputra
E.	Central Province	5. Taxila

	A	B	C	D	E
(a)	5	1	2	3	4
(b)	1	2	1	3	5
(c)	2	3	1	4	5
(d)	3	2	1	4	5.

48. The Harappan civilization does not have homogeneity or uniformity in

(a) Weights and Measures
(b) Serial crops

(c) Burial practices
(d) Both (b) and (c) above.

49. The entry point for trade between the Indus trading centres and Mesopotamia was

(a) Elam (b) Oman
(c) Bahrain (d) Afganistan.

50. The Harappan cities were ruled by

(a) Monarch (b) Priest king
(c) Merchants Oligarchy (d) Not known.

ANSWERS

1.	(c)	2.	(d)	3.	(c)	4.	(b)
5.	(d)	6.	(b)	7.	(c)	8.	(a)
9.	(a)	10.	(c)	11.	(a)	12.	(c)
13.	(c)	14.	(a)	15.	(c)	16.	(a)
17.	(b)	18.	(c)	19.	(d)	20.	(a)
21.	(a)	22.	(c)	23.	(d)	24.	(c)
25.	(c)	26.	(a)	27.	(c)	28.	(d)
29.	(c)	30.	(b)	31.	(b)	32.	(a)
33.	(a)	34.	(d)	35.	(c)	36.	(d)
37.	(b)	38.	(c)	39.	(b)	40.	(c)
41.	(a)	42.	(a)	43.	(b)	44.	(d)
45.	(d)	46.	(c)	47.	(a)	48.	(d)
49.	(c)	50.	(d)				

SET III
ASSESS YOURSELF

1. In Ancient India the State promoted trade through
   (a) Foundation of market towns
   (b) The making and maintenance of roads
   (c) Ensuring security on trade routes
   (d) All the above.

2. In the promotion of expansion of trade and commerce, the greatest contribution was made by the
   (a) Mauryas
   (b) Indo Greeks, Sakas, Kushanas, etc.
   (c) Sungas
   (d) Imperial Guptas.

3. In early Ancient India, the largest urban centre was
   (a) Kausambi (b) Champa
   (c) Paltliputra (d) Taxila.

4. The history of Ancient Indian trade rightly begins from the ----period
   (a) Harappan (b) Later Vedic
   (c) Buddhist (d) Mauryan.

5. The industries in early ancient India were concentrated in the areas where
   (a) Raw materials and markets were available
   (b) The craftsmen were concentrated
   (c) The foreign merchants could easily arrive
   (d) The state pursued the policy of free trade.

6. The socio-economic significance of the trade and craft guilds was that
   (a) They maintained the business and occupational monopoly of particular varnas
   (b) They turned into castes
   (c) They enforced a social discipline
   (d) They provided economic support and organisation to trade and crafts.

7. Kautilya's Arthashastra's chapter on Kantakasodhana is mostly devoted to
   (a) Regulation of profits, wages, and prices
   (b) Regulations against adulteration of goods
   (c) Strict control of artisans and traders by the state
   (d) Measures for the protection of merchants and artisans by the state.

8. The great increase in the number of crafts resulted in
   (a) Mass production of goods
   (b) Greater specialisation in production techniques
   (c) Both (a) and (b) above
   (d) Stiff competition among craftsmen.

9. The great Royal Road mentioned by Megasthenes ran from------to-------
   (a) The Indus to Pataliputra
   (b) Pataliputra to Prayaga
   (c) Prayaga to Ujjaini
   (d) Pataliputra to Taxila.

10. The main land route between India and Western Asia passed through
   (a) The pass of Khyber and the valley of Kabul
   (b) The passes of Khyber and Balan
   (c) Taxila, Peshawar, and Kabul
   (d) Kabul and Bamiyan.

11. Which of the following had the monopoly of iron deposits?
    (a) Kalinga (b) Kashi
    (c) Magadha (d) Vatsa.

12. In the Mauryan and post Mauryan periods, the most important emporium of trade in Western India was
    (a) Bharukachchha (b) Suparaka
    (c) Kalyana (d) Chaul.

13. Which of the following was not the main product of South India?
    (a) Musk and Saffron
    (b) Spices
    (c) Sandalwood
    (d) Gold and Precious stones.

14. Sind Sauvira was famous in Ancient India as the home of
    (a) Fine swords and daggers
    (b) Horses and asses
    (c) Woollen textiles
    (d) Leather goods.

15. According to Patanajali, Mathura was specially famous for its textile industries. Which of the following varieties of textile was the speciality of Mathura?
    (a) Dukula (b) Sataka
    (c) Kshauma (d) Chinasunka.

16. The balance of trade was very unfavourable to the West and resulted in a serious drain of gold from the Roman empire, which of the following lamented the degenerate habits of the Romans of his day, which resulted in this drain?
    (a) Pliny (b) Ptolemy
    (c) Nero (d) Strabo.

17. What was the reason for India becoming an intermediary in the silk trade between China and the West?
    (a) The Chinese were *persona non grata* in the Western Countries

(b) After the building of the Great Wall by Shi Huang Ti, the relations between the Chinese and the Roman empire were estranged
(c) On account of Roman conflict with Parthia the latter prevented Chinese merchandise from reaching the West directly
(d) India had the best expertise in silk weaving.

18. There are records of several embassies from Indian kings to the caesars. To which of the following was an Indian embassy not sent?
(a) Augustus (b) Nero
(c) Antoninus (d) Pius.

19. The main items of export from India to the Roman empire were
(a) Agricultural commodities
(b) Raw materials for Industries
(c) Luxury goods
(d) Capital goods.

20. Which of the following was not one of the countries regions with which India had trade relations during the early centuries of the Christian era?
(a) Roman empire (b) Japan and Korea
(c) Malay Peninsula (d) North-east Africa.

21. The first to establish trade contracts with the Roman empire were
(a) Kushanas
(b) Tamil and Chera Kingdoms
(c) Western Sakas
(d) Vakatakas.

22. Which of the following categories of crafts were regarded as lower in status?
(a) Those which used perishable commodities for raw material
(b) Those associated with destruction of life

(c) Those producing goods meant for poor people
(d) Those employing untouchables as hired labourers.

23. Which of the following was not responsible for the thriving trade between India and the Western World in this period?
(a) Discovery of the monsoon winds by the Greek Sailor Hippalus in the first century A.D.
(b) Foreign invasions and external contacts
(c) Decline in production of fashion goods in the Western World
(d) Emergence of the Roman empire as paramount and most prosperous in the Western World.

24. The most interesting thing about the punchmarked coins is that they
(a) Remained in circulation for about five centuries
(b) Were in circulation in the North and South both
(c) Have various religious symbols on them
(d) Do not bear the name of any ruler.

25. Which of the following is said to have introduced Indian culture in Cambodia?
(a) Kharevela
(b) Kaundinya
(c) Kshemeshvara
(d) Kumargupta.

26. Which of the following was not one of the luxury and fashion goods of export to the Roman empire?
(a) Perfumes and spices
(b) Jewels and Precious stones
(c) Fine textiles
(d) Hair dyes, wigs, ivary combs etc..

27. Who constructed the Royal highway from pataliputra to Taxila, the most widely used highway?
(a) Mauryas (b) Kusanas
(c) Sakas (d) Guptas.

28. In return for her exports, which of the following was not one the items imported by India from the Roman empire
    (a) Wine (b) Tin and Lead
    (c) Iron (d) Linen.

29. On account of the use of which of the following items imported from India did the Roman ladies become a menace to the city's morals?
    (a) Pearls (b) Muslin
    (c) Silk (d) Perfumes.

30. Which of the following works does not help us in teaching Ancient India's trade contacts with the Western World?
    (a) The book of Duarte Barbosa
    (b) Strabo's Geography
    (c) Pliny the Elder's Natural History
    (d) Ptolemy's Geography.

31. From which point in the north-west did roads go in different directions to countries outside India?
    (a) Taxila (b) Shakala
    (c) Kabul (d) Kandahar.

32. Which of the following did not lie on the same route taking off from Kabul?
    (a) Kandahar (b) Bactria
    (c) Herat (d) Ecbatana.

33. Which of the following towns was not connected by land route from India?
    (a) Persepolis (b) Susa
    (c) Seleucia (d) Alexandria.

34. From the branch road connecting kausambi and Bharu-kachchha, the main route to the South took off from Ujjaini. Which of the following did not lie on this route to the South?
    (a) Vidisha
    (b) Pratishthana
    (c) Matupalti
    (d) Madurai.

35. Exchange of merchandise led inevitably to an exchange of ideas. Which of the following was not the result of this interaction with the west?
    (a) The borrowing of wards, largely of a technical kind on both sides
    (b) Conversion of foreigners to Hinduism and of Indians to Christianity
    (c) The emergence of the hybrid Indoa Greek style of Gandhara art
    (d) Adoption of Indian folk tales and fables in European literature.

36. The primary reason for the extension of India's trade with South east Asia was
    (a) The Roman need for spices could not be met entirely by localy supply, and this led Indian merchants to venture as middlemen into South East Asia
    (b) The merchants of South-east Asian countries wanted to develop trade relations with the Roman empire through
    (c) Te spirit of adventure of the Indian people and the religious zeal of the Buddhist monks combined to take them to South East Asian countries
    (d) India had direct land and maritime routes to South east Asia.

37. Which of the following towns did not lie on the Royal Highway?
    (a) Varanasi (b) Kausambi
    (c) Vidisha (d) Mathura.

38. From which point on the Royal Highway did a branch take off for the part of Bharukachchha (Broach)?
    (a) Kausambi (b) Varanasi
    (c) Mathura (d) Taxila.

39. Which of the following was not one of the leading guilds of the period?
    (a) Potters (b) Stone-cutters
    (c) Metal workers (d) Carpenters.

40. Which of the following rules were not fixed by the guilds?
   (a) Social conduct
   (b) Quality of goods
   (c) Prices of commodities
   (d) Sale of commodities.

41. Which of the following parts was on the Indus Delta?
   (a) Tamralipti (b) Barygaza
   (c) Barbaricum (d) Muziris.

42. At which of the following places was a trading station/ monastery not set up in Central Asia by Indiaan merchants/ Buddhist missionaries?
   (a) Yharkand (b) Kabul
   (c) Miran (d) Kashgarh.

43. The part known to the author of Periplus Maris Erthreal as Padouke was
   (a) Arikamedu (b) Tamralipti
   (c) Korkai (d) Barbaricum.

44. An early ancient Indian city, which was a nodal point for trade routes from east to west and from north to south, was
   (a) Mathura (b) Vidisha
   (c) Ujjaini (d) Pratishthana.

45. The oldest and the largest entrepot on the Western coast of India, which handled the bulk of trade with Western Asia, was
   (a) Barbaricum (b) Barygaza
   (c) Suparaka (d) Patala.

46. At which of the following parts have a sizable Roman settlement and a Roman factory been discovered?
   (a) Tamralipti
   (b) Muziris or Mushri
   (c) Kaveripattanam
   (d) Arikamedu.

47. The merchant groups of which of the following towns did not issue coins?

(a) Taxila (b) Prayaga
(c) Kausambi (d) Vidisha.

48. Arikamedu was the most important Indo-Roman trading station because

(a) Its coast was ideal for the anchorge of Roman ships
(b) It produced fine muslins and other fashion goods according to the Roman taste and specifications
(c) Both (a) and (b) above
(d) It was the first part of call for the Roman ships.

49. About which of the following South Indian cities are thre descriptions in early Tamil literature to the effect that, the Yavana ships used to arrive with their cargoes and that the Yavana section of the city over flowed with prosperity?

(a) Arikamedu
(b) Kaveripattanam
(c) Mamallapuram
(d) Muziris.

50. Which of the following was not one of the reasons for the vast majority of artisans joining the guilds?

(a) The membership of a guild provided social status
(b) It offered a degree of general security
(c) It was difficult for them to complete as individuals against the guilds
(d) Without the membership of a guild, the craftsmen were not eligible for various concessions offered by the state.

ANSWERS

1.	(d)	2.	(b)	3.	(c)	4.	(a)
5.	(a)	6.	(a)	7.	(c)	8.	(c)
9.	(a)	10.	(a)	11.	(c)	12.	(a)
13.	(a)	14.	(b)	15.	(b)	16.	(a)
17.	(c)	18.	(b)	19.	(c)	20.	(b)

21.	(b)	22.	(b)	23.	(c)	24.	(d)
25.	(b)	26.	(d)	27.	(a)	28.	(c)
29.	(b)	30.	(a)	31.	(c)	32.	(b)
33.	(b)	34.	(a)	35.	(b)	36.	(a)
37.	(c)	38.	(a)	39.	(b)	40.	(d)
41.	(c)	42.	(b)	43.	(a)	44.	(b)
45.	(b)	46.	(d)	47.	(b)	48.	(b)
49.	(b)	50.	(b)				

SET IV
ASSESS YOURSELF

1. The behaviour of the guild members was controlled through
   (a) The elder
   (b) Members of the Council
   (c) Guild court
   (d) Conduct committee.
2. Which of the following statements about the organisation of the guilds is not correct?
   (a) The guild was headed by a chief, usually called the elder
   (b) The elder was assisted by a small council of senior members
   (c) The office of the elder was usually elective
   (d) The guilds had a corporate life symbolished by the banners of each guild
3. Which of the following is not one of the facts testifying to the importance of the guilds?
   (a) The had their own insignia, banner and seals
   (b) In several cities they seemed to have issued coins
   (c) They sometimes acted as trustees and bankers
   (d) The Elders of the guilds were appointed to important political post.
4. Which of the following was not one of the probable reasons for lack of political ambition on the part of guilds?

(a) The king appears to have had financial interest in the guilds ensuring their well being
(b) The caste rules effectively prevented the coming together of different guilds for political purposes
(c) Anticipating the possible threat of his position from the guilds, the king took steps to thwart other political ambitions
(d) They were mainly socio-economic organisations.

5. The donation made by which of the following guilds is recorded in a famous inscription?
(a) Mandsor silk weavers
(b) Vidisha ivory workers
(c) Nasik weavers
(d) Corn dealers.

6. The great meeting ground of the Indian and Western merchants during the early centuries of the christian era was
(a) Dedesiya (b) Alexandria
(c) Taxila (d) Palmyra.

7. On numismatic evidence, the administration of which of the following towns is believed to have been carried on by the corporation of merchants on the eve of the Greek occupation of north-west India?
(a) Taxila
(b) Kausambi
(c) Vidisha
(d) Mahishmati.

8. What was the possible reasons for the guilds to employ hired labour (both free labour and slaves) in addition to artisans?
(a) Increasing prosperity
(b) To meet greater demand
(c) The desire for greater freedom
(d) Directives of the state.

9. Artisans and craftsmen were largely drawn from
   (a) Vaisyas (b) Sudras
   (c) Venas (d) Rathakaras.

10. Which of the following was not one of the important centres of guilds of artisans according to available inscriptions?
   (a) Mathura region in the north
   (b) Magadha in the east
   (c) Gourdhana in the western Deccan
   (d) Mandasor in central India.

11. Apart from the guild, there were other worker's bodies, such as workers, cooperatives which of the following correctly describes the composition of the workers cooperatives in Ancient India?
   (a) These mainly consisted of untouchables who were not admitted to guilds
   (b) These were non-economic organisations serving purely social purpose
   (c) These generally included artisans and enterprise, e.g. architects and masons
   (d) These cooperatives consisted of the workers of particular profession, caste and locality.

12. Before the establishment of Indo-Greek rule in India, the coins were issued by the
   (a) Rulers
   (b) Individual merchants
   (c) Merchant corporations
   (d) All the above.

13. The most commonly used coin, during the Mauryan period, was
   (a) Nishka (b) Suvarna
   (c) Karshapana (d) Kakini.

14. The metal, in which the karshapana coins were minted was
   (a) Gold and Silver (b) Copper
   (c) Lead (d) Silver or copper.

15. Which of the following coins was issued in silver?
    (a) Nishka (b) Pala
    (c) Shatamana (d) Kakini.

16. Imported coins were mostly used as
    (a) Items of Jewellery (b) Legal tender
    (c) Foreign exchange (d) Bullion.

17. The most unusual item(s) of exporst from India to the Roman world was/were
    (a) Singing and talking birds
    (b) Wild and pet animals, such as monkeys
    (c) Both (a) and (b) above
    (d) Mineral water and Himalayan herbs.

18. The rate of interest in Ancient India varied according to the venture and also perhaps according to the venture and also perhaps according to the caste of the borrower. For which of the following was the rate of interest the highest?
    (a) Unsecured loan taken by sudras
    (b) Loans taken by overland caravan traders
    (c) Loans taken by seafaring merchants
    (d) Short-term Loans for commercial ventures.

19. Which of the following was not one of the terms used to describe professional bankers and money lenders?
    (a) Srenis (b) Chettis
    (c) Chettiyars (d) Sresthins.

20. Which of the following institutionss did not act as bankers?
    (a) Trade guilds (b) Royal treasury
    (c) Larger temples (d) Village assemblies.

21. The largest number of Roman coins have been formed from
    (a) Kerala
    (b) Tamil Nadu
    (c) Both (a) and (b) above
    (d) West Bengal.

22. Seaborne trade between India and Rome received great impetus during the reign of Roman Emperor
    (a) Clayldius (b) Augustus
    (c) Trajan (d) Nero.

23. Which of the following banking functions was not performed by the trade guilds of the period?
    (a) Accepting money as fixed deposit
    (b) Granting loans to the members of the guild
    (c) Accepting safe deposits
    (d) Issuing demand drafts and promissory notes.

24. The most widely exported metals from India was
    (a) Gold (b) Iron and Steel
    (c) Copper (d) Brass

25. The gold standard was introduced in Ancient India on account of
    (a) Increase in the Price of commodities
    (b) Decline in the value of gold vis-a-vis silver
    (c) India's favourable balance of trade
    (d) Global scarcity of silver.

26. Which of the following towns was not an important commercial centre in early Ancient India?
    (a) Bharukachchha in the west
    (b) Patala in the Indus delta
    (c) Push Kalavati in the north-west
    (d) Malaimandalam in south India.

27. The Satavahanas issued their coins predominantly in lead because
    (a) Lead coins were suitable for economic transaection
    (b) In the absence of silver in the south the lead was the only alternative
    (c) They wanted to maintain a balance between two currency system of copper in the north and of silver in the west
    (d) Both (a) and (b) above.

28. Which of the following Indian commodities was not exported to Rome?
    (a) Spices-specially pepper
    (b) Indian parrots, exotic birds, lions and tigers
    (c) Ivory articles, perfumes and costly timber
    (d) Indian sculptures.

29. Ashoka's contribution to the promotion of trade during the Mauryan and post Mauryan period was that
    (a) By pursuing his pacific policies he created an ideal climate for the growth of trade
    (b) By sending embassies to the Hellenic states, he indirectly encouraged brisk commercial intercourse
    (c) He promoted the policy of free trade
    (d) By sending the Buddhist missions outside India he opened the channels of trade.

30. From the first century A.D. India's foreign trade was mainly carried on by sea, because of
    (a) Disruption of land route on account of foreign invasions
    (b) Obstacles to India's trade by the Arab merchants
    (c) Increase of India's trade with the eastern Roman empire
    (d) Discovery of monsoon winds.

31. Ships plying in mid ocean took rows with them for
    (a) Keeping them alert about attack by pirates.
    (b) Helping the navigations in locating the right direction
    (c) Sending messages to homeland
    (d) Protecting the ships from being overturned by whales and sharks.

32. The first Indian rulers to issue gold coins on the Roman pattern were
    (a) Sungas (b) Indo Greeks
    (c) Kushanas (d) Guptas.

33. Which of the following was perhaps the most advanced industry of the period?
    (a) Textile (b) Pottery
    (c) Jewellery (d) Metal work.

34. Which of the following was not one of the varieties of textiles produced during the period?
    (a) Silk (b) Cotton
    (c) Velvet (d) Calico.

35. Which of the following cities of North India was regarded as the best producer of silk?
    (a) Taxila
    (b) Patliputra
    (c) Kausambi
    (d) Varanasi.

36. Which of the following was not one of the reasons for a decline in the production of silk towards the later Gupta Period?
    (a) An important guild of silk weavers in western India discontinued its traditional vocation and took to other occupations
    (b) With larger quantity of Chinese silk reaching the western countries, the demand for Indian silk declined
    (c) With other varieties of textiles becoming available in the market, the local demand for silk declined
    (d) Justinian laws regulated silk prices all over Byzantine empire.

37. The Pandyan kings employed as bodyguard the Romans who were called, in the Tamil works, 'dumb-muchhs'; because
    (a) They were not allowed to talk to anybody
    (b) They could not communicate with the Indians
    (c) The Pandyan security rules did not allow the bodyguards to mix with anybody
    (d) One security grounds, dumb Romans were employed as bodyguards.

38. The rulers of an Ancient Indian ruling dynasty who issued the coins representing as many as thirty five deities worshipped by different peoples living in their kingdom, were the
    (a) Mauryas
    (b) Sakas
    (c) Kushanas
    (d) Guptas.

39. Indian maintained connection with Egypt through the
    (a) Red Sea route
    (b) Persian Gulf route
    (c) Indian Ocean route
    (d) Mediterranean sea route.

40. The term a Kshayanivi signifies
    (a) A permanent endowment with a guild or a banker
    (b) The guilds spent the profits or interest on the deposits according to the terms stated by the depositors
    (c) Both (a) and (b) above
    (d) The fixed deposits of the people with the banker or guild.

41. The term srusthi-kulika-nigma was like a
    (a) Federation or central guild of Bankers, Craftsmen and Guilds
    (b) Chamber of Commerce and Industries
    (c) Merchants and Craftsmen Organisation
    (d) Central Guild of all leading crafts guilds.

42. In Ancient India the guilds, besides being the organisation of Craftsmen and merchants also acted as
    (a) Banks receiving public deposits
    (b) Agencies receiving public deposits as trust properties
    (c) Agencies spending the interests on deposits for specified religious or charitable purpose
    (d) All the above.

43. Capitalistic methods of production and distribution were prevalent during this period along with the age old domestic system. Which of the following was the extreme form of capitalism prevalent in this period?
    (a) High rate of interest
    (b) Centralised production
    (c) Employment of forced and slave labour
    (d) Monopoly of means of production.

44. For which of the following purposes was hired labour not used?
    (a) Agriculture
    (b) Industry and trade
    (c) Protection of king's person
    (d) Animal rearing.

45. References to several public deposits with the guilds indicate
    (a) That guilds were the only banking organisations
    (b) Public confidence in the solvency and honesty of the guilds
    (c) That guilds were performing multifarious functions
    (d) All the above.

46. What was the main reason for expansion of internal trade during the Gupta period?
    (a) Technological advancement in commodity production
    (b) Greater prosperity of the people
    (c) Peace and order on account of a strong Gupta rule
    (d) Better organisation of guilds.

47. With the Huna invasion of the Roman empire India's trade with it came to an end. In which direction did the Indian traders mainly look for business there after?
    (a) Sri Lanka
    (b) China
    (c) South East Asia
    (d) Africa.

48. Which of the following was not one of the reasons for general decline of foreign trade during the later Gupta period?
    (a) Decline and fall of the Roman empire
    (b) Decline in the quality of goods produced
    (c) Arabs and Chinese outstripped the Indians in the art of shipbuilding
    (d) Indian law makers declared it a great sin for a Hindu to travel by sea.

49. Which of the following acted as bankers and moneylenders?
    (a) Sarthavahas (b) Sresthis
    (c) Nagarsresthins (d) Nagarakas.

50. Which of the following seem to have monopolised trade in silk?
    (a) Chinese (b) Arabs
    (c) Persians (d) Sinhalese.

ANSWERS

1.	(c)	2.	(c)	3.	(d)	4.	(c)
5.	(a)	6.	(b)	7.	(a)	8.	(b)
9.	(b)	10.	(b)	11.	(c)	12.	(d)
13.	(c)	14.	(d)	15.	(c)	16.	(d)
17.	(a)	18.	(c)	19.	(a)	20.	(b)
21.	(b)	22.	(a)	23.	(d)	24.	(b)
25.	(c)	26.	(d)	27.	(d)	28.	(d)
29.	(b)	30.	(d)	31.	(b)	32.	(c)
33.	(a)	34.	(c)	35.	(d)	36.	(c)
37.	(b)	38.	(c)	39.	(a)	40.	(c)
41.	(a)	42.	(d)	43.	(c)	44.	(c)
45.	(b)	46.	(c)	47.	(c)	48.	(b)
49.	(c)	50.	(c)				

SET V
ASSESS YOURSELF

1. The Sufi saint and his followers who loved to call themselves Rishis and not Sufis were the followers of Shaikh Nuruddin Rishi of
   (a) Bengal (b) Kashmir
   (c) Delhi (d) Gujarat.

2. The Sufi order which was popularised in India by the first Mughal emperor Babur was
   (a) Naqshbadiya (b) Qudiriya
   (c) Suhrawardi (d) Chistiya.

3. Dara Shikoh the eldest son of Shah Jahan was the follower of the ---------Sufi order------
   (a) Qadiriya (b) Chistiya
   (c) Suhrawardi (d) Naqshbadiya.

4. Who gave the Islamic equivalents for the features of the Krishna legand?
   (a) Malik Muhammad Jayasi
   (b) Mir Abdul Wahid
   (c) Shaikh Nasirudin Chirag-i-Dehlvi
   (d) Baba Farid.

5. A Sufi saint who is considered to be the first poet of Punjabi literature and whose compositions are in corporated in the Adi Granth was
   (a) Amir Khusrau
   (b) Baba Farid

(c) Baba Shafeuddin
(d) Shaikh Nizamuddin Aulliya.

6. Banis were the hymns and poems composed by
(a) Guru Nanak (b) Kabir
(c) Dadu (d) Narahari Mehta.

7. A Bhakti saint who like Jesus, Christ, believed that "only those who considered themselves reach before God attained salvation" was
(a) Kabir (b) Nanak
(c) Dadu (d) Chaitanya.

8. Which of the following was not a great contemporary of the Saint poet Tulsidas?
(a) Surdas (b) Nand Das
(c) Vitthalnath (d) Dadu.

9. After Kabir's death his tomb was built at
(a) Varanasi (b) Gorakhpur
(c) Magahar (d) Basti.

10. Chaitanya's great disciple who tried to root out the evils of the caste system from Bengal was
(a) Raghunath Das (b) Bhagavatacharya
(c) Nityanand (d) Jiva Gosain.

11. A woman saint of medialval India, who was a great shaivite was
(a) Lalla of Kashmir
(b) Mirabai of Rajasthan
(c) Sita, the queen of Pipa
(d) Jambai of Maharashtra.

12. Bhakti saint who with great aversion for the saktas said, "The Saktas and dogs are both brothers" the one is asleep while the other barks", was
(a) Kabir (b) Guru Nanak
(c) Chitanya (d) Tulsidas.

13. Guru Nanak's concept of religion was
    (a) Severely practical (b) Ethical
    (c) Both (a) and (b) (d) Purely spiritual.

14. The basic objective of Kabir's teachings was/were
    (a) To preach a religion of love
    (b) Promotion of unity among all castes and creeds
    (c) Both (a) and (b)
    (d) To free society from all hypocrisy and external formalities.

15. The most famous and the earliest biographer of Chaitanya who wrote Chataniya Charitamrita was
    (a) Sunderdas (b) Kritivasa
    (c) Madhavacharya (d) Krishnadas Kaviraj.

16. The cordinal doctrines of sufism were expounded by
    (a) Ibnal Arbi
    (b) Abdul Karimal Ji
    (c) Abu Hashim of Kufa
    (d) Mansural Hollaj.

17. Who founded the Varkari sect in Maharashtra?
    (a) Tukaram (b) Namdev
    (c) Visoba Khechar (d) Eknath.

18. Namdev, a great Bhakti saint of Maharashtra was the disciple of
    (a) Jnaneshwar (b) Visoba Khechar
    (c) Tukaram (d) Eknath.

19. Of the Bhakti saint who was/were cobbler by profession?
    (a) Dadu (b) Raidas
    (c) Both (a) and (b) (d) Malukdas.

20. Which of the following propounded the philosophy of Shuddhaadvaita?
    (a) Vallabhacharya (b) Chaitanya
    (c) Nimbarka (d) Ramanuja.

21. The first Bakti saint to use Hindi, the language of the masses, for the propagation of his doctrines, was
    (a) Ramananada (b) Kabir
    (c) Tulsidas (d) Mirabai.

22. Who said, "God knows man's virtues and inquires not his caste in the next world there is no caste"?
    (a) Kabir (b) Guru Nanak
    (c) Chitanya (d) Ramananda.

23. Which of the following was a great satirist and ridiculed all the institutions of his time?
    (a) Kabir (b) Nanak
    (c) Ramananda (d) Chaitanya.

24. In the following pairings of Bhakti saint the states to which they belonged the one which is not property matched as
    (a) Shankaradeva (b) Kabir
    (c) Narsi Mehta (d) Tukaram.

25. Which of the following was not one of the Sufi saints of the period?
    (a) Shaikh Muinudin Chisti
    (b) Baba Fariduddin Ganj-i-Shakar
    (c) Shaikh Nizammuddin Aulliya
    (d) Muhammad bin Bakhtiyar Kaki.

26. Which of the following ideas of the Bhakti and Sufi saints inspired Akbar to propound his doctrine din-i-ilahi?
    (a) Leaves a means of achieving union with God
    (b) Unity of all religions
    (c) The role of a fair or a guru in facilitating relationship of God
    (d) The need to unite with god.

27. What was the term used by the Sufis for the successor nominated by the teacher of a particular order or Silsilah?
    (a) Pir (b) Murid
    (c) Wali (d) Khanqah.

28. Which of the following established the Chisti order in India?
    (a) Shaikh Salim Chisti
    (b) Khwaja Muinuddin Chisti
    (c) Nizamuddin Auliya
    (d) Fariduddin Ganj-i-Shakar.

29. In which region of India was the Firdusi order popular?
    (a) In and around Delhi
    (b) Sind
    (c) Bihar
    (d) The Deccan.

30. Which of the following was not one of the three chief sufi orders in India?
    (a) Shultari (b) Chisti
    (c) Suharawardi (d) Firdusi.

31. Which of the following religions did not make any contribution of the growth of sufism?
    (a) Hinduism (b) Jainism
    (c) Buddhism (d) Christianity.

32. Which of the following was not a feature of society against which the sufis reacted by isolating themselves from society?
    (a) The Vulgar display of wealth
    (b) Degeneration of morals
    (c) Rationalist philosophy
    (d) Religious dogmatism.

33. Which of the following did not make use of Hindi in his/her devotional literature either fully or partly?
    (a) Mirabai (b) Nanak
    (c) Narsi Mehta (d) Ramananda.

34. What was the language employed by Surdas for his devotional songs?
    (a) Hindi (b) Maithili
    (c) Avadhi (d) Brijbhasha.

35. Which of the following was translated in to Bengali by Kritivasa?
   (a) Mahabharata
   (b) Ramayana
   (c) Gita
   (d) Bhagavata Purana.

36. Poet Chandidas contributed to the popularisation of
   (a) Bengali (b) Hindi
   (c) Marathi (d) Gujarati.

37. The use of which of the following regional languages was popularised by the Bhakti leader Shankardeva?
   (a) Bengali (b) Brij Bhasha
   (c) Avadhi (d) Assamese.

38. Which of the following was not a features of the literature produced in regional languages?
   (a) It was spontaneous and imbued with genuine sentiment
   (b) Its terms were of common interest to people of various regions
   (c) It was largely confined to religious treaties
   (d) Literary innovation travelled quickly and widely in the regional literature of North India.

39. Who said "Abide pure amidst the impurities of the world thus shalt thou find the way of religion"?
   (a) Kabir (b) Nanak
   (c) Namdev (d) Surdas.

40. Who said "one stone is adored another is trodden under post if one is god the other is also a God"?
   (a) Kabir (b) Namdev
   (c) Tukaram (d) Tulsidas.

41. Which of the following Bhakti saints was regarded by his followers as an incarnation of Vishnu?
   (a) Ramananada (b) Ramanuja
   (c) Namdev (d) Chaitanya.

42. The philosophy of which of the following exponents of Bhakti cult degenerated to earn the epithet. "The Epicureanism of the east"?
    (a) Ramananda (b) Krittivasa
    (c) Vallabhacharya (d) Narsi Mehta.

43. The monism preached by which of the following leaders of the Bhakti movement is known as Suddha advaita or 'Pure non Duality?
    (a) Ramanuja (b) Vallabhacharya
    (c) Ramananda (d) Chtanya.

44. The Bhakti saint who had twelve disciples including a butcher, a barber, a cobbler and Muslim weaver, was
    (a) Vallabhacharya (b) Ramananda
    (c) Kabir (d) Surdas.

45. The Bhakti saint who was not a worshipper of Krishna was
    (a) Vallabhacharya (b) Mirabai
    (c) Surdas (d) Ramananda.

46. One of the following leaders of the Bhakti movement who was greatly influenced by Islam was
    (a) Ramanuja (b) Namdev
    (c) Chaitanya (d) Ramananda.

47. The Bhakti saints come from a diversity of back ground. By and large their adherents were
    (a) Artisans (b) Merchants
    (c) Middle class (d) Lower class.

48. The earliest Vaishnava Bhakti Saints from the south were
    (a) Alvars (b) Nayanmaras
    (c) Bhagavatas (d) Virashaivits.

49. The Cult of Bhakti has been fully enunciated in the
    (a) Katha and svetaw atara upanishads
    (b) Bhagavad Gita
    (c) Bhagavata Purana
    (d) Commentry on Brahma Sutra.

50. The concept of Bhakti centres around the thought of
    - (a) Devotion to one formless God
    - (b) Love and devotion to one personal God
    - (c) Total self surrender to God
    - (d) All of the above.

51. Which of the following was not one of the common concepts of the advocates of the Bhakti movement?
    - (a) Fundamental equality of all religious
    - (b) The unity of God head
    - (c) Condemnation of caste system
    - (d) Denunciation of polytheism and idolatry.

52. Which of the following was not a common teaching of Kabir and Nanak?
    - (a) The ideas of both were drawn from Bhakti and Islami sufi traditions
    - (b) Both emphasised the doctrine of Karma
    - (c) Both believed in the formless God
    - (d) The objective of both was only to reform Hindu society.

53 One of the Bhakti saints who first joined the Sufi but later left them was
    - (a) Kabir (b) Nanak
    - (c) Namdev (d) Tukaram.

54. The first Sufi saint to propound the view that the divine knowledge of God can be achieved by faith, devotion and meditation was
    - (a) Mansural Hallaj
    - (b) Shaikh Shahabuddin
    - (c) Ibnal Arabi
    - (d) Shaikh Muinuddin Chisti.

55. The most famous work of Dara Shikoh in which he proved that the Islamic Sufi concepts were identical with those of the Hindus was
    - (a) Sakinatul-awliya (b) Hasnatul
    - (c) Majmul (d) Munqizmin.

ANSWERS

1.	(b)	2.	(a)	3.	(a)	4.	(b)
5.	(b)	6.	(c)	7.	(c)	8.	(c)
9.	(c)	10.	(c)	11.	(a)	12.	(a)
13.	(c)	14.	(c)	15.	(b)	16.	(b)
17.	(a)	18.	(b)	19.	(c)	20.	(a)
21.	(a)	22.	(b)	23.	(a)	24.	(d)
25.	(d)	26.	(b)	27.	(c)	28.	(b)
29.	(c)	30.	(a)	31.	(b)	32.	(d)
33.	(c)	34.	(d)	35.	(b)	36.	(a)
37.	(d)	38.	(c)	39.	(b)	40.	(b)
41.	(d)	42.	(d)	43.	(b)	44.	(b)
45.	(d)	46.	(b)	47.	(b)	48.	(a)
49.	(c)	50.	(d)	51.	(b)	52.	(d)
53.	(b)	54.	(c)	55.	(c)		